Collins · THE EGYPTIAN ELITE

ISLAMKUNDLICHE UNTERSUCHUNGEN · BAND 99

herausgegeben von

Klaus Schwarz

KLAUS SCHWARZ VERLAG · BERLIN

ISLAMKUNDLICHE UNTERSUCHUNGEN · BAND 99

Jeffrey G. Collins

THE EGYPTIAN ELITE UNDER CROMER, 1882 - 1907

KLAUS SCHWARZ VERLAG · BERLIN · 1984

© Dr. Klaus Schwarz, Berlin 1983
ISBN 3-922968-99-6
Druck: aku-Fotodruck GmbH, Eckbertstr. 19, 8600 Bamberg

iii

To my wife and father.

TABLE OF CONTENTS

Introduction

This dissertation presents a study of Egyptian society during the
first twenty-five years of the British occupation, with special
attention focussed on the Egyptian elite. The object of this study is
to uncover the basic dynamics behind the evolution of an entire
national society in the Middle East during a quarter of a century.
Because the scope of this study is so broad, despite limitations
imposed by the choice of methodology, the conclusions offered in the
final chapter must be regarded as somewhat tentative.

This study assumes that important social transformations take
place because of changes on the levels of political and economic
relationships. It is also assumed that such transformations are not a
result of changing intellectual currents. Although I would be the
last to deny the vitality or importance of intellectual life in Egypt
during the period of rule by Cromer, 1882-1907, the topic is
peripheral to the focus of this dissertation. Instead I chose to
analyze the vast quantitative data available in archives and published
sources in order to peel back layer upon layer of economic and
political structures in Egypt as they evolved from 1882 to 1907.
During this period Egypt formed an extremely complex and rapidly
growing national organism of about ten million people. Bound together
by history, the Nile and the political borders of the time, this
energetic populus would defy the descriptive efforts of historians
were it not for the tendency of government and private bureaucracies

in Egypt to churn out myriad records of the passage through time of
this collective national being.

The methodology utilized in this study can best be seen as the
basis for its organization. Chapter one outlines the demographic
background to our inquiry. The people who lived in Egypt form the raw
material for this study. Changes in the size, composition and
geographical distribution of population offer clues to the evolution
of a society but cannot furnish the root causes for such
transformations. Wealth and power appeared to shift along three axes
in Egyptian society: rural versus urban, local versus foreign and
Muslim versus non-Muslim. However, the chapter on demography serves
more to raise questions than to answer them.

Chapters two through five describe the evolution of economic
structures in Egypt in the broadest sense, on the assumption that
economic relationships constitute a basic level of dynamic causation
whose effects radiate throughout society. The general approach in
these chapters is to move from levels of effect to those of essential
causation.

Chapter two documents the evolution of foreign trade and
commerce, signalling the importance of cotton cultivation throughout
this period. Chapter three describes the dual nature of
manufacturing, with an archaic structure in the hands of many small
proprietors and a modern sector, as in commerce, controlled by
foreigners and minority sect Egyptians. The deepest levels of

movement appear in the organization of production where pre-modern structures such as the last vestiges of the guild system were replaced by wage labor. Chapter four focusses on changes in the distribution of property and the organization of production in Cairo, which alone constituted almost sixty percent of Egypt's urban sector. Here great attention is paid to the social implications of changing relationships in manufacturing and commerce, made tangible in Cairene society by shifting configurations of occupation and property distribution. Quantitative analysis of property tax records makes it possible to describe urban society as a four tiered structure consisting of (1) the great majority of urban dwellers owning little or no real property, (2) small scale merchants or lower level civil servants, (3) middle ranking functionaries, professionals and employees and (4) high government officials, merchants, industrialists, financiers and successful professionals in the liberal arts. Chapter five applies the same approach to the distribution of agricultural land and the organization of production in the rural sector. Were the dissertation to end at the conclusion of chapter five, we would be left with the impression that economic relationships constituted the unique level of primary evolution in Egypt under Cromer.

Chapter six and seven stress the primacy of politics, thus offering a different approach to an understanding of the evolution of Egyptian society during the first twenty-five years of the British occupation. These two chapters present a picture of changes flowing from the top down through the hierarchy of the Egyptian state to the village and neighborhood level. The British rulers at the helm of government are depicted as the dynamic elements in a process that was not exactly modernization, but more one of a division of labor. This study argues that the British made almost all important political decisions and that these were actively or passively approved by the Egyptian political elite which acted as a "native screen" that served to legitimize foreign rule. The political changes promoted by the British, e.g. a more professional bureaucracy with many Europeans, proteges and minority sect Egyptians in the upper ranks, greater centralization of power and a rationalized budget process, all tended to make the state apparatus into a formidable instrument for the projection of British power down to local levels. The state did not promote modernization in public education, which received little funding or attention until the end of Cromer's rule and the state actively intervened to impede the formation of a modern textile industry. However, the state invested massively in the modern infrastructure that transformed Egypt into an ever more productive cotton farm. The political quietism of indigenous Egyptian elites ended in 1906 or 1907 when national representative institutions provided a forum for demands for greater local power. The concluding chapter of this dissertation describes the interaction of the political and economic transformations taking place and argues for the primacy of politics under Cromer.

The framework of analysis employed in this dissertation is essentially structural it should now be clear, but this is implemented

with the tools of quantitative analysis. Although I would not
describe the approach as radical empiricism, it is my belief that when
a historian makes a broad statement about wealth and political power,
he should be able to substantiate it with figures when data is
available, as is certainly the case for nineteenth century Egypt. The
reader should bear in mind that this study attempts to establish a
benchmark for the study of Egyptian social history in the nineteenth
and early twentieth centuries. No previous studies have made such
wide use of the quantitative data available. Because of the ground
breaking nature of this dissertation, there are unfortunately no
comparable statistics or analyses for the preceding and following
periods. The basic quantitative techniques used in this study, from
growth rates to the Chi Square test, are explained as they are
employed in the text. Primary sources for the quantitative study of
Egyptian society from 1882 to 1907 are vast.

The researcher is overwhelmed by an embarrassment of riches.
This introduction will now provide an overview of the most important
primary sources, concentrating on those utilized in this study. These
fall into the rubrics of published sources, both private and
governmental, and archival sources.

As in other Islamic regions, nineteenth century Egyptians had a
strong prediliction for biography, which is a delight to the student
of elite history. Zaki Muhammad Mujahid's <u>Biographies</u> <u>of</u> <u>Famous</u> <u>Men</u>
<u>of</u> <u>the</u> <u>Orient</u>, Cairo, 1949, is merely the best organized of a
series of relevant biographical dictionaries treating important

Egyptians of all occupations. These furnish birth and death dates,
education, career history, religion, titles, an indication of wealth,
and in many cases the names and occupations of prominent relatives.
Some, like 'Abd al-Rahman Zaki's <u>Prominent</u> <u>Men</u> <u>of</u> <u>the</u> <u>Egyptian</u> <u>Army</u>
<u>and</u> <u>Navy</u> <u>in</u> <u>the</u> <u>Nineteenth</u> <u>Century</u>, are of greater value than the
titles might lead one to believe because of great mobility between
different positions for the elite. All are in Arabic. Even more
valuable is a strange compilation by a Christian printer who brought
out the first business directory in modern Egypt, <u>Guide</u> <u>to</u> <u>Cairo</u>,
by Yusuf Assaf, Cairo, 1891 (Arabic). It lists the holders of all
major positions in the Egyptian government that year, almost 1000, as
well as most important men in every field of business for Cairo, the
other major towns and the provincial capitals. His listing is most
complete for Christians and for government employees. I suspect he
had access to both the <u>Official</u> <u>Journal</u> and to official lists of
the ministries.

'Ali Mubarak's enormous <u>al-Khitat</u> <u>al-Tawfiqiyya</u> is an
encyclopedia for the political and economic history of nineteenth
century Egypt. Even though it was compiled from government sources by
a Minister of Public Works, it cannot be treated as an alternative
source to the Egyptian archives themselves. On the other hand it must
not be overlooked because of its many biographies, family histories
and descriptions of property held by individuals.

Most important officials of the government in Cairo, whether
English, French or Egyptian, did not resist the temptation to write

lengthy memoirs. Some, like Cromer's <u>Modern Egypt</u> or <u>Abbas II</u>,
came out quickly and have a polemic or journalistic quality. Others,
like Qallini Fahmy's <u>Memoirs</u> (Arabic), show a patient taste for
research and are essentially biographical dictionaries spiced with
gossip. T.R. Russel's <u>Egyptian Service</u>, 1902-1946, London, 1949,
was among many written during the leisure of retirement in England
that are valuable for insight into the organization of government.
The memoirs of Abbas II's private secretary, Ahmad Shafiq, form a
diary of day to day political intrigue often useful to settle points
about the Egyptian viewpoint toward British acts. The private letters
of political figures sometimes help to understand opposition practices
and the reactions of the government, e.g. Mustafa Kamel Pasha,
<u>Egyptian-French Letters</u> (<u>Addressed to Mme Juliette Adam</u>),
<u>1895-1908</u>, Cairo,1909.

Though government documents are of prime importance, private
contemporary analyses are sometimes helpful in describing government
structures and the changing role of law, e.g. Charles Royle, "The
Administrative Machinery of Egypt," in <u>The Nineteenth Century</u>
(1881),9. The main source for the changing structure and role of the
Egyptian government is a semi-official publication by a secretary to
the Minister of Justice, Philippe Gelat Bey, <u>Répertoire général</u>
<u>annoté de la législation et de l'administration égyptiennes</u>
<u>1840-1908</u>, Alexandria,1909, in four volumes.

Economic groups competed within the changing legal framework
described by contemporary analyses. The <u>Répertoire général</u>

mentioned directly above is the fullest source here, but is
supplemented by a variety of commentaries by private parties that
allow one to observe the complex web of economic structures, as for
example, relations of property. The Right of Landed Property in
Egypt, by Yacoub Bey Artin and translated by Edward Van Dyck,
London, 1885, traces property law and taxation down to 1880. Lands
and Taxes (Arabic) by Sadiq Hanain, Cairo, 1904, duplicates this
description and continues it down to 1903. These two major works are
supplemented by a series of pamphlets and articles, mostly in Arabic.
A series of texts on Egyptian agriculture bring us to a finer level of
economic relations in the countryside, providing generalizations about
farming techniques, land values, wages, profits and lease agreements.
Here one of the most detailed treatments is by Raoul de Chambert,
Enquête sur la condition du fellah égyptien au triple point de vue
de la vie agricole, de l'éducation, de l'hygiène et de l'assistance
publique, Dijon, Imprimerie Darantiere, 1909. Some information on
industry and commerce appears in comtemporary accounts such as Sugar
in Egypt and Elsewhere, but the major sources here are governmental.

Al-Mu'ayyad was the only newspaper used extensively in this
study. From it were extracted obituaries of approximately one
thousand elite members who died between 1901 and 1910. Al-Watan
furnished a few obituaries beginning in 1885, but the obituary column
only became a regular feature of Egyptian newspapers beginning in 1901
with al-Mu'ayyad. These notices not only enable us to fix the date
of death but also provide information on occupation for men.

Official government publications must be ranked as second only to
archival sources for their detail and variety. The entire Egyptian
government carefully documented its own structural evolution during
the British occupation. The <u>Official</u> <u>Journal</u> of the Egyptian
government is the single most valuable source for both nominations to
public posts and for information about the structure of the
bureaucracy. It was published three or four times a week both Arabic
and in a combined English and French version. Because most
complementary sources were in Arabic, to avoid confusion arising from
transliteration I used the Arabic edition and was able to extract the
names of all holders of top posts in the twenty-one ministries and
departments from 1882 to 1907. The Official Journal also published
annual budgets, summaries of the tax revenue collected and due for
each province, the state of the public debt, and occasionally
biographies of prominent officials. Most orders from the central
government in Cairo to outlying branches at the <u>mudiriyya</u>, <u>markaz</u>
or village level were also published in the <u>Official</u> <u>Journal</u>.

The <u>Annuaire</u> <u>Statistique</u>, first issued in 1909, contains
aggregate data for the period 1882 to 1908 on almost all topics of
interest to the Egyptian government: population, international trade,
taxation, the distribution of agricultural land, annual budgets, the
state debt, the numbers and tasks of employees in all government
departments and public education at all levels. It is therefore the
essential starting point for analysis of econmic groups and the role
of the state. However, because it merely summarizes information

collected and published elsewhere, and because full explanations are
not given of just how the data was collected or summarized, the
Annuaire Statistique must be used with caution and compared with
other data sources whenever possible.

The separate ministries and departments of the government also
documented their activities and evolution in a long series of official
publications. Units like the Department of Direct Taxes reported
regularly on changes in the structure of urban and rural property.
The most valuable single publications here are two lists of back taxes
owed by large landowners in 1884 and 1885.

The yearly reports of the Domains Commission provide a basis for
interpretation of the archival records of the sale of about 283,000
feddans from 1879 to 1907. The Daira Saniyya Commision also issued
detailed reports on its management and eventual sale of 324,000
feddans during the same period. Because these sales accounted for
such a large block of the cultivated land of Egypt, they are vital to
an understanding of changing economic structures. A European parallel
of equal significance is the confiscation and sale of church lands by
Henry VIII of England.

Though foreign trade is fully documented in the annual report of
the Customs Administration, manufacturing and internal trade are more
difficult to trace in detail despite the lists published by the
statistical department of the Ministry of Finances, for example that
of 295 Joint Stock Companies Operating Chiefly in Egypt, December 31,

1907, Cairo, 1909. The numerous other publications of various
departments of the Egyptian government need not be mentioned here, but
will be evaluated as necessary in footnotes or appendices.

No valid study of modern Egyptian society can be written unless
it is based on the vast archival sources located in London and Cairo.
Though the French archives are perhaps more valuable prior to 1882,
after the British occupation the archives in London take precedence
over all other European collections.

The British archives house two distinct categories of information
about the economics and politics of modern Egypt. In the first case,
British civil servants collected and forwarded to London information
about topics of special interest to the Foreign Office. In the second
case, the British archives can best be treated as a summary or
overview of the archives in Cairo. Because they controlled the
Egyptian government after 1882, the British extracted data from
various departments in Cairo and again sent it to the Foreign Office.
In both cases these holdings were eventually stored in the Public
Record Office. Some of the documents were reproduced in the House of
Commons Sessional Papers or in briefs known as the Confidential Prints
F.O. 407, for use at the periodic meetings of the British cabinet.
These are available in some research libraries in the United States.

Because Egypt funtioned as a large cotton plantation for English
textile interests, British civil servants in Cairo compiled detailed
reports on Egyptian agriculture long before the Egyptian government

gave this responsibility over to a separate ministry. Documentation
on politics was even more extensive because Egypt was a "veiled
protectorate" and not a colony. To manipulate affairs indirectly
without full colonial powers the British had to be very well informed
about Egyptian politics. Reports were forwarded to London almost
daily about Egyptian personalities and nominations to high posts.

The British archives contain summaries of data compiled by the
Egyptian government dealing with economic structures and political
institutions. Though the <u>Annuaire</u> <u>Statistique</u> of 1909 shows the
distribution of land holding by size of plot for Egypt taken as a
whole, a report compiled in 1907 breaks this down for each <u>mudiriyya</u>
and compares the situation in 1896 and 1906. The best description of
Egypt's representative institutions is, of course, a report to the
Foreign Office by the man who planned them singlehandedly, Lord
Dufferin. The role of Europeans in the Egyptian administration is
summarized in three reports by Fitzgerald, Wilson and Lord Cromer.
Intelligence reports on the practices of different social groups are
interspersed in the continuous flow of documents over the entire
twenty-five year period beginning the British occupation.

Most of the important detailed information about the economic and
political structures of Egypt during the beginning of the British
occupation comes from the archives in Cairo. They are overwhelmingly
in Arabic and this study is among the first to utilize them
systematically. The archives of the Ministry of Finance, known as Dar
al-Mahfuzat, house most of these records.

The Dar al-Mahfuzat holds a vast collection of records which document the distribution of urban and rural property. For example, the Mixed Court of Cairo recorded 3541 acts of mortgage on land and houses from January 1, 1876 to November 14, 1883 and these are stored in Dar al-Mahfuzat.

The Domains Commission managed approximately half a million feddans of the best agricultural land in Egypt after the Law of Liquidation of 1880 and from 1879 to December 30, 1906 sold 283,195 feddans. The yearly reports of this commission furnish the name of purchaser, location by village, price, area and date for each sale. The Daira Saniya Commission managed another ten percent of Egypt's cultivable land in 1879, amounting to 505,098 feddans. These lands were then transferred to a private land company based in London in return for payment of L.E. 6,431,500 which equalled the outstanding mortgage on the lands. The Dar al-Mahfuzat has full information on the management and disposal of these lands and it is used extensively in chapter five.

The tax records for Cairo of 1894 are the major source for urban property distribution used in this study. The Egyptian government decided to levy house taxes in 1875, but systematic collection did not begin until 1880. Complete records are available in Dar al-Mahfuzat for taxes on Cairo property beginning in 1894, and include the name and occupation of the owner, yearly rental value of the property, street address, type of building, and the residence of the owner.

These records form the major archival source for statements about the social structure of Cairo and the distribution of urban property under Cromer.

Many of the sales of Domains or Daira Saniya land were made in exchange for the pension rights of former government employees. This study utilizes records of all pension exchange sales made from November 11, 1886 to July 5, 1891. These records served as a valuable check on the Domains and Daira Saniya sales records.

The pension records stored in Dar al-Mahfuzat furnish full career biographies for government employees accorded a pension throughout the first twenty-five years of the British occupation and beyond. The typical pension file gives names, date of birth, occassionally place of birth and knowledge of foreign languages, but almost always a complete career biography from first to last employlment with the government, including position, administrative division, salary, starting and ending date, years, months and days in the position and often rank. From the 16,000 pension files compiled from 1882 to 1914, I copied two hundred for the highest ranking employees, from Prime Minister to Judge of the Native Courts. The pension files then, in combination with the nominations to posts of the Official Journal, furnished extremely full information on the holders of important political posts and their career patterns.

These published and archival sources make it possible for this study to offer a new synthesis within the context of the social

history of the modern Middle East. The combination of a structural
approach, quantitative methodologies and new archival material should
ensure that this dissertation will incite some controversy among
concerned historians. My intent however, is to avoid the pitfalls of
evaluating contributions by those scholars of Egyptian history who
have gone before me. Moreover, such evaluations would add many pages
to an already lengthy work and some might wrongly be interpreted as
ad hominem judgments. Instead, I invite interested students and
interpreters of history to share and to comment upon the fruits of my
intellectual endeavors in modern Egyptian history.

Chapter One

The Demographic Background

This chapter treating demographics will set the background for
the entire study of Egyptian society under Cromer. Demographic
material can point out significant trends but the root causes of major
shifts in a society do not often lie within the realm of demographics
alone. For this reason this chapter forms a preliminary investigation
into the mechanics of Egyptian society during the first twenty-five
years of the British occupation. It will point out demographic
evidence of three major shifts in Egyptian society and subsequent
chapters will seek to explain them in more depth.

The population of Egypt grew considerably during the first
twenty-five years of the British occupation but not all sectors grew
at the same rate. Differences in the growth rate point to several
significant changes in the compostion and balance of power within
Egyptian society. Population and power shifted along three major axes
of of Egyptian society: urban versus rural, foreign versus Egyptian
and Muslim versus non-Muslim.

Censuses were taken for Egypt in 1882, 1897 and 1907. The 1882
census was inaccurate because it grossly underestimated the national
population. Before addressing the basic questions of demographics, we
must analyze and compensate for flaws in the 1882 census data. From
the two more recent censuses Justin McCarthy has calculated the growth
rate for each province or major governorate, and then shown that the

1882 figures imply an implausibly high increase for the period from
1882 to 1897 for most areas. Hypothesizing that growth rates would
not change substantially from 1882 to 1907, McCarthy has established a
corrected population estimate for Egypt of 7,840,271 in 1882. The
breakdown by area is given in the footnotes to this chapter.[1]

Following McCarthy's argument, the total population of Egypt was
probably as follows:

1882	7,840,271
1897	9,734,405
1907	11,287,359

We may conclude that the overall rate of increase for the period
1897-1907 was most likely near the figure of .0149118 per annum.
McCarthy has calculated that the annual rate of increase was .015246
for the period 1897-1907. Then deaths caused by epidemics were
deducted. My rate of increase, .0149118, is based on the net change
over the decade. Annual rates of change in this study will be
calculated on this basis. Following McCarthy's argument, the rate for
the period 1882-1897 was probably as high, though below the rate of
.017143 for 1846-1882. These rates take into account a series of
epidemics detailed by McCarthy.

Although the censuses of 1897 and 1907 may be accepted as
relatively accurate, the census of 1882 poses additional problems.
Not only was the overall population undercounted but some segments
were less likely to be counted than others, introducing systematic bias

into the data. The country was in the midst of a power struggle
between the Khedive, the army officers under Ahmad 'Urabi and their
supporters and the European powers headed by England and France.
Relations were so tense that British warships arrived in Alexandria
harbor two weeks after the census was taken and a few weeks later
anti-European riots broke out in the city. It is probable that
Europeans would make every effort to be counted in this situation, as
they were calling for European intervention to protect their
privileged status against nascent Egyptian nationalism. On the other
hand, the native population probably saw little advantage to be
derived from an accurate census and in a time of crisis the Egyptian
peasant in the nineteenth century always dreaded conscription.
Moreover, rural Egyptians were largely illiterate and mistrusted both
the census taker and the tax collector, whom they may well have
confused. For these reasons, the foreign community as recorded in the
1882 census is probably counted with some accuracy and the Egyptian
population is most likely undercounted. With these qualifications in
mind about the census of 1882, we can proceed to analyze the changes
in the structure of the Egyptian population during the first
twenty-five years of the British occupation.

The rural population increased more rapidly than the urban
population. On the basis of the uncorrected 1882 census, the
population was distributed as follows.[2]

Raw Census Data 1882

Urban Population (total)	1,022,521	15.02%
Governorates	708,052	10.40%
Provincial Capitals (14)	314,469	4.62%
Rural Population (total)	5,783,860	84.98%
Lower Egypt (urban and rural)	3,296,436	
Upper Egypt (" " ")	2,801,893	
Total Population of Egypt	6,806,381	100.00%

In the above table, the figures for all but the provincial capitals were taken from the 1882 census. The population of the 14 provincial capitals was calculated from the 1897 figure for these cities of 384,013. This was calculated to be theoretically 362,237 in 1882 on the basis of a constant rate of increase from 1882 to 1907 equal to the observed rate of .0038995 for the period from 1897 to 1907. Then 362,237 was multiplied by (6,806,381/7,840,271), that is, the rate of underestimation of the 1882 population as calculated by McCarthy. The result is an estimated population of 314,469 for the provincial capitals in 1882. This calculation was made necessary because the census itself was no longer available for consultation.

We can also estimate the balance of urban and rural population in 1882 on the basis of the corrected figures of McCarthy. The difference between the population of Cairo in 1882 in the census and as estimated is 88,576. The difference for Alexandria is 25,525.

Damietta was a governorate in 1882 but was made part of the province of Daqahliya in 1907 so we cannot calculate a rate of annual increase for the period from 1897 to 1907. For this reason it seemed best to estimate the population of the governorates by adding the difference in the populations of Alexandria and Cairo to the total for the governorates in the 1882 census. The population of the provincial capitals was calculated to be 362,237 as explained on the previous page. Using these corrected population estimates did not substantially change the balance of urban and rural population as is evident in the following table.

Egypt in 1882 (Estimated)

Urban Population (total)	1,184,390	15.11%
Governorates	882,153	10.49%
Provincial Capitals (14)	362,237	4.62%
Rural Population (total)	6,655,881	84.89%
Total Population of Egypt	7,840,271	100.00%

In 1897 and 1907 the balance of urban and rural population was as follows.[3]

	1897		1907	
Urban Pop.	1,355,688	13,95%	1,509,373	13.37%
Govnts.	971,675	10.00%	1,110,373	9.84%
Prov.Caps.	384,013	3.95%	399,253	3.54%
Rural Pop.	8,361,540	86.05%	9,777,985	86.63%
Lower Egy.	4,719,335	48.57%	5,519,194	48.90%
Upper Egy.	4,026,218	41.43%	4,658,045	41.27%
Total Pop.	9,717,228	100.00%	11,287,359	100.00%

It is clear that the rural population increased more than the urban population and that the population of Lower Egypt increased more rapidly than that of Upper Egypt. By observing the percentage figures in the two tables directly above, it becomes clear that these were continuing trends from 1882 to 1907. The provincial capitals grew least of all, as can be seen in the following table of annual rates of increase for the period 1897 - 1907.

<u>Area</u>	<u>Annual Rate of Increase (1897 - 1907)</u>
Governorates	.0134093
Provincial Capitals	.0038995
Rural Egypt	.0157722
Urban Egypt	.0107964
Lower Egypt (urban and rural)	.0158341
Upper Egypt (urban and rural)	.0146952
All Egypt[4]	.015091

From 1882 to 1897, the foreign population increased only slightly more rapidly than the total population of Egypt, as nearly as can be estimated. Population tables for foreigners are presented in Appendix 1. The foreign population recorded in Alexandria shrank by 3,575 or 7.19%. Although some of this loss may be due to undercounting in 1882, it appears that Cairo acted as a magnet for foreigners in the first fifteen years of occupation. Certainly by the 1890's it became clear that withdrawal was not near[5] and Europeans could feel secure living in the capital because of the large British garrison. The great majority of the net influx of foreigners was absorbed by Cairo and Alexandria. As late as 1897, less than thirteen percent of the foreign comunity lived outside these two cities, most of them in the provincial capitals. Europeans lived in the towns of Egypt because they were engaged almost exclusively in commerce, as the director of the census remarked in the census of 1882: "L'Européen se livre presque exclusivement au commerce et à l'industrie; il n'est pas attiré en Egypte par les travaux agricoles...."[6]

From 1897 to 1907 the foreign population of Egypt grew more than twice as rapidly as the total population. On the average, the foreign community grew by almost four thousand persons each year. Eighty-seven percent of the net increase in the European population ended up in Cairo alone. As late as 1907, the foreign population outside the governorates was minimal, accounting for about three-tenths of one percent of the population of Lower Egypt. Yet in the larger cities, contemporary observers remarked that the influx of

Europeans was detrimental to the Egyptian inhabitants of certain

quarters. The Census of 1907 states that,

> There is one important point which must be borne in mind
> when looking at the increase, not only in Cairo and Alexandria,
> but also in several other of the larger towns of Egypt; and that
> is the effect that an influx of Europeans has upon the town
> populations as a whole. It is believed that in portions of many
> urban areas the native residents have actually been replaced by
> foreigners, and that in many cases where the new arrivals are
> sharp-witted, pushing individuals on the look-out for employment,
> the result has been to actually drive a portion of the indigenous
> community not to other quarters of the same town, but altogether
> out of the urban area.[7]

Many Egyptians were driven out of al-Muski in Cairo in the decade

from 1897 to 1907, to cite one example. In 1897, al-Muski had a

greater percentage of foreigners than any other neighborhood in Cairo,

29.0% compared to 21.8% for al-Azbakiyya and 11.9% for Hulwan. The

1907 census does not give a breakdown by nationality for the quarters

of Cairo, but this can be approximated using the breakdown by

religion. In 1907 the population of the al-Muski was classed by

religion as shown in the following table in the left column.

Population of al-Muski in 1907

Religion	N	Egyptians	Foreigners
Muslim	9,716	9,716	0
Coptic (total)	952	952	0
Orthodox	443		
Catholic	509		
Protestant	0		
Roman Catholic	2,746	723	2,023
Protestant	176	0	176
Greek Orthodox	4,445	0	4,445
Eastern Orthodox	1,078	0	1,078
Jewish	2,918	1,459	1,459
Total	22,031	12,850	9,181

The right side of the table uses religion to approximate
nationality. The categories of Roman Catholic and Jewish deserve some
explanation. On a national level, half of all Jews in Egypt held
foreign nationality in 1897, or 12,507 out of 25,200. Jacob Landau
attests to the fact that this was normal for the nineteenth century.[8]
Therefore I assumed that half of the Jews in al-Muski were foreign.
In 1897 there were 61,051 Catholics in Egypt, of which 4,630 were
Copts. Of the remaining 56,421 non-Coptic Catholics, 13,406 were
foreign. In 1907 there was a total of 57,774 Catholics in Egypt, and
assuming the Egyptians in non-Coptic Catholic churches increased at
the national rate, they would number a little over 15,000. Therefore
I assumed about 15/57 Catholics in Egypt would be Egyptians. Hence

2,746 (15/57) = 723 Egyptian Roman Catholics probably lived in
al-Muski in 1907. Of the 16,504 Egyptians who lived in al-Muski in
1897, constituting 71.0% of the total population there, only 12,850
remained in 1907, when they comprised only 58.3% of the total. Had
the Egyptians in al-Muski decreased at the overall rate for the
quarter, they would have numbered 15,642 at the end of the decade. We
may conclude that approximately 2,792 Egyptians were forced out of
al-Muski by the influx of foreigners from 1897 to 1907. Used to more
spacious living conditions, the incoming 2,447 foreigners displaced
more than an equal number of Egyptians.

Although these calculations are only approximate, it is clear
that the foreign population of al-Muski expanded from 29% to over 40%
during the decade. Thus a detailed examination of the 1897 and 1907
censuses confirms the observation that Egyptians were being forced out
of certain neighborhoods in the larger cities.

The different religious communities in Egypt grew at suprisingly
differing rates during the first twenty-five years of British
occupation, especially during the period from 1897 to 1907. The
Muslim majority declined somewhat relatively, the Christian groups
generally grew and the Protestant and Catholic Coptic sects increased
at the expense of the Orthodox Coptic church from 1897 to 1907. These
shifts within the religious communities of the Egyptian population can
be observed in the table located in Appendix 2.

Had the Muslim population increased at the national rate of

.0140328 from 1897 to 1907, it would have reached 10,320,131. In
actuality, the Muslim population was 50,686 lower than this in 1907.
There is every reason to believe that the Muslim population, living
predomiantly in the villages where the rate of increase was greater
than in the towns, would have risen more quickly than the national
average. Since the primary and secondary sources treating this period
mention no substantial emigration, we can only suppose that
nutritional and health conditions were significantly worse for Muslims
than for other Egyptians.

Two striking shifts occured within the Christian population.
Firstly, the non-Coptic Orthodox population almost doubled, mostly
because of the influx of Orthodox Greeks. The Greek community
expanded from 38,208 in 1897 to 62,973 in 1907, an increase of 24,765
or 64.82%. If we add this net immigration to the non-Coptic Orthodox
population of 1897, combined with the expected increase at the
national rate, the total is as follows:

Non-Coptic Orthodox Population of 1897	53,381
Net Greek Immigration	24,765
Expected Increase in Orthodox Population	7,982
Total	86,128

This leaves an unexplained increase of 18,762 (104,890 minus
86,128) in the non-Coptic Orthodox population. Some of this probably
reflects the immigration of Orthodox Christians from the Levant.
Perhaps some Copts joined the Greek Orthodox church during this

decade.

The second major shift within the Christian population occurred within the Coptic community, which grew at almost exactly the national rate. The Orthodox Coptic population grew more slowly than the national average, taking immigration into account. The native Egyptian population increased at a rate of .014903 per year from 1897 to 1907.[9]

Had the Orthodox Coptic community grown at the national rate for the native population, it would have totalled 686,817 in 1907, or 19,781 more than observed. It is clear that most of the discrepancy is accounted for by the movement of Orthodox Copts to the Protestant Coptic and Catholic Coptic churches. At the rate for Egyptians, the Protestant Coptic population should have reached 14,501 in 1907 and the Catholic Coptic population should have reached 5,368 at that date. The discrepancies can be summarized in the following table.

		Expected	Observed	
Copts	Pop.'97	Pop.'07	Pop.'07	Difference
Orthodox	592,374	686,817	667,036	-19,781
Protestant	12,507	14,501	24,710	+10,209
Catholic	4,630	5,368	14,576	+ 9,208 [10]

Here the discrepancies are almost completely accounted for. Slightly less than twenty thousand Orthodox Copts apparently joined the Protestant Coptic or Catholic Coptic churches from 1897 to 1907. An explanation for this striking shift will be presented in the concluding chapter of this thesis.

Within the non-Coptic communities of Egypt, both the Protestant
and Catholic sects grew very little during the decade that ended in
1907. The census of 1897 indicates that there were 18,036 Egyptian
Catholics in Egypt that year and 4,630 Coptic Catholics. Therefore
13,406 Egyptians belonged to non-Coptic Catholic churches. There were
56,421 non-Coptic Catholics in Egypt, thus 43,015 were foreigners. If
the Egyptian community in non-Coptic Catholic churches expanded at the
annual rate for Egyptians, .014903, it would have numbered 15,543 in
1907. Yet only 57,744 total members of non-Coptic Catholic churches
are listed in 1907,despite heavy net immigration from the "Catholic"
countries of Europe into Egypt during the decade, as shown in the
following table.

The Foreign Population of Egypt from Selected
Countries, 1897-1907 [11]

	1897	1907	Increase
France	10,277	11,685	1,408
Italy	24,454	34,926	10,472
Spain	765	797	32
Total	35,496	47,408	11,912

Subtracting the expected Egyptians from the non-Coptic Catholic
churches of 1907, (57,744 - 15,543) the total foreign Catholic
community should have been approximately 42,201 in 1907. Yet three
Catholic countries of Europe, France, Italy, and Spain, theoretically

accounting for only 35,496 divided by 43,015 = 82.52% of the foreign Catholic community in 1897, numbered far more in 1907 than the entire population of the foreign Catholic community. This apparent contradiction leads one to think that a large proportion of the net immigration from Europe into Egypt was Jewish. This would fit nicely with the rising tide of anti-Semitism in Catholic Europe apparent in the Dreyfus affair at the end of the century. Moreover, Jews arriving in Egypt would find their position markedly improved; fleeing Christian anti-Semitism in Europe they would benefit from the legal privileges offered foreigners in Egypt by the Capitulations and the Mixed Courts.

The rapid growth of the Jewish community corroborates this observation. From 1897 to 1907 the Jewish population increased 53.41%. Had it grown at the annual rate for Egyptians, the Jewish community would have numbered 28,301 rather than 37,446 in 1907. The difference of 9,145 must be accounted for by this immigration, chiefly from the "Catholic" countries of Europe. The slow growth of the non-Coptic Protestant community reflects the lack of major immigration from the Protestant countries of Europe.

The geographical distribution of the various sects became slightly more accentuated during the decade that ended in 1907. Jews lived almost entirely within the governorates and provincial capitals. Christians were concentrated in the governorates and in Upper Egypt. In 1897 they formed only 7.51% of the total population, but constituted 12.0% of the populus of Upper Egypt and 13.63% of the

governorates. These percentages had increased to 7.88, 12.05 and
18.54 by 1907. Catholics were even more concentrated in the
governorates, accounting for .63% of the total population, but 5.13%
of the governorates in 1897. These increased to .65 and 5.27 by 1907.
As remarked by the editors of the 1907 census, Copts appear to have
been squeezed into a narrower band of sub-provinces or _markaz-s_ from
1897 to 1907, where they constituted over 25% of the population in
areas of Assyut, Girga and Minia.[12]

This final section on demography will outline changes in
population by province, concentrating on the differences in growth
rate during the first twenty-five years of the British occupation.
Following McCarthy's argument, we can probably assume that all
provinces were equally undercounted in 1882 except Daqahliya and
Girga. With these problems in mind, we can rank the provinces by rate
of increase in population for the period from 1882 to 1897. See
Appendix 3.

Because of changes in _mudiriyya_ and national boundaries, Aswan
should be eliminated from this ranking. We can conclude that growth
was relatively rapid in some provinces of both Upper and Lower Egypt.
Since there was no major influx of rural dwellers into the provincial
capitals or governorates form 1882 to 1897, an explanation for the
divergent growth rates must be sought elsewhere than purely in
demography. The growth rate is not correlated with the percentage of
foreigners or with the increase of the foreign population. Demography
indicates these shifts, but cannot explain them. The rankings for the

period from 1897 to 1907 are basically the same, as shown in Appendix 4.

Though the growth rates appear to fall after 1897 for most provinces because of the undercounting of 1882, the rank of most provinces changed little. Qena should be eliminated from this ranking because the 1882-1897 figures from McCarthy are not compatible with the census figures for 1897-1907. Following McCarthy's argument above, we can probably assume Daqahliya was undercounted less than the other provinces in 1882, thus giving it a lower ranking for 1882-1897 than it should have. Indeed, the ranking for 1897-1907 rose to seventh. Likewise Girga in thirteenth position moved up to eighth for the second period.

We can conclude that the rural population grew more rapidly than that of urban areas and Lower Egypt grew faster than Upper Egypt. Up to 1897 the foreign community grew somewhat faster than the total population and then increased at twice the national rate up to 1907. Egyptians were forced out of some desirable urban neighborhoods such as al-Muski in Cairo. The Muslim majority declined somewhat relative to other groups while the Chrisitan population increased significantly. The Protestant Coptic and Catholic Coptic sects grew at the expense of the orthodox Coptic community from 1897 to 1907. The non-Coptic orthodox population almost doubled during this period because of the influx of Greeks. Among the non-Coptic Christian communities of Egypt, Protestant and Catholic sects grew little from 1897 to 1907. The Jewish community grew, probably due to immigration

from Europe. The rural Coptic community was squeezed into a narrower
band of sub-provinces during this period. Finally, some provinces
grew much more rapidly than others. These differing growth rates will
be analyzed in a subsequent chatper.

Where there was demographic growth, especially relative to other
groups within Egyptian society, we might be tempted to read in shifts
in wealth or power. As we shall see in succeeding chapters, this was
true in some cases. The decline in the Muslim majority population
relative to Christians reflected a major structural transformation as
did the shift away from orthodox Coptic communities to non-orthodox
Coptic sects. The rapid influx of foreigners after 1897 again
mirrorred real shifts in national wealth and power. On the other
hand, though the rural sector grew in population it suffered a real
decline in economic power and political influence relative to the
urban sector. Thus demographic data enable us to focus our attention
on three axes of structural shifts in Egypt under Cromer but cannot
explain them: urban versus rural, foreign versus Egyptian and Muslim
versus non-Muslim.

Footnotes: Chapter One

1.   Population of Egypt in 1882, 1897 and 1907

Province	'82 Pop.	'97 Pop.	'07 Pop.
Cairo	374,838	570,062	654,476
Alexandria	231,396	319,776	370,009
Beheira	415,234	636,825	792,242
Daqahliya	586,033	780,480	912,428
Gharbiya	936,276	1,297,656	1,484,814
Minufiya	646,013	864,206	971,016
Qalubiya	271,391	371,602	434,575
Sharqiya	464,655	748,972	886,346
Beni-Suef	219,573	312,115	372,412
Fayoum	228,709	371,006	441,583
Giza	283,083	401,234	460,080
Minya	314,818	550,971	663,144
Asyut	562,137	782,720	907,435
Girga	521,413	688,011	797,940
Qena	386,249	626,869	685,653
Aswan Mark.	13,962	67,440	75,532
Edfu Mark.	57,441	86,218	101,694
Esna Mark.	51,475	84,588	95,196

The figures for Qena were corrected by McCarthy. Justin McCarthy, "Nineteenth Century Egyptian Population," Middle East Studies, v.12, n.3, October, 1976, p.27.

2. Egypte. Ministere de l'Interieur. Direction du Recensement, _Recensement Général de l'Egypte_, Cairo Imprimerie nationale de Boulaq, 1884, v.1,p.ix. This census will be cited hereafter as _Census of 1882_.

3. Egypt. Ministere des Finances. Department du Cadastre. _Recensement générale de l'Egypte ler juin 1897 , ler moharrem 1315_. Vol. 1, p.xii. Cairo, 1898. Egypt. Ministry of Finances. Census Department. _The Census of Egypt Taken in 1907_. Cairo, 1909. These will be cited as hereafter as _Census of 1897_ and _Census of 1907_.

4. The figures for 1897 that are used in the preceding two tables do not correspond exactly to those of the 1897 census because of adjustments to reflect certain boundary changes. The updated figures for 1897 are drawn from the census of 1907 and are reproduced in the _Statistical Yearbook of Egypt for 1909_, Cairo, 1910, p.22.

5. Afaf Lutfi al-Sayyid, _Egypt and Cromer_, p.81.

6. _Census of 1882_, v.1, p.ix.

7. _Census of 1907_, p.28.

8. Jacob Landau "The Jews in Nineteenth Century Egypt, Some Socio-Economic Aspects", in P.M. Holt, ed., _Political and Social Change in Modern Egypt_, p.207-8.

9. The native population in 1897 numbered 9,717,228 - 112,574 =

9,604,654. The second figure refers to the foreign community. The
native population in 1907 numbered 11,287,359 - the foreign community
of 151,414 = 11,135,945. The tenth root of 11,135,945 divided by
9,604,654, minus one equals .014903.

10. As usual, all observed populations are derived from the
respective censuses, while expected populations were calculated by the
author.

11. The figures in the first two columns are taken from the
censuses of 1897 and 1907; the increases were calculated by the
author.

12. <u>Census</u> <u>of</u> <u>1907</u>, pp.119,124.

Chapter Two

Foreign Trade and Commerce in Egypt, 1882-1907

The structure of Egytian foreign trade has been thoroughly
investigated for the period from 1882 to 1907. Moreover, the analysis
of a nation's foreign trade reflects the productivity of that country
and its role within the international division of labor, but cannot
proceed very far in explaining either. For these reasons only a brief
summary of Egyptian foreign trade will be given, and it is intended to
raise questions rather than to answer them.

Egypt's foreign trade and commerce indicate the accelerating
growth of a dual economy under Cromer: a modern and productive export
sector managed by non-Egyptians and clients of the royal family and a
domianted sector of small scale production and commerce run by Muslim
Egyptians.

During the first twenty-five years of the British occupation,
Egypt shipped increasingly large quantities of cotton abroad and
cotton accounted for an almost continually rising share of export
earnings, rising from 57.10% for the period from 1885 to 1889 to
71.41% for the period from 1904 to 1907. See Appendix 5.

The domination of Egyptian export by cotton becomes even more
obvious if we list cotton seed separately from "other goods," as in
the table directly below. Combined with cotton, cotton seed accounted
for 67.70% of the value of all exports in the first period and had

risen to 78.29% in the final period. Excluding the export of specie,
these percentages jump to 80.94 and 89.70. We shall take up later the
question of why Egypt was increasingly transformed into a large cotton
farm.

Period	Cotton Seed L.E.	Export %	Cotton & Seed as % Export	Cotton & Seed as % Exports minus Specie
1884-5				
1888-9	1,395,669	10.60	67.70	80.94
1889-90				
1893-94	1,662,408	11.00	67.66	79.18
1894-95				
1898-99	1,350,530	8.83	72.91	83.92
1899-1900				
1903-04	1,813,360	8.81	77.94	87.49
1904-05				
1906-07	1,925,416	6.88	78.29	89.70 [1]

Egypt's other traditional exports, wheat, barley, maize, rice and
beans, shrank or shifted entirely into import items while cigarettes
remained the only manufactured product of any importance among
exports. The value of cigarette exports increased from about 1895
until 1900, then began to decline slightly.[2] Egypt's imports also

increased greatly from 1882 to 1907, in fact, slightly more so than

exports, and the difference was made up by an inflow of private

capital, especially from 1903 to 1907.[3]

As stated by Owen,

> Very generally, Egyptian imports can be divided into four
> groups: manufactured goods; industrial raw materials, such as
> coal, petrol, and building wood; raw materials for working up in
> Egypt, such as tobacco; and food. Egyptian trade was thus not a
> simple question of exporting primary products in return for
> manufactured goods; much of its export earnings were spent on a
> variety of raw materials which it needed for its own development
> or to feed its own population.[4]

Egypt became a net importer of cereals in about 1900. The

imports of short-staple cotton, once grown in Egypt and then replaced

by long-staple cotton for export, increased rapidly after 1900 and was

consumed in both small workshops and modern textile mills until the

latter were closed by pressure from British authorities. This

question will be treated in detail in the following chapter on

manufacturing. In general, investment goods imported into Egypt

averaged about 2.6 million Egyptian pounds between 1885 and 1889,

while consumption goods stood at 5.3 million pounds in this period.

Then investment goods increased 300% over the next twenty years, while

imports of consumption goods expanded only half as quickly.[5] On the

basis of the available evidence marshalled by Owen, it appears that

the terms of trade moved against Egypt in the 1890's and then became

more favorable after 1900.[6]

Because of Egypt's large debt held abroad following the Law of

Liquidation of 1880, debt payments played an important role in Egypt's
international position throughout the period under study. From 1884
to 1907, Egypt's public debt stood at an average 102,326,000 L.E.
Payments abroad on this debt aveaged 4,860,000 L.E. per year, as can
be seen in Appendix 6.

Though the public debt shrank after 1897, private debt grew very
rapidly beginning in 1903, though even in the period from 1903 to
1907, public debt outweighted private debt by a factor of 3.76.
Egypt's massive cotton exports served largely to pay tribute to the
Ottomans, service the staggering interest on the debt and even reduce
the debt, though much of the reduction was also due to the sale of
former royal lands. Although the ratio of interest payments on debt
to exports remained mostly unchanged from 1884 to 1907 - an average of
35.19% of exports went to pay creditors - the ratio of exports to debt
held abroad increased dramatically, moving from about 1/9 to almost
1/5.

Great Britain continued to be Egypt's main trading partner
throughout the first twenty-five years of the British occupation,
though its share of both imports and exports shrank slightly over the
period, as is illustrated in the following table.

Country	Percentage of Value of Imports into Egypt		of Exports from Egypt	
	1885-6	1907	1885-9	1907
Great Britain	38.5	33.4	62.8	54.4
Turkey	17.6	10.3	3.5	1.2
France	10.9	12.5	8.16	7.29
Aust-Hungary	10.9	7.8	6.5	4.7
Germany	.5	5.5	.13	8.0
Russia	5.2	2.6	9.1	5.7
Italy	3.4	5.3	6.8	2.8
British Possessions [7]	5.5	5.1	.15	.44

Competition among the European nations was stiff, and the rise of Germany as a great economic and industrial power is reflected in the rapidly rising percentage of its trade with Egypt. British political and military domination of Egypt, therefore, was not automaticially translated into commercial advantage during the British occupation, even after the entente with France in 1904.

The commerce of Egypt was shaped by a basic investment decision made in the first years of the occupation by the British rulers of Egypt who decided to launch a program of irrigation to increase the country's agricultural output. The result was an expanding commercial sector devoted especially to the financing, production, transportation and export of cotton. This export sector of the Egyptian economy was organized on the most modern European lines except in the fields and

was backed by the legal authority of the Mixed Courts. The large
scale commerce of Egypt was dominated by Europeans, Levantines,
minority group Egyptians given foreign status under the Capitulations
and a few Muslim Egyptians who were members of the royal family or
high government officials. Our examination of commerce will treat
export houses, banks and mortgage companies, land investment companies
and a final category that can only be described as miscellaneous.

Ninety-six percent of Egypt's export trade and almost ninety
percent of its imports passed through the port of Alexandria during
the first decades of the occupation, principally because it offered
the only port capable of accomodating large ships.[8] Four foreign
houses exported almost half of the cotton crop in the season of 1910
and 1911.[9] Of these three were English and the largest and oldest was
Italian.[10] All were companies or subsidiaries of companies based
outside Egypt and only one was listed in the Statistical Yearbook
for Egypt for 1909 as among the 295 joint stock companies operating
in Egypt.

Credit for cotton and other agricultural production was provided
by banks and financial houses, the largest of which were limited
liability companies whose board members had foreign status, belonged
to the royal family, or were high government officials. Of the
thirteen banking, financial and mortgage companies in the list of
firms operating in Egypt in 1901 drawn up by the British Chamber of
Commerce of Egypt, the only companies including board members native
to Egypt were the National Bank of Egypt, the New Egyptian Company and

the Credit Foncier Egyptien. The only Egyptians were members of the royal family like prince Hussein Pacha Kamil, ministers such as Boghos Pasha Nubar or Egyptian Jews with foreign status like Raphael Suares.[11]

The growth of banks and mortgage companies is summarized in the following the following table.

Paid-Up Value of Shares and Depentures of Companies

in Egypt   (L.E. 1000)

	1883	1892	1897	1902	1907
Mortgage Companies	3,826	4,547	5,968	10,525	36,680
Annual Growth Rate [12]	-	.0193683	.0558951	.1201564	.283647

Mortgage companies grew slowly up to 1897, then expanded with great speed thorugh 1907 until the crash of that year. The holdings of banks shrank rapidly in the first five years of the occupation, remained stable up to 1897, and then expanded rapidly, reflecting the rise in land values that began slowly in the 1890's and then picked up speed after 1898 as agricultural products drew higher prices.[13] The following table lists the value of the cotton exports that dominated Egyptian commerce.

Value of Cotton Export from Egypt

Season	L.E. 1000	Annual Growth from Previous Season
1883-4	8,101	----
1892-3	9,597	.0190076
1897-8	10,451	.0171956
1902-3	17,721	.111389
1907-1908	23,159	.0549851 [13]

The capital invested in Egyptian mortgage companies closely
mirrored the value of cotton exports from the season of 1883-4 to that
of 1907-8; the correlation is .9091459.[14] The capital invested in
banks and financial companies followed the rise in cotton values less
closely, with a correlation of .8713604. This is probably a result of
the skepticism of bankers and the fact that the occupation took on
permanent status only in the 1890's. Moreover, the unit value of
cotton exports began a prolonged rise only with the season of
1899-1900, after a long descent from 1880-81, as can be seen in
Appendix 7.

The Credit Foncier Egyptien dominated the mortgage industry
throughout the first decades of the occupation. The company was
founded in 1880 by a group of French financiers and Cairo and
Alexandria bankers.[15] The president was Raphael Suares, an Egyptian
Jew who was probably, along with Ernest Cassel, one of the two most
powerful financiers in Egypt before World War I. From its foundation
to 1900, its capital was set at 3,086 million Egyptian pounds, of

which one quarter was paid up in 1900.[16] On October 31, 1900, its

debentures stood at 4.766 million Egyptian pounds. Thus paid up

capital and debentures totalled 5.538 million Egyptian pounds in 1900

and 6.857 in 1902, or 65.14% of the total paid up capital and

debentures of all mortgage companies operating in Egypt in that

year.[17] in 1902, 5,543,000 L.E. out of a total of 5,968,000 L.E.

of capital and debentures of mortgage companies operating in Egypt, or

92,88%, was held outside the country.[18] Most of the capital and

debentures of the Credit Foncier Egyptien not held abroad was in the

hands of foreign residents of Egypt.

In 1889, the Honorary President of the Credit Foncier Egytien was

Blum Pasha, the Under Srecretary of the MInistry of Foreign Affairs,

the Vice-President was Raphael Suares, and the Director was Carlo

Beyerle. Mahmud Bey Riaz, the son of the Prime Minister Riaz Pasha,

and two Egyptian Jews also sat on the board of directors, as well as

eight Europeans.

In 1900 the local board of directors grouped together the summit

of the financial elite of Egypt; none was of Egyptian nationality and

none was Muslim. It is pertinent to recall here that Muslims

constituted 92.23% of the national population in 1897. The local

board was as follows in 1900.

R. Suares   President
C. Beyerle   Vice-President and Managing Director
Board Members: F. Suares, S. Rolo, M.Cattaui, J.Barois,

C.Adda, M.Bretschneider, W.Pelizaeus, E.Cattaui, A.
Pestel, Baron de Lassus de St.-Genies, and Sir E. Palmer

The last mentioned board member was also the Financial Advisor to
the Egyptian Government, who made all important financial decisions
for the state, though under the watchful eye of Lord Cromer. Such a
dual role for the chief financial officer of the nation might
constitute ethical problems in normal circumstances, but Egypt during
the British occupation presented a different pattern.

The Credit Foncier Egyptien, like all other large mortgage
companies, offered loans chiefly to large landowners. From 1880
through 1907, the Credit Foncier made most of its loans in amounts
over 500 L.E., far beyond the reach or need of the average peasant.
In 1907 land was held by 1,267,403 "owners" and of those, 1,117,925 or
88.21% were native Egyptians who owned an average of 1.18 feddans.[19]

In the annual report for 1906 Lord Cromer observed that the
figures for rural land distribution were not accurate because a
landowner would be counted once for each village where he owned
property. Moreover, the process of land registration tended to
inflate the increase in the number of small proprietors between 1896
and 1906 for two reasons.

> In the first place, the Survey has recorded separately a
> certain number of small proprietors who were originally shown in
> the land-tax register as being in partnership with others, and,
> in the second place, the reduction of registration dues has,
> without doubt, enabled many small proprietors to register their
> deeds of purchase.[20]

On the other hand, the smallest landowners usually held property
in only one village. Thus the 1.18 feddan figure is most likely
rather accurate. The land owned by these smallholders was probably
worth considerably less than 60-80 L.E., the price of good land in the
delta.[21] Even at the high price of 60 L.E., typical peasant could
not hope to mortgage all of his land for more than 60% of its
value.[22] This amount, though far below the average Credit Foncier
loan, was still larger than the small sums borrowed annually by the
peasants from the village money lenders, usually about ten Egyptian
pounds,[23] or less. The Credit Foncier did not cater to the vast
majority of Egypt's land owners, as is obvious in Appendix 8.

Although the size of loan made frequently was between 500 and
1000 L.E., the average sum loaned over the entire period was 3,278
L.E. Only .05% of the total was in amounts under 100 L.E. and only
3.23% in amounts under 500 L.E.

To provide credit for small holding farmers, the Egyptian
government began to loan its funds on an experimental basis and in
1898 transferred the task to a private bank given official
encouragement, The National Bank of Egypt. This bank was formed with
an initial capital of 1,500,000 L.E. in 150,000 shares, fully paid
up. The bank possessed the right of note issue guaranteed by a
deposit of half the amount in gold and half in securities approved by
the Egyptian government. The governor of the bank was none other than
the British financial advisor, Sir Elwin Palmer, and he was assisted
by two government commissioners from the Ministry of Finances. the

local board, plus important local bankers from the Armenian, Jewish and Italian financial communities of Cairo and Alexandria.[24]

> By 1902 the operations of the National Bank had grown so
> large that a separate Agricultural Bank was created with L.E.
> 2,500,000 capitalization. Its loans were divided into two
> categories: those for less than L.E. 20, secured by the
> borrower's note of hand; and those not exceeding L.E. 500,
> secured by a first mortgage on land. Loans were to be negotiated
> by government agents whose payment was to be 1 percent of the
> interest and principal being collected by tax collecting agents
> at the same time that taxes were collected.[25]

Most of the loans made by the bank up through 1907 were between twenty and fifty pounds so some owners of small and middle sized farms benefited from the government sponsored program while most small holders remained at the mercy of village money lenders who charged from twenty-five to over forty percent per year.[26] Egyptian landowners resented the high profits made by foreign commercial agents and money lenders. In May of 1888, Mr. Garstin wrote in his agricultural report to Lord Cromer, Evelyn Baring at the time,

> As an Egyptian land-owner said to me the other day, 'There
> are two worms in our country far worse than the cotton worm: one
> is the Syrian and the other is the Greek, and these two worms are
> gradually eating up our country.' [27]

In 1904 the Bank made the following loans:

Size of Loan (L.E.)	Number of Loans
.5 - 1	1,060
1 - 5	6,776
5 - 20	9,662
20 - 50	96,234
50 - 100	13,207
100 - 150	3,934
150 - 500	9,334
Total	140,207 [28]

In 1907 the Agricultural Bank made 22,594 small loans against promissory notes that averaged 9.61 L.E. each. At the same time 1,309,127 L.E. was loaned against mortgages to 24,487 borrowers for an average loan of 53.46 L.E.[29]

Although the Agricultural Bank made a credible attempt to free smallholders from debt to usurious money lenders, the loans of 1907 show that was merely a modest beginning. Only 22,594 smallholders received loans from the bank that year when the Cadastral Survey Office estimated that there were 1,117,925 Egyptian "owners" of under five feddans in Egypt. Moreover, after the crisis of 1907 the Egyptian economy began to falter, credit was reduced and borrowers began to defalt on their loans.[30]

It is clear that Europeans dominated the large financial

institutions that furinished capital for agricultural production in
Egypt in the first decades of the occupation. In his <u>Who's Who</u> of
Egypt for 1889, Yusuf Assaf listed eleven insurance companies in
Cairo. All were headed by Europeans. Apparently life insurance had
not spread beyond the European sector of the populus at that date.[31]
The primary and secondary sources suggest that Levantine, Greek and
Jewish middle men and money changers continued to dominate the field
of small loans to the peasants despite the attempts of the
Agricultural Bank. Some Muslim merchants like Mustafa Manzalawi acted
as intermediaries between cotton cultivators and foreign exporters in
Alexandria.[32] On the other hand, census figures lead one to believe
that European control over small day-to-day transactions was far from
complete. The further we proceed down the scale of Egypt's financial
institutions, the more Egyptians and the more Muslims we find.

In 1897, there were 49,492 men working as employees in
"commerce,industry,etc." The financial professions were broken down as
follows.

Professions of Men in Egypt in 1897

Profession	Egyptians	Foreigners	Total
Courtier			
(Stock Broker)	2,666	557	3,223
Magasinier			
(Warehousing)	623	108	731
Négociant,			
Banquier	31,059	5,261	36,320
Total[33]	34,348	5,926	40,274

Thus foreigners accounted for 14.71% of the financial professions in 1897, despite their much smaller percentage in the population as a whole, 1.34%. Unfortunately the census of 1907 does not break down the professions by religion or by nationality. One is left with the impression that small scale finance, though heavily dependent on European sources of capital, was left in the hands of many Egyptian and Muslim clerks and money lenders who dealt directly with urban artisans and the peasants in the countryside.

Although the mortgage industry was dominated by European run joint stock companies, the amount of land mortgaged to all companies and individuals was approximately nine percent of the total value of Egyptian land. Alfred Eid estimated the total borrowings upon rural land at 38,997,720 L.E. in 1907, broken down as follows.

Mortgages of Rural Land by Creditor

	L.E.	%
Banks and Mortgage Companies	20,600,000	52.82
Insurance Companies and European Capitalists	2,200,000	5.64
Private Loans	5,445,000	13.96
Sums Due on Long Term Purchases	10,752,720	27.57
Total	38,997,720	100.00

Thus private parties held only 13.96% of the mortgages in Egypt in 1907. Most long term purchases were handled by the Credit Foncier Egyptien, the largest mortgage company, so the first and final categories could be lumped together. If we accept Eid's estimation of the total theoretical value of Egyptian rural land, 415.8 million L.E., then only about nine percent of the land was mortgaged in 1907.[34]

The six irrigation and agricultural companies listed by the British Chamber of Commerce of Egypt in 1901 had a total paid up capital of 1,528,505 L.E. One was managed by local proteges, two by Englishmen and three by mixed boards of Europeans and proteges. Until 1902, most capital and debts of agricultural and urban land companies operating in Egypt were held locally. Then the majority came to be held abroad and next shifted back to local ownership, as is clear in the list located in Appendix 9.

The flow of foreign capital into companies in this group began to
swell after the increase in land prices and cotton at about the turn
of the century, while local capital grew only after 1902.

The Egyptian Land Investment Company, founded in 1905 with an
initial capital of 25,000 L.E., offers a good example of the pattern
of management within a locally owned land company. The table below
lists the name, nationality and capital of the eight owners at the
time of incorporation.

Ownership of the Egyptian Land Investment Company, S.A.

Name	Nationality	Paid-up Capital
Abraham Bartan Pasha	Russian protege	20,250 (L.E.)
Isma'il Pasha Yeken	Egyptian	1,250
Kalil Pasha Kayat	Portugese protege	750
Cmdr. Augusto Luzzato	Austro-Hungarian	625
Tigrane Gamsaragan	Ottoman	1,250
Michel Rezian Bey	Ottoman	250
Yranthe Agathon	Ottoman	250
Emmanuel Struss	Austro-Hungarian	375
Total [35]		25,000

The only Egyptian board members of companies in this category
were foreign proteges, high government officials or relations of the
royal family, as was the case with Isma'il Pasha Yeken in the above
list. Armenian Egyptians on the board of the Egyptian Land Investment
Company, who made up half of the total membership, held foreign

nationality as did the Egyptian Copt, Khalil Pasha Khayat.

The greatest coup scored by foreign capital in the first quarter
century of the occupation was the purchase for resale of approximately
300,000 feddans belong to the Daira Saniyya, former royal land. With
an initial investment of only 600,000 L.E., the stockholders of the
Daira Saniyya Company,Ltd.,gained control of approximately four
percent of Egypt's cultivable land which was then resold for a
comfortable profit. The shares offered at 5 L.E. in 1898 went as
high as 8 L.E. in 1900. The board members were all Europeans and
mostly English, with the exception of the ubiquitous Raphael Suares
and his coreligionist, Rolo Bey.[36]

As in the category of banks and mortgage companies, land
companies were managed largely by Europeans and minority group
Egyptians, and most of the capital and debts were held abroad or by
foreign residents of Egypt. Although these land companies had paid-up
capital and debts of over nineteen million Egyptian pounds in 1907,
this sum represented a very small percentage of the hypothetical value
of Egyptian rural land, 361,000,000 L.E., and urban property,
54,823,000 L.E., in the estimation of Alfred Eid.[37]

Taking into consideration Samir Radwan's[38] approximation for
the net fixed capital stock in Egyptian agriculture in the same year,
23,056,000 L.E., it becomes clear that joint stock companies
controlled the largest single blocks of capital invested in Egyptian

land, but that these constituted a small percentage of the whole.

Joint stock companies were used by European investors to limit the risk of holding urban commercial property in Cairo and Alexandria. Of seventeen such companies listed by the British Chamber of Commerce of Egypt in 1901, nine were managed by Europeans, one by local proteges, one by a British dominated board that included Prince Hussein Kamil Pasha as chairman and Boghos Nubar Pasha as member, another by Europeans that included Prince Said Halim as President and five by boards of Europeans and local combined. Though Europeans and elite Egyptians controlled these companies, they held a small percentage of Egyptian real property.[39]

The European dominated joint stock companies that invested in urban property controlled only a small share of the market. For a full discussion, see Appendix 10. Most mortgages were held by individuals. The distribution of urban property will be treated in chapter four.

Of the thirteen transport companies listed in 1901, one was directed by local proteges, three by Englishmen, one by Frenchmen, one by a combination of proteges and Europeans, five by combinations of Muslim Egyptians and Europeans and two by Europeans other than Englishmen or Frenchmen. The total paid up capital of these companies amounted to 2,566,802 L.E. Crouchley lists the total paid up capital and debentures of transport and canal companies at 2,218,000 L.E. in

1897 and at 3,970,000 L.E. in 1902. As elsewhere, this growth was a
response to rising agricultural prices and greater productivity in the
rural sector.[40] In 1897, 88.73% of the paid up capital and
debentures of these companies was foreign held. In 1902 this had
increased to 91.81%.[41]

One of the great coups of foreign capital under Cromer, dwarfed
only by the Daira Saniyya sale, was the purchase of the Egyptian
government's fleet of steamships, docks and buildings by the Khedival
Mail Steamship and Graving Dock Company,Ltd., in 1898. The board
members were entirely English. With Cromer's and Earnest Cassel's
obvious approval, the company acquired the government shipping
interests for less than 494,000 L.E.[42]

The parallel Tawfiqiyya or Nile Navigation and Commercial
Company, though it included two Muslims on the board in 1901, was
headed by Alexander Biancardi. Of the ten employees listed in 1889,
one was European, five were Muslim and four were Copts.[43]

Unlike the field of urban commercial property, these few joint
stock companies managed almost all transportation in Egypt above the
level of animal transport and motor cars, and outside the government.
Though the Societe Anonyme des Chemins de Fer de la Basse Egypte owned
109 kilometers of track and the Fayoum Light Railways, Ltd. 168
kilometers in 1902, most railroad mileage was owned and managed by the
Egyptian government.[44]

Small scale transport, employing a large proportion of those

involved in the field, rested mostly in the hands of individuals or
partnerships. See Appendix 11. Large scale shipping, agricultural
railways, tramways and omnibuses were mostly controlled by European
dominated joint stock companies, while the Egyptian government managed
the national railways, roads, telegraph and canal systems, all of
which were greatly developed from 1882 to 1907 as part of the effort
to provide an adequate infrastructure for cotton export.[45]

The Cairo, Alexandria and Tanta water companies were managed by
mixed boards Europeans and Egyptians in 1901, when they had a total of
of 795,887 L.E. capital, fully paid up. Twelve miscellaneous
companies were listed by the British Chamber of Commerce of Egypt as
having 1,284,575 L.E. capital, and of these, five had English boards
of directors, two were managed by other Europeans, three by mixed
boards of proteges and Europeans and two by Europeans with one Muslim
Egyptian member, Prince Hussein Kamil.[46]

Egypt's foreign trade and internal commerce were increasingly
dominated by cotton during the first twenty-five years of the British
occupation. The trend toward a dual economy accelerated during this
period. Large scale commerce and the lucrative export sector were
dominated by foreigners, proteges, minority sect Egyptians and clients
of the royal family. Small scale commerce remained in the hands of
Muslim Egyptians. Egypt exported cotton, imported manufactured goods
from Europe and exported a few locally manufactured goods abroad such
as cigarettes. By 1900 the country became a net importer of foods.
Though Great Britain remained Egypt's major trading partner, its

overall share of imports and exports declined. Government
institutions made some progress supplying credit to middle level
agricultural producers after 1898 although small farmers remained at
the mercy of local money lenders who charged usurious rates.

Footnotes: Chapter Two

1. <u>Statistical</u> <u>Yearbook</u> <u>of</u> <u>1909</u>, p.100.

2. Owen, <u>Cotton</u>, p.308.

3. This summary of trade is heavily drawn from Owen, <u>Cotton</u>,
pp.307-311.

4. <u>Ibid</u>., p.309.

5. <u>Ibid</u>., p.310.

6. <u>Ibid</u>., p.311.

7. Imports in the above table signify goods only, excluding
tobacco products. Exports include tobacco products. <u>Statistical</u>
<u>Yearbook</u> <u>for</u> <u>1909</u>, pp.92-93.

8. A.E. Crouchley, <u>The</u> <u>Economic</u> <u>Development</u> <u>of</u> <u>Modern</u>
<u>Egypt</u>, London, Longmans, Green and Co., 1938, p.173.

9. Owen, <u>Cotton</u>, p.221.

10. <u>Ibid</u> ,p.386.

11. <u>List</u> <u>of</u> <u>Financial</u>, <u>Manufacturing</u>, <u>Transport</u> <u>and</u> <u>Other</u>
<u>Companies</u> <u>Established</u> <u>in</u> <u>Egypt</u>, <u>Prepared</u> <u>by</u> <u>the</u> <u>British</u> <u>Chamber</u> <u>of</u>
<u>Commerce</u> <u>of</u> <u>Egypt</u>, Alexandria, June, 1901, pp. 1-8.

12. Crouchley, <u>Investment</u>, pp.147,155. The annual growth
rates were calculated by the author. For example, the growth rate for

the period 1883-1892 is stated as .0193683.

13. Owen, <u>Cotton</u>, pp.107, 241-242. The rates of increase were
calculated by the author.

14. A correlation is a statistical method for evaluating the
relationship between two sets of figures. For example, if a man with
two children earns five thousand dollars per year, a second with two
children earns ten thousand and a third with three children earns
fifteen thousand, the correlation between the number of children and
annual income for these men is 1.000. If the two sets of figures
increase together, the correlation will be positive. If one increases
while the other decreases, the correlation will be negative. All
correlatioins fall into the range between plus one and minus one.

15. Owen, <u>Cotton</u>, p.277.

16. <u>List of Financial</u>..., p.7.

17. Credit Foncier Egyptien, <u>Rapports du Conseil
d'Adminstration et des Censeurs- Résolutions de l'Assemblée</u>,
<u>Exercise 1902</u>, Cairo, Typ. Bochme et Anderer, 1903, p.19; <u>Ibid.</u>,
1901, p. 17; Crouchley, <u>Investment</u>, p.147.

18. <u>Ibid.</u>, p.44.

19. <u>Statistical Yearbook for 1909</u>, p.266.

20. Great Britian, House of Commons Sessional Papers, HCSP,
<u>Annual Report on Egypt and the Sudan for 1906</u>, Cd. 1999, cxii,

p.979.

21.   Owen, Cotton, p.242.

22.   Alfred Eid, La Fortune Immobilière de l'Egypte et sa
Dette Hypothécaire, Paris, Felix Alcan, 1907, p.131. 1.18 x .6 x 60
= 42.48 L.E.

23.   Lord Cromer, Annual Report for 1906, p.980.

24.   List of ..., pp.4-5.

25.   Robert Tignor, Modernization, p.237. This is drawn
largely from Crouchley, Investment, pp.54-55.

26.   Hamid, Nizam, p.145; Cromer, Report of 1906, pp.979-980.

27.   Mr. Garstin to Mr. Baring, Inclosure in No.54, PRO,FO,
407/73, 14 May, 1888.

28.   Cromer's Annual Report for 1904, cited in De Chamberet, Le
Fellah Egyptien, p.65.

29.   Walid Kazziha, Thesis, p.49; citing Gorst to Grey, PRO,FO,
368/284, 20 March, 1909. The averages were calculated by the author.
30.   PRO,FO, 368/284/18359. I am indebted to both Walid Kazziha and
Roger Owen for this citation.

31.   Yusuf As af, Dalil Misr li-'amay 1889 1890 (Guide to
Cairo, 1889-1890), (Cairo, 1889), pp.164-165.

32. Owen, Cotton, pp.132-134.

33. Census of 1897, v.1, p.xxiii.

34. Eid, La Fortune Immobilière, pp,129,19; 39/415.8 = 9.38%.

35. Egypt, Journal Officiel, 21 January 1905.

36. This sale will be treated in detail in a later section concerning the distribution of rural land.

37. Eid, La Fortune Immobilière, pp.19,53.

38. Radwan, Capital Formation in Egyptian Industry and Agriculture 1882-1967, Oxford, 1974, pp.63,251. Here the figure given by Radwan is in 1960 prices and is 144,100,000 L.E. This was multiplied by his price deflator for 1907, 16/100 to give 23,056,000 L.E.

39. List of Financial..., pp.9-20.

40. Crouchley, Investment, p.44; List of Financial ..., pp.30-58.

41. Crouchley, Investment, p.44.

42. List of Financial..., p.37.

43. Asaf, Dalil, p.170.

44. Owen, Cotton, p.215.

45. This discussion excludes figures on the capital and
debentures of the Suez Canal company.

46. <u>List</u> <u>of</u> <u>Financial</u>..., pp.45-53.

Chapter Three

Manufacturing in Egypt

Egyptian industry in the first decades of the British occupation
was marked by many of the traits of a colonial or dual economy. Most
modern production was oriented toward the agricultural export sector,
construction and luxury goods for the urban rich. Elsewhere the level
of technology was archaic, depending largely on human or animal energy
sources. The evolution of a fully modernized manufacturing sector was
blocked during the first decades of the occupation. The impediments
of the guild system were replaced by fluid wage labor in the towns,
but though traditional manufacturing declined, the emergence of fully
developed modern industry was blocked by Britain. This chapter will
offer a brief description of Egyptian manufacturing organized along
the following lines: output, ownership and management, employment and
relations of production.

The small modern sector of Egyptian industry continued under the
British along the lines established under the Khedive Isma'il. The
concentration upon the processing of agricultural products,
fabrication of construction materials and production for affluent
urban consumers is obvious in a list of manufacturing companies in
Egypt in 1901 and 1908 provided in Appendix 12.

All thirty-six companies listed in Appendix 12 fall into three
general categories with one exception. These are (1) the processing
of agricultural products, chiefly cotton, sugar and tobacco , (2) the

construction of building materials, and (3) the production of luxury goods for the urban rich. The exception is the Egyptian Swiss Iron Works, which was founded sometime between 1901 and 1908, but which probably played a minor role in Egyptian industry because it is not mentioned in the files of the Companies Registration Office of London and it appears nowhere in the secondary literature that has come to my attention.

Though it is true that "Egyptian trade was thus not a simple question of exporting primary products in return for manufactured goods"[1], a close analysis of the structure of Egyptian manufacturing in the first decades of the occupation shows that no local heavy industry developed. The government joined with private industry to create a modern export sector, with massive investment in infrastructure, especially irrigation, transport, and in the primary processing of agricultural products, for example cotton ginning and the refining of sugar. However, there were no foward or backward linkages to sectors of the economy other than the production of beverages, cigarettes and houses for the urban rich. The fact that many of the cigarettes rolled in Egypt were exported has no impact on this discussion.[2]

Egypt did not develop even a minimal industrial sector to help the balance of payments through import substitution of agricultural machinery. Those who would argue that Egypt's industrial development was impeded by poor "factor endowment" ,i.e. few natural resources, must have a hard time explaining the presence of massive industry in

Japan in the 1980's because of Japan's limited natural resources.
Arguments based solely on "factor endowment" are clearly fallacious.
Others who argue that Egypt formed no native entrepreneurs must
therefore explain why foreign investors who set up large textile mills
at the turn of the century were forced to close down operations.
Purely economic explanations are not sufficient. We must put off
further analysis of the lack of development in Egyptian industry until
politics can be examined in following chapters.

Though the modern sector of Egyptian industry was restricted to
the narrow areas outlined above, the capital, debts and output in
manufacturing grew rapidly during the first twenty-five years of the
occupation, as can be observed in the table below.[3]

Year	Capital and Debts (L.E.)	Annual Growth Rate (from former period)	Absolute Change(L.E)
1883	474,000	-	-
1892	1,223,000	.111063	749,000
1897	3,540,000	.2368452	2,317,000
1902	5,731,000	.1011473	2,191,000
1907	11,691,000	.1532521	5,960,000
1911	12,810,000	.0231148	1,119,000

From a small base, Egyptian industry expanded rapidly during the
first fourteen years of the occupation, then somewhat less quickly up
to the turn of the century when rising agricultural prices and rapid
expansion of the foreign population began a boom that lasted until the

crash of 1907. Overall, industry expanded much more rapidly than the
national population or even the foreign population. This expansion
was somewhat speculative and ran ahead of the rise in export earnings.
The correlation is -.5560201. If export earnings are averaged from
1895 to 1899 to provide a more representative figure for 1897, the
correlation between export earnings and industrial investment is still
only -.4487125. These two negative correlations between export
earnings and investment show in any case that there was not a close
relationship between the two. This investment increased in response
to hopes of future profits, not as a steady response to Egypt's main
source of profit, agricultural exports. The shifts in export values
are outlined in the following table.[4]

Year	Value of Exports	Rate of Increase	Absolute Change
1883	12,553,313	-	-
1892	13,505,796	.0122636	952,483
Average of 1895-			
1899	13,308,097	-.0029449	-197,699
1897	12,552,639	-.014531	-953,157
1902	18,046,939	.07531	5,494,300
1907	28,013,185	.0919224	9,966,246

Net fixed capital stock in Egyptian industry also grew rapidly,
rising from 89 million L.E. in 1899 to 143 million in 1907 in
constant 1960 prices. Appendix 13 shows the growth of capital
formation and capital stock during this period of expansion.

The average annual growth rate was 6.23% between 1899 and 1907,
and 6.68% between 1902 and 1907. The annual rate of increase of net
fixed capital was .117904 between 1902 and 1907, somewhat behind the
rate of increase of paid-up capital and debts in Egyptian industrial
corporations, .1532521, but ahead of the rise in the value of exports,
.0919224. Thus the rise in capital and debts was rather speculative,
as became clear after the crash of 1907, when 2,251,000 L.E. of
capital from abroad in Egyptian industrial, commercial and mining
companies was liquidated.[5]

Large scale industry in Egypt was owned and managed largely by
Europeans. In a country dominated by cotton production, cotton
ginning was naturally a lucrative field for investment in industry.
At the start of the twentieth century there were approximately 105
ginning factories in Egypt with 3,521 gins. Two-thirds of the gins
were owned by Europeans and the rest by Egyptians or Syrians. The two
largest cotton pressing companies, founded in 1889 and 1892 by
European cotton exporters, were joined by a third large German concern
in 1906. These three companies re-presssed all cotton shipped out of
Alexandria using the most modern machinery. Roger Owen's calcultions
suggest that cotton ginners earned up to 376,650 L.E. in return for
their services, out of a total value for exported cotton of 27,532,000
L.E. in the 1911-1912 season,[6] or 1.37% of the total. These five
ginning or export companies held 14.88% of the total capital and debts
of all industrial companies listed by the British Chamber of Commerce

as operating in Egypt in 1901.[7]

Aside from cotton ginning and pressing, eighteen other industrial companies were listed in 1901. Of these, one was managed by local proteges, six by English entrepreneurs, one by French industrialists, five by proteges and Europeans and four by other Europeans. Management could not be determined for one company. No Muslim Egyptians sat on the boards of directors of these eighteen industrial companies.[8]

The great majority of shares and debts of Egypt's industrial mining and commercial companies was held abroad throughout the first twenty years of the occupation, as is obvious in the following table.[9]

Capital and Debts of Industrial, Mining and Commercial

Companies   (L.E. 1000)

Year	Held Abroad	%	Held Locally	%	Total
1883	669	100	0	0	669
1892	915	71.99	356	28.01	1,271
1897	2,974	83.00	609	17.00	3,583
1902	5,418	83.11	1,101	16.89	6,519
1907	7,170	50.86	6,928	49.14	14,098

During the speculative boom that lasted from 1900 to 1907, local capital flowed into Egyptian companies outside the traditional area of

investment, namely real estate. Figures on industrial capital alone
are available for 1909, when residents of Egypt held 29,948,000 L.E.
out of a total of 101,031,000 L.E., or 29.64%.[10] It should not be
forgotten that most "residents of Egypt" investing in local industry
were foreigners or minority group Egyptians who benefited from foreign
status under the Capitulations.

The largest block of capital in Egyptian industry was invested in
sugar manufacturing. The twenty-three manufacturing companies listed
by the British Chamber of Commerce of Egypt in 1901 had total capital
of 3,580,676 L.E. Of these, the two sugar companies, La Société
Générale des Sucreries et de la Raffinerie d'Egypte and the Egyptian
Sugar and Land Company, Ltd., had combined capital and debts of
1,834,437 L.E., or 51,23% of the total.[11] During the first decades
of the occupation, ownership of much of the country's sugar refining
capacity was transferred from the Egyptian government to French and
English investors.

Egypt's modern sugar industry was the creation of Khedive
Isma'il. In 1876 this industry was mostly transferred to the Daira
Saniyya Administration, a mixed administration controlled by the
board's English and French directors. Others of the Khedive's sugar
refineries were dismantled. In the early years of the occupation
output rose and unit costs declined, which attracted investors to set
up a number of new plants. The largest companies were French,
controlled by the sugar magnate Leon Say, and these combined in 1897
to form the Société Générale des Sucreries. Five local companies, of

which two were set up by Copts and two by Muslim Egyptians, did not
survive the decline in sugar prices that began in 1901. In the
following year the Daira Saniyya Administration sold all of Isma'il's
survivng sugar factories and railways to the Sucreries. This
enterprise experienced extreme difficulties in 1905 caused by
mis-management and over capacity, as rising cotton prices brought
about a decline in acreage under sugar. By closing outmoded plants
the company survived a second crisis in 1908 and was making healthy
profits by the start of World War I.[12]

Though Europeans controlled the modern sector of Egyptian
industry where large blocks of capital were invested, employment
figures demonstrate that most manufacturing activity was small scale
and used traditional methods. This pre-modern sector of the economy
depended on human and animal sources of energy, was labor rather than
capital intensive and was mostly owned and run by native Egyptians.
Appendix 14 breaks down activity in this sector by occcupation for
1897 and 1907.

The census figures enabled us to approximate male activity in
manufacturing at 231,732 in 1897 and 276,342 in 1907. This represents
7.29% of the active male population in 1897, totalling 3,176,788 and
7.99% of the active male population in 1907, which reached 3,458,494
that year. Activity in manufacturing for men thus grew at an annual
rate of .0177617, somewhat more rapidly than the total growth rate for
the male population, .0149903.[13]

The percentage engaged in manufacturing in 1897 is probably

somewhat inflated, as the category "persons without occupation" was

only added in the census of 1907, when it included 905,206 men. We

can draw the general conclusions that manufacturing, in both the

modern and traditional sectors, employed a small percentage of

Egyptian men and that it grew little between 1897 and 1907, scarcely

faster that the male population. For purpose of comparison, men

employed in manufacturing in the United Kingdom in 1891 constituted

34.58% of the total active male population.[14]

Woodworking and construction employed the largest group of men in

both 1897 and 1907, moving from 34.46% to 40.29% of those in

manufacturing. The annual rate of increase was quite high, .0308414.

This reflects the sharp rise in consumption by bureaucrats, foreign

investors and cotton growers and landlords. The last two groups moved

increasingly to the larger cities. Much of the wealth earned by

cotton exports came into the hands of the urban elite and flowed in

two basic directions: (1) it was used to bid up the price of

agricultural land and (2) it was invested in urban residences,

especially in Cairo and Alexandria. The sharp increase in woodworking

and construction employment was mirrorred by the growth in building

permits and buildings subject to tax, as illustrated in the table

below.[15]

Indices of Urban Construction in Cairo and Alexandria

Year	Cairo	Bldg.Permits	Rate	Year	Alex.Bldgs.	Rate
1895		1,703		1902	16,941	
1907		3,017	.0488098	1907	20,730	.0411949

The building trades did not constitute a popular occupation among the property holding elite of Cairo in 1894. Of the 2,414 property owners in Cairo that year who paid a minimum of four L.E. on real estate, or were in prominent government positions, occupation could be determined for 802. The average tax paid by the entire group was 20.32 L.E.; the median or middle value was 7.2 L.E. and the mode, the most common tax, was 5.4 L.E. Of the 802 whose occupation could be determined, only 21 or 2.62% were in the building or woodworking professions. Their taxes were about average, eleven falling below and ten above the mean as shown in the table below ranking tax by quartiles.[16]

Real Estate Tax Paid by Those in Woodworking
   and Construction in Cairo, 1894

Annual Tax(L.E.)	Total Cases	Woodworking & Construction
0-4.6	604	3
4.7-7.2	603	8
7.3-14.9	604	5
15.0-top	603	5

Of these twenty-one, fifteen were Muslim, five Christian and one
either Muslim or Christian. Muslims thus were under-represented,
constituting at most 76% of this group, but more than eighty-four
percent of the population of Cairo in 1897.

The textile industry employed the second largest block of men in
both 1897 and 1907. This sector expanded considerably faster than
either the national population or manufacturing in general, increasing
at an annual rate of .0266628 and moving from 31.41% of manufacturing
to 34.26%. Though two modern textile firms were established in 1899,
both failed due to government opposition and the great majority of
activity in textile manufacture was traditional.

The Egyptian Cotton Mills Company was founded with a capital of
160,000 L.E. and was managed by an entirely English board.[17] It
built a factory in Cairo that began operations with 20,000 spindles in
1901. By 1907 it was forced to close, partly because of
undercapitalization but basically because Lord Cromer ordered it to
pay a tariff of eight percent ad valorem as if its goods were imported
from abroad. The Anglo-Egyptian Spinning and Weaving Company,Ltd.
was formed with a capital of 125,000 L.E. and registered in
Liverpool. The board of directors included most of the directors of
the Credit Foncier Egyptien and prominent members of the royal family.
It was headed by Sir Elwin Palmer.[18]

Apparently Palmer interceded with his superior, Lord Cromer, when
the company was unable to pay an installment of the excise duty of

eight percent due in 1908. Cromer agreed to remove the duty for five years but the company was barely able to survive the aftermath of the crisis of 1907. Its factory in Alexandria contained 22,000 spindles and 400 looms and employed 700 workers.[19] Thus the two concerns probably employed less than 1,500 workers combined, or less than two percent of those engaged in textile manufacturing in 1907. Due to government interference, the modernized sector of Egyptian textile manufacturing remained very small.

In both 1897 and 1907, Egypt exported raw cotton and imported cotton, wool, linen, silk and jute thread from Europe. Omitting re-exports, thread valued at 383,000 L.E. was imported in 1897 and 587,000 L.E. worth was imported ten years later. Then the *thread*, supplemented by some of local production, was worked into fabric all over Egypt using the most primitive methods. Over 66 of Egypt's 94 <u>markaz</u>-s employed more than 100 weavers in 1907. The largest weaving centers are listed in Appendix 15. Since the fourteen largest <u>markaz</u>-s or governorates employed only 23,377 out of Egypt's total of 42,365 weavers or 55.17%, it is clear that the industry was widely dispersed.[20]

Most weavers bought their thread from abroad or through Cairo importers. The looms were primitive affairs of local manufacture, powered by foot pedal. Wages varied between four and ten piasters per day, though some silk workers received higher wages. In some of the larger cities, local entrepreneurs employed as many as thirty weavers under one roof, but in smaller centers like Abou Kerkas in Minya, for example four businessmen employed most of the town's 400 weavers who worked at home, in a putting out system where each isolated weaver was aided by a child.[21]

It appears as if the difficulties in purchasing thread gave entrepreneurs control of the industry except in areas like Qalyubiya where local sheep furnished the wool from which thread was spun in the village itself. There individual weavers could control the supply and act independently.[22] Atyya Chenuda adds that linen weaving was also organized as was the weaving of wool.

> Pour le tissage de la laine et du lin, l'instruction technique se fait par transmission de père en fils, car ces deux matières sont en usage dans les villages plutot qu'ailleurs, de plus, il n'y a pas d'atelier ou l'on apprenne le tissage. Pour la soie et le coton, l'instruction se fait le plus souvent par apprentissage dans les ateliers: les enfants y entrent d'abord comme garcons de tisserands; des qu'ils commencent à se rendre vraiment utiles on leur donne de petites récompenses; leur apprentissage ne finit qu'au bout de six ans au moins et ils deviennent alors tisserands et travaillent chacun pour soi.[23]

Despite the closing phrase "each for himself", this picture of the training of weavers seems to indicate that some wool and linen weavers worked on a family basis, while cotton and silk weavers were sometimes gathered together into workshops and received wages or were paid for piece work. Others were employed in a putting-out system.

In Assyut, boys began to learn weaving at the age of eight and slowly became piece work weavers who earned six piasters per day.

> The usual course is for boys to enter the shops (20 in Assyut with about 70 looms) at the age of eight, when they work in preparation of the treads, and have to learn what they can. There is no system of apprenticeship, nor does the trade run in families in general. The employees are are men or boys, Egyptians,and no foreigners are to be found employed in the workshops. They are on piece-work and their average earnings are about 6 piaster per day, which they receive weekly. The boys get from 3 to 6 piasters per week.[24]

We can draw the general conclusion that textile manufacturing in
the early twentierh century was no longer regulated by guilds, but
took on several forms of wage labor: family shops, piece-work or
salaried production in worshops, or the putting-out system.

As in textiles and the building trades, almost all manufacturing
activity in Egypt up through 1907 was small scale artisanal
production. This was true for all categories from iron and metals
through glass making in the list in Appendix 14, with the exception of
some food industries and sugar refining mentioned in the list of
European industrial concerns above. This sector of manufacturing can
be variously described as artisanal, petit-bourgeois, or following
Rene Maunier, "la petite industrie".

> Le caractere peut-être fondamental de l'économie égyptienne
> est la prédominance presque absolue de ces formes d'industrie que
> l'économie politique appelle l'industrie domestique et le metier,
> et le language courant réunit sous le nom de petite
> industrie.[25]

In his preface to a description of apprenticeship in Egypt in
1912, Maunier went on to deplore the gradual disappearance of
craftsmanship in local artisanal production, with the notable
exceptions of textiles and pottery. Comparing the employment figures
for 1897 and 1907, textile manufacturing expanded only slightly,
accounting for 31.41% of manufacturing in 1897 and 34.26% a decade
later. Wood and construction increased from 35.46% to 40.29%, leather
and shoes remained almost unchanged at 7.14% and 6.82%, jewelry was
stable at 2.16% and 2.12%, while artisanal production in iron and

other metals shrank from 16.06% to 10.87%. Production of terra-cotta products grew, though the job categories grouped together in the two censuses are not perfectly comparable. It is clear that Maunier's remarks about the exceptional nature of production in textiles and pottery are significant. Unlike most other groups, employment there did not decline or merely remain stable. Even more strikingly, in the production of iron and other metal articles, employment declined precipitously, although the importation of machinery and parts grew from a valuation of 232,549 L.E. per year in the period 1885-1889, to 357,898 L.E. for 1895-1899 and stood at 1,069,537 L.E. in 1907.[26] While employment in this sector declined 19.27%, imports rose 298.84% from 1897 to 1907. Egypt's national textile manufacturing capacity was obviously being subordinated to the needs of European firms to obtain lucrative export markets for their goods.

Though employment in manufacturing as a percentage of male employment rose somewhat from 7.29% to 7.99%, there were important shifts within the manufacturing sector away from goods produced in Europe by modern capital intensive methods such as metals and machinery, and towards bulk artisanal products like pottery or construction materials where high transport costs limited the dangers of competition from outside Egypt. In other words, capital allocation and employment in Egyptian industry were restructured less by indigenous economic factors than by international and political constraints, especially tariff schedules.

Moving from the structure of employment in industry to the

internal organization of artisanal production, the evidence is less

clear. Rene Maunier summarizes the consensus of scholarship to date

that the vestiges of guild organization disappeared between 1882 and

1907 and were supplanted by small scale wage labor.

> Ces corporation ont cessé depuis 1882 d'avoir aucun rôle
> économique; un décret de 1890, en venant affirmer le principle du
> libre exercice de l'indusrie, leur a porté le dernier coup; elles
> ne sont plus que des confréries religieuses.[27]

Maunier's observation is confirmed by legal evidence gathered by

Gabriel Baer who showed that nine important guilds were officially

recognized for the last time between 1870 and 1896, and that between

1889 and 1903 there were either decrees by the Egyptian government

abolishing these guilds or official regulations treating the

occupation without reference to the guild.[28]

A close examination of the occupations of urban property holders

in Cairo in 1894 confirms the gradual disappearance of the guilds at a

time when references abound to small scale wage labor.[29]

Of the 2,414 owners who paid four pounds or more of tax on urban

property in Cairo or were members of the political elite in 1894,

occupation could be determined for 802. Of these, ten were the heads

of the following guilds: grain merchants (2), coimmission agents (2),

butchers (2), tailors (1), cooks (1), Luxor merchants (1), and

coppersmiths (1). They owned between one and 23 units of taxable

property and they paid annual taxes ranging from 1.7 L.E. to 91.2

L.E. Taking tax as an index of wealth, they can be ranked as follows:

Guild	Tax	Property Units	Tax/Unit
Commission Agent	1.7	1	1.7
commission Agent	4.6	3	1.53
Grain Merchants	5.3	10	5.3
Grain Merchants	6.8	7	.83
Luxor Merchants	7.7	3	2.57
Butchers	11.7	10	1.17
Cooks	17.6	9	1.96
Butchers	22.9	23	1.00
Tailors	32.6	22	1.48
Coppersmiths	91.2	5	18.24

Of the ten, six were deceased or retired according to the tax records which were lax in recording such traits. The wealthiest man ,Mustafa al-Maligi, was a member of the General Assembly and though he was listed as president of the Guild of Coppersmiths in 1889,[30] he probably spent the majority of this time managing his properties and participating in politics. The most valuable piece of property in which he had an interest was shared by Hassan Pasha Hilmi. When Mustafa al-Maligi was made Bey in 1887, he was mentioned as "a notable of Cairo" without reference to his position in the Coppersmiths' Guild. Out of a total of 802 property owners in Cairo with known occupations in 1894, only three were basically identified as active heads of guilds.

We can conclude that guilds were no longer an important form of artisanal organization by that time. Even though six of the ten guild heads were retired or dead in 1894, the information about these ten men can be used to compare this occupational grouping with all other Cairo property owners if one bears in mind that the comparison will probably reflect the state of affairs in the one or two decades preceding 1894.

The guild heads possessed the title of Bey in about the same proportion as the entire body of urban property holders in 1894, twenty per cent versus 16.86% for all others. None was called Effendi or Pasha, titles given respectively to 18.0% land 16.0% of the larger group. Two were called mu'allim out of a total of twenty-two in the entire population of 2,414 property owners. This is only natural inasmuch as mu'allim can mean master craftsman as distinguished from subyan or 'usta, i.e. apprentice in the guild structure. All ten guild heads were Muslim though Muslims constituted only 73.49% of the total population of tax payers. All were Egyptian nationals, whereas Egyptians made up only 88.28% of the larger group. All were male, while women made up 15.16% of all taxpayers. The ten guild heads fit into the job classification schema of the Census of 1907 as compared with all owners as follows:

	Guild Heads	%	1894 Property Owners	%
Manufacturing	4	40	155	19.33
Trade	5	50	63	7.86
Domestics, Hotels	1	10	6	.75
Other	0	0	518	72.07

Guild heads clearly over represented their job categories within the general population of urban property owners. They tended to live in the more popular quarters of Cairo as compared with other property owners, as can be seen in Appendix 16.

One guild head lived in the fashionable quarter of 'Abdin where property owners were most concentrated. The head of a guild also lived in each of the popular quarters of Bulaq and Misr al-Qadima where property owners were very under represented. Guild heads were concentrated in the older popular quarter of Sayeda where property owners were somewhat over represented, surprisingly enough. Al-Darb al-Ah mar also drew more than its share of guild heads where property owners were evenly distributed with the general male population.

The general pattern seems to be that guild heads lived near where they worked, in the areas where their trades were traditionally concentrated. For example, the coopersmiths had their shops in Bayn al-Qasrayn, now called Coppersmiths' Street, or in Khan al-Khalili.[31] Indeed, Mustafa Bey al-Maligi lived in al-Darb al-Ahmar though his political role might have drawn him closer to 'Abdin. The two grain merchants lived in the port areas of Misr al-Qadima and Bulaq and both commission agents lived in the commercial area of Sayeda Zaynab.

The ten heads of guilds did not fit into any one level if wealth is judged by real estate, though 40% were gathered in the top quartile.

Urban Tax	Prop. Holders		Known Occup.		Guild Heads	
L.E.	N	%	N	%	N	%
0-4.6	603	25.0	191	23.82	2	20.0
4.7-7.2	604	25.0	202	25.19	2	20.0
7.3-14.9	603	25.0	198	24.69	2	20.0
15.0-top	604	25.0	211	26.31	4	40.0
Total	2414	100.0	802	100.00	10	100.0

The guild heads in the top quartile were a cook, a butcher, a tailor and a coppersmith. In his list of disappearing guilds, Gabriel Baer stated that the butchers' guild of Cairo was last officially recognized in 1887 but that by 1893 the occupation was regulated without reference to the guild.[32] The butcher in question was one of the three active men in the list of ten, which would seem to support the observation that the butchers' guild was one of the last to disappear. Though guild heads fall into the upper range of property holders in Cairo in 1894, it is perhaps more significant that there were only ten within the entire urban elite and only three active. Only seven guilds were thus represented in the elite of 1894. The many other guilds must have lost power long before that date. Of the 2,414 elite property holders, only twenty-two were described as master craftsmen, mu'allim. The guilds had almost disappeared from Cairo in 1894.

We can conclude that manufacturing in Egypt during the first

decades of the British occupation was marked by many of the traits of
a colonial or dual economy. Most modern production was oriented
toward the agricultural export sector, construction and luxury goods
for the urban rich. Elsewhere the level of technology was archaic,
depending largely on human or animal energy sources. Large blocks of
capital in industry were almost completely owned and manged by
foreigners, proteges, a few high government officials and members of
the royal family. In relation to the entire work force, employment in
manufacturing grew little from 1882 to 1907. Attempts to modernize
the textile industry were obstructed by the British governors of
Egypt. It appears that the last vestiges of the guild system of
artisanal production disappeared by 1907 and were replaced by modern
wage labor, at least in the larger towns where information is
available.

Footnotes: Chapter Three

1. Owen, _Cotton_, p.309.

2. This classical dependency argument is well stated by Charles Issawi in "Egypt since 1800: a study in lop-sided development, _Journal_ _of_ _Economic_ _History_, March, 1961.

3. Crouchley, _Investment_, p.105; the rates and absolute changes were calculated by the author.

4. Direction general des douanes egyptiennes, _Le_ _Commerce_ _extérieur_ _de_ _l'Egypte_ _pendant_ _l'année_ _1909_, Alexandria, 1910, pp.vii,lvii. The rates of increase and absolute changes were calculated by the author.

5. Crouchley, _Investment_, p.66.

6. Owen, _Cotton_, pp.219-221,229.

7. 532,740/3,580,676 L.E. = 14.88%. _List_ _of_ _Financial_..., pp.18-21, 26-36.

8. _List_ _of_ _Financial_..., pp.26-36.

9. Crounchley, _Investment_, pp.148.155.

10. _Ibid._, p.152.

11. _Ibid._, pp.26-36.

12. Owen, _Cotton_, pp.295-297; Crouchley, _Economic_

Development, pp.167-168.

13. The tenth root of 276,342/231,732 -1 = .0177617; the tenth root of the total male population for 1897, 4,883,601 minus one equals .0149903.

14. B. R. Mitchell, European Historical Statistics, 1750-1970, Columbia University Press, New York, 1975,p.163. Men working in manufacturing in 1891 totalled 3,460,000 out of 10,007,000 active men.

15. Owen, "Cairo Building Industry", p.338,344. The rate above refers to the annual rate of increase calculated from the preceding date.

16. The distribution of urban property and the tax records will be treated in more detail below.

17. List of Financial..., p.29.

18. List of Financial..., p.27.

19. Owen, Cotton, pp.222-224.

20. Sidney H. Wells, "Note preliminaire sur l'industrie du tissage en Egypte", Egypte Contemporaine, November, 1910, No.4, p.578-581.

21. Ibid., January, 1911, No.5, p.72.

22. Ibid., No.5, p.54.

23. Attya Chenouda, "Notes sur l'industrie du tissage," <u>Egypte Contemporaine</u>, January, 1910, No.1, p.189.

24. W.V. Shearer, "Report on the Weaving Industry in Assiout," <u>Egypte Comtemporaine</u>, v.1, Jan., 1910, p.185.

25. Rene Maunier, "L'Apprentissage dans la petite industrie en Egypte", <u>Egypte Contemporaine</u>, v.11, May, 1912, p.341.

26. <u>Statistical Yearbook for 1909</u>, p.96.

27. Maunier, <u>Op.Cit.</u>, p.344.

28. <u>Egyptian Guilds in Modern Times</u>, Jerusalem, 1964, pp.144-149.

29. Cf. especially the articles by Sidney Wells on weaving cited above.

30. Asaf, <u>Dalil</u>, p.151.

31. Andre Raymond, <u>Artisans et Commerçants au Caire au XVIIIè Siècle</u>, Damascus, 1973, v.1, p.359.

32. Baer, <u>Egyptian Guilds</u>, P.148.

Chapter Four

The Distribution of Urban Property and the Social Structure of
Cairo

This chapter will present a detailed analysis of property holding
in Cairo from 1882 to 1907 that indicates a massive flow of wealth and
power in the city away from Muslim Egyptians and to the benefit of
foreigners, proteges, and minority sect Egyptians. The only Muslims
whose relative status did not decline were members of the royal family
and top government officials.

As detailed in Appendix 17 all the information in the property
tax registers was recorded for (1) all owners of property who were to
pay four pounds or more and (2) all members of the political elite,
who can be described briefly here as all government employees and
representatives who held the title of Bey, Second Class, or above.
The entire sample yielded a list of 2,414 urban property holders.
This elite thus constituted 13.51% of the total estimated property
holders in 1894. Of these 2,414, 85 were included merely by virtue of
their political role and were assessed less than 3.5 L.E. tax. There
were 1,997 who were assessed over 3.5 L.E. The remaining 332 property
owners were included for a varity of reasons: (1) possession of a
title by the property owner, that of Bey Second Class or above,
accorded as recognition of activity outside the government or merely
as a sign of membership in a prestigious family or (2) election or
appointment to national, _markaz_, or provincial assemblies or (3) a

close blood relationship to some prominent member of the economic or political elites. For a discussion of aggregate statistics on the distribution of urban property in Cairo, see Appendix 18.

The 2,414 members of the urban elite paid an average tax of 19.02 L.E. The total tax levied on this group amounted to 45,907.896 L.E., or 56.37% of the total property tax assessed in Cairo in 1894! It is interesting to recall that they constitued only 13.51% of the estimated property holders of that year. Even among this elite, property was distributed very unevenly, as can be seen in the histogram below.

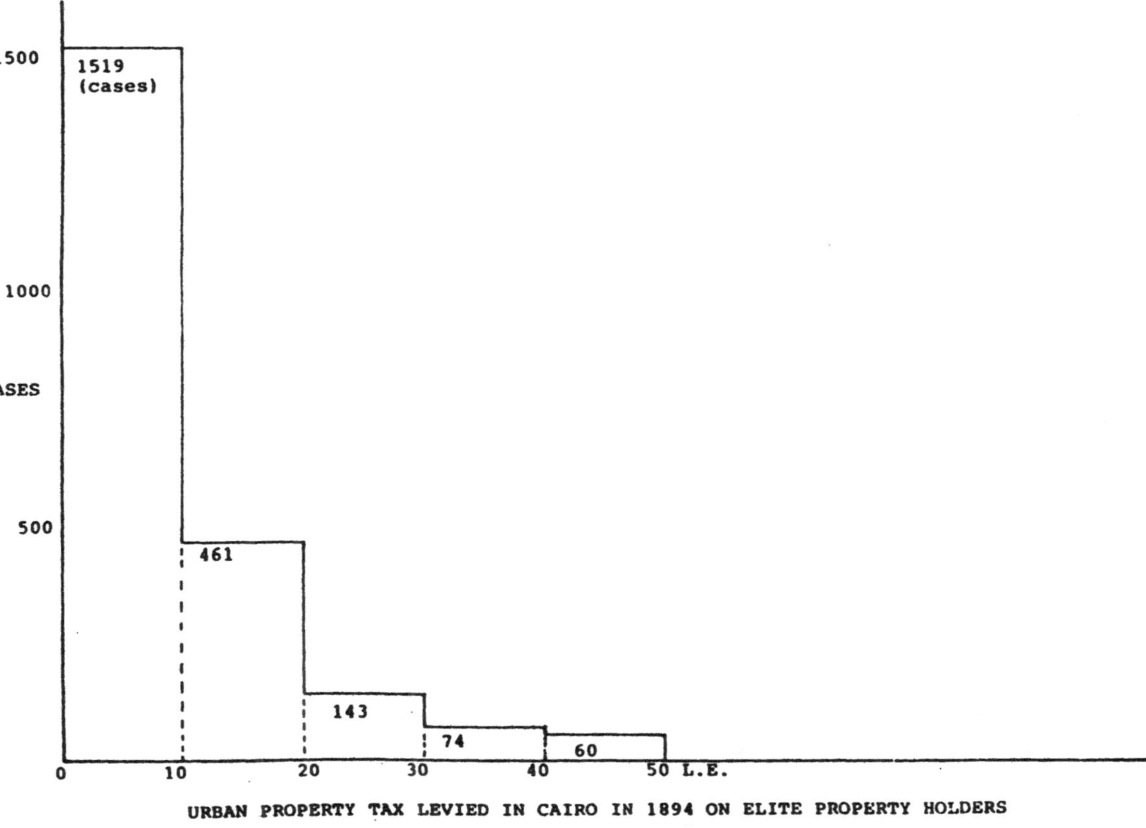

URBAN PROPERTY TAX LEVIED IN CAIRO IN 1894 ON ELITE PROPERTY HOLDERS
(157 cases above 50 L.E. were excluded.)

With most of the values bunched at the lower end of the scale, it
is clear that the distribution is extremely uneven. Most Cairenes
held little taxable property and a few owned a great deal. In
statistical terms, the curve is far from normal. Because the total
2,414 property owners contain several distinct groups, it is best to
factor out the main sub-groups and analyze their histograms so as to
understand the composition of the urban elite. A varible which was
coded as property type allows us to separate the urban elite at the
beginning of the occupation from the elite members alive in 1894.
These two groups will be called the old and new urban elites.
Property type was broken down into (1) heirs (2) waqf (3) business (4)
personal property shared with co-proprietors (5) heirs and
co-proprietors (6) heirs and waqf (7) personal property and waqf and
(8) personal property.[1]

Selecting owners by the above categories numbered one, two, five
and six, produced a list of 732 property owners most of whom were
alive at the beginning of the occupation but who were dead by 1894.
There were a few exceptional cases such as the waqf of Sultan Inal,
but most such waqfs were not taxed and were administered by the
Department of Awqaf (Waqf-s). This group of 732 property owners may
be labeled as the old urban elite.

The histogram below, labeled H1, shows the taxes paid by the
first 631 property owners, who paid between .4 and 29.9 L.E. The
remaining 101 paid thirty pounds or more and are not shown because
their holdings were so extreme that it would have made the shape of

the curve difficult to see. First of all, the curve is not normal but
is skewed to the right, again indicating that the richest owners held
far more than their share of property. Looking more closely, we can
see that the urban elite of Cairo was composed of at least two
distinct groups. This is so because the curve has two peaks, which
indicates that it contains two distinct sub-groups, each of which has
a curve that looks more like a normal curve than the composite curve.
The first peak seems to occur at 1.5 L.E. and the second at about six
pounds. It also appears as if the more normal part of the second
curve might end at about twenty L.E. If this pattern is not merely a
coincidence, but a more permanent characteristic of late nineteenth
century Egyptian society, it should recur for property owners alive in
1894. The new urban elite of 1894 grouped together 1,682 property
owners whose holdings are pictured in the histogram below labeled H2.

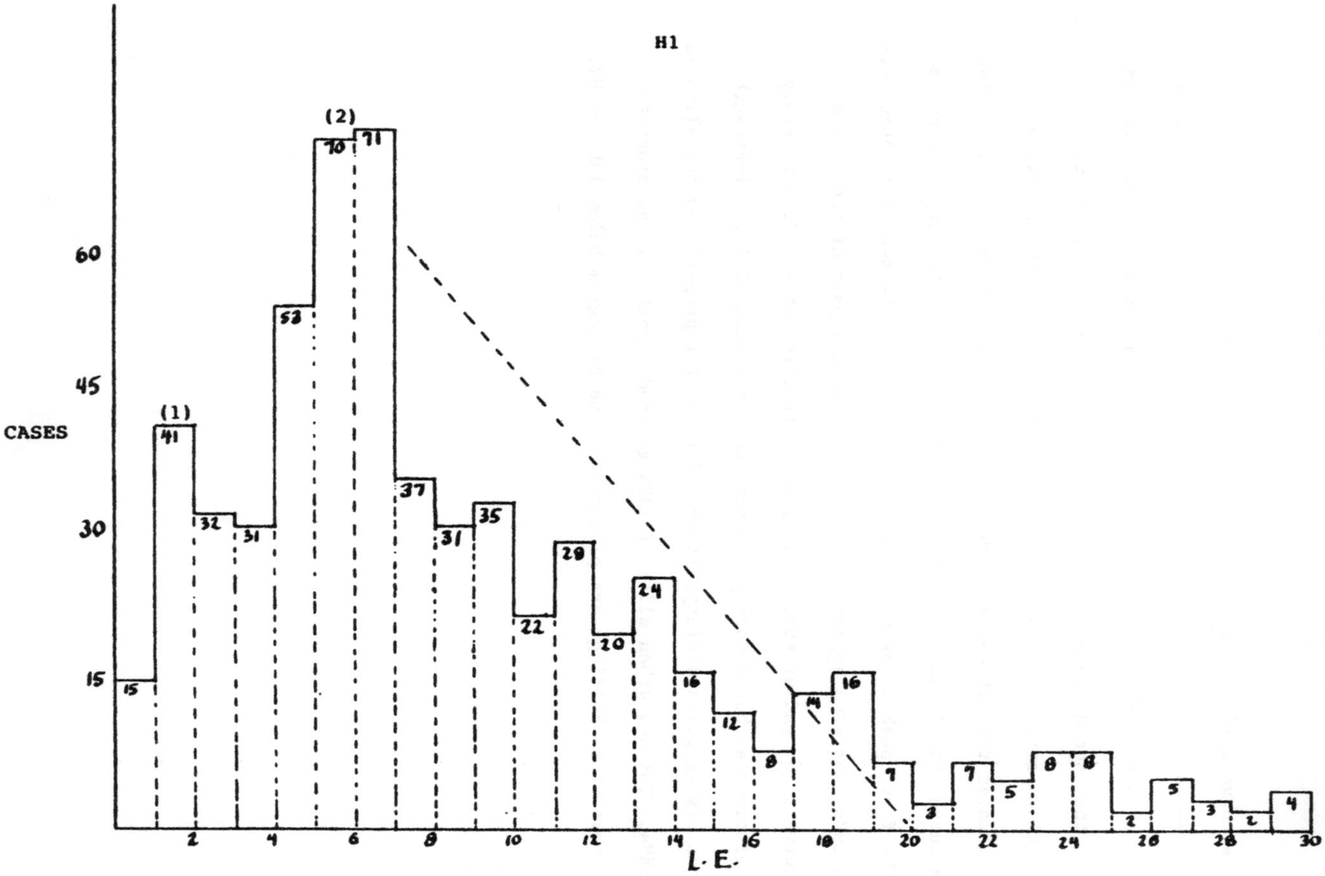

CAIRO URBAN PROPERTY TAXES OF OWNERS, HEIRS OR WAQF, IN 1894

92

H2

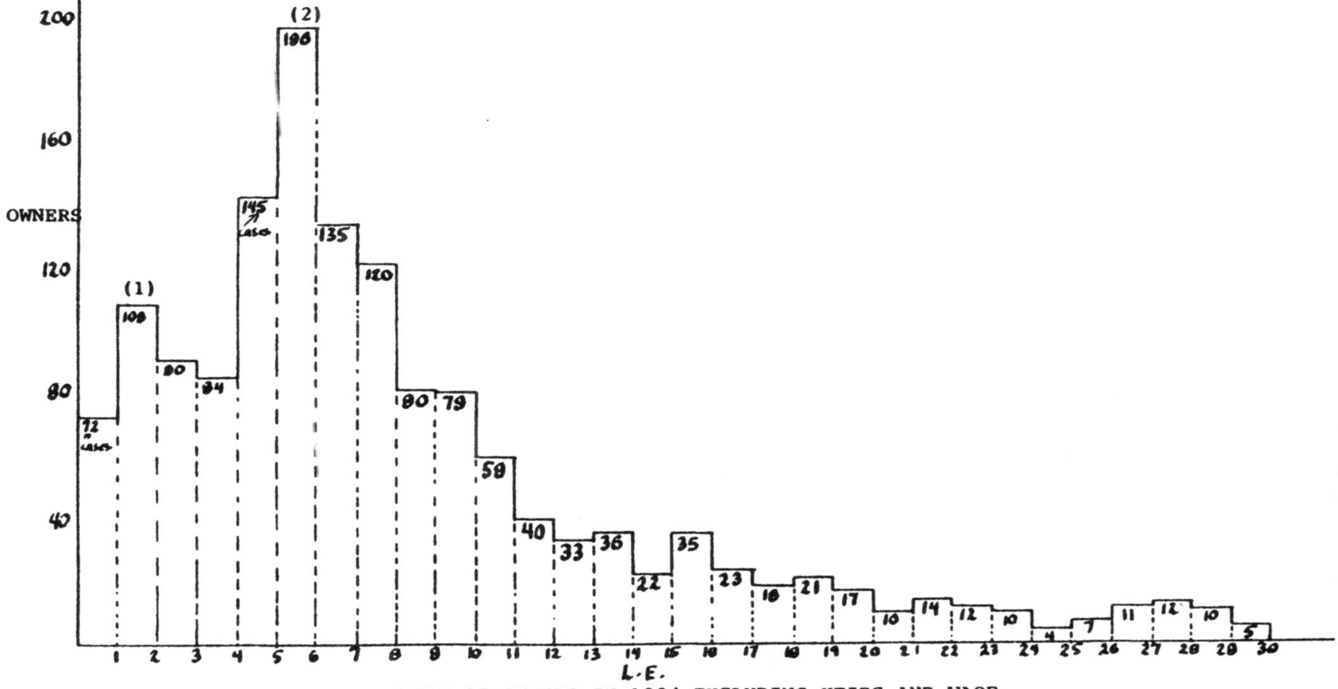

CAIRO URBAN PROPERTY TAX OF OWNERS IN 1894 EXCLUDING HEIRS AND WAQF

The resemblance to the previous histogram is striking. Again, there are peaks at about 1.5 and six L.E. It appears as if there was a tightly grouped social class of small urban property holders, paying up to about 3.5 L.E. per year in tax. Since the tax set at one twelfth of the annual rent, the maximum rental value of property held by this group would be about 42 pounds. The rental value of a building as calculated by Eid was about six percent of the total value,[2] so the maximum property of this group probably stood at around 700 L.E. or 875 L.E. if we accept Eid's observation that rental values were normally undervalued 25%. The more finely divided histogram below, labeled H3, seems to confirm the imprssion that we are dealing with a distinct group, because the curve from 0 to 3.5 L.E. looks almost normal.

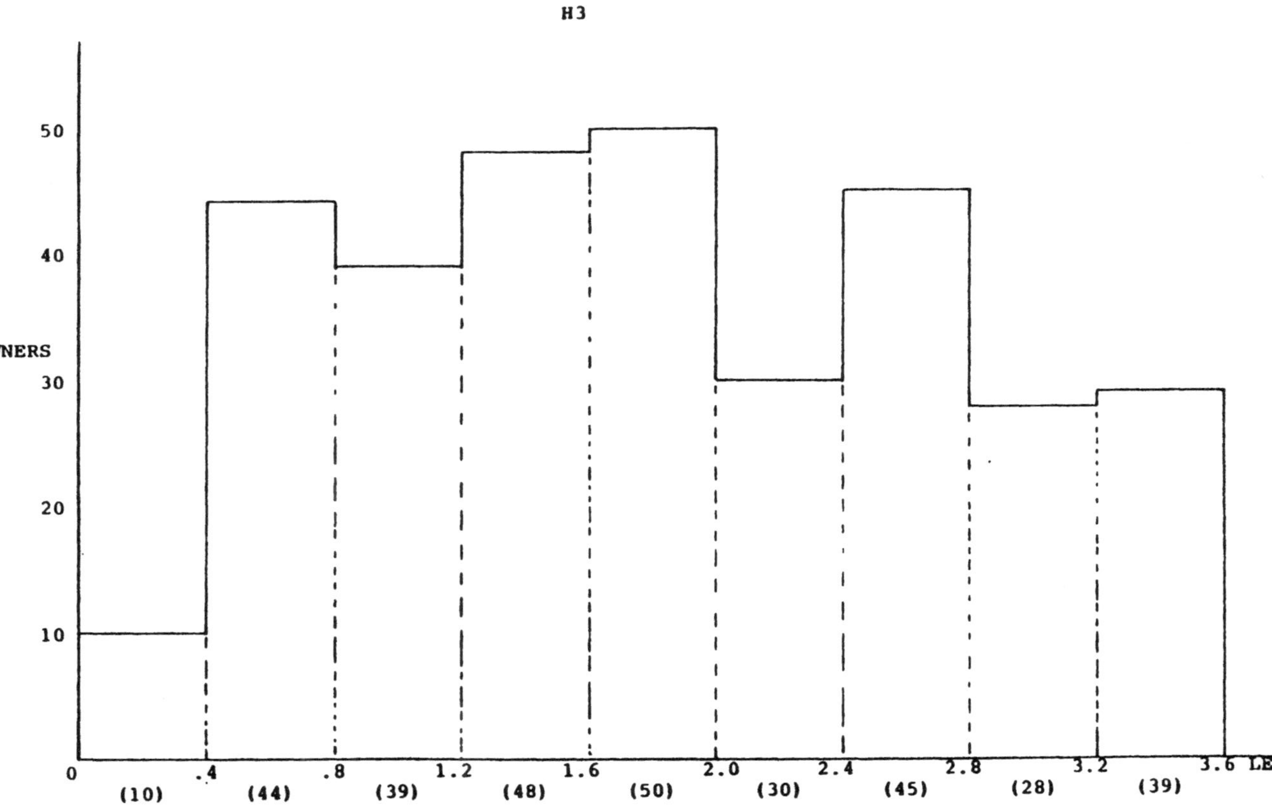

URBAN PROPERTY TAXES FOR OWNERS ALIVE IN 1894, CAIRO

Inspection of the raw frequencies between 3.2 dand 3.8 confirms the impression that 3.5-3.6 is the cut off point.

Cairo Property Owners Alive in 1894

N	Annual Property Tax (L.E.)
13	3.2
6	3.3
8	3.4
6	3.5
19	3.6
9	3.7
6	3.8

Two important problems remain that could vitiate this picture of sub-groups among the urban elite. Firstly, due to the results of the original selection of every fiftieth adjacent property, a theoretical cut off point of four pounds was adopted but in practice almost all units above 3.0 L.E. were recorded. Perhaps the shape of the curve of our 2,414 property owners is merely a result of the sampling process. If a histogram of the orginal 176 raw taxes is drawn and it fails to conform to the curve of the lower range of the urban elite, then the analysis would be rather doubtful. As the histogram below labeled H4 makes clear, there is a real break between groups of property owners above and below a point somewhere around three pounds.

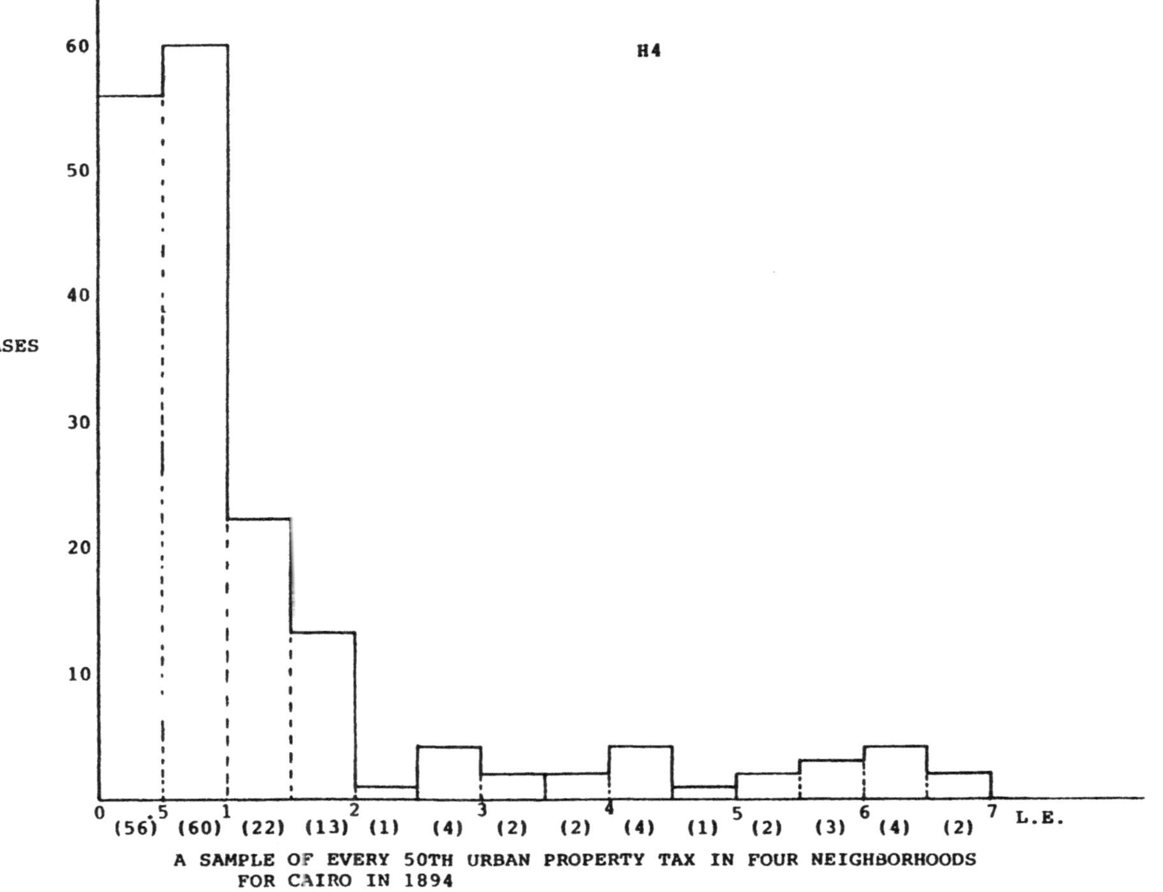

A SAMPLE OF EVERY 50TH URBAN PROPERTY TAX IN FOUR NEIGHBORHOODS
FOR CAIRO IN 1894

97

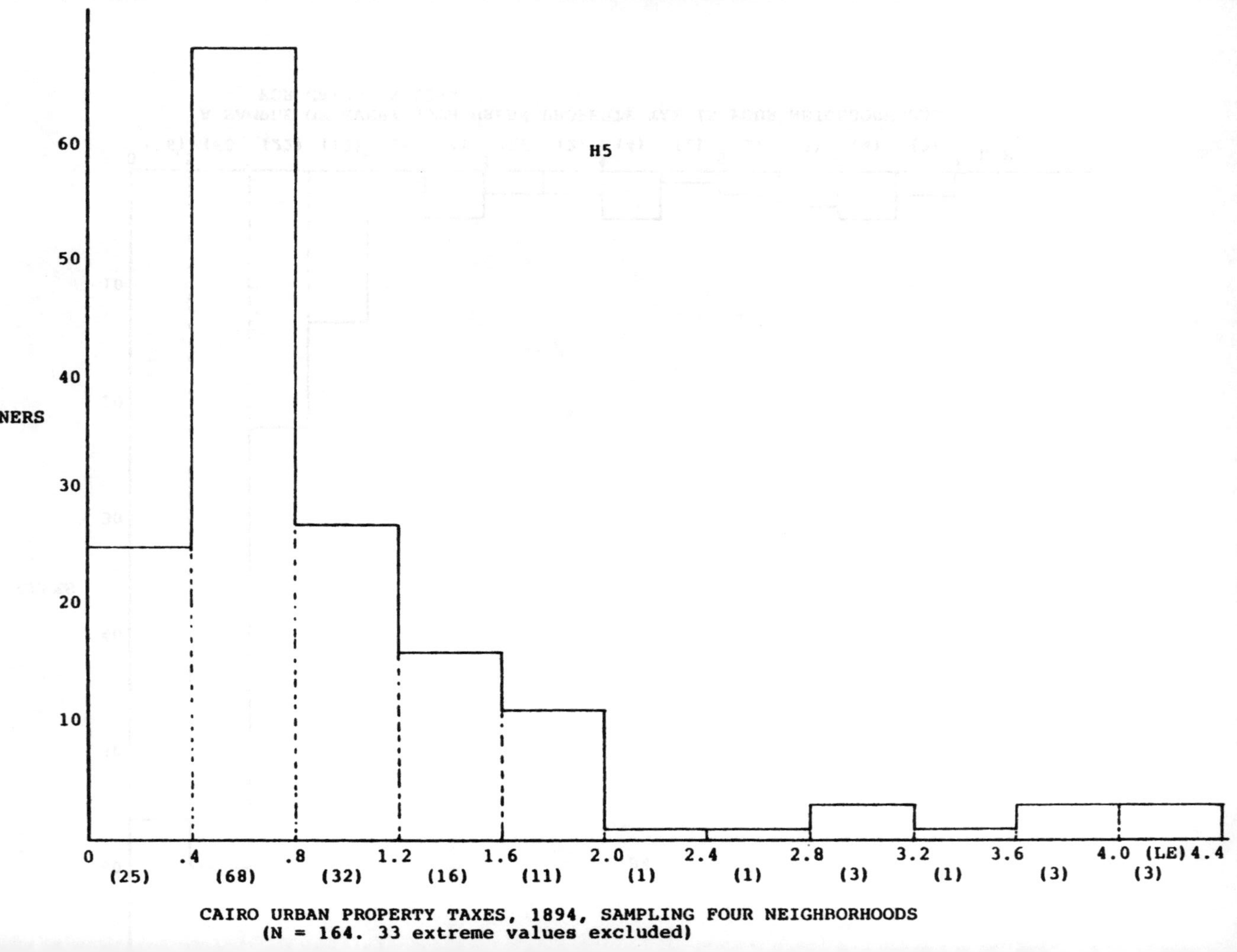

CAIRO URBAN PROPERTY TAXES, 1894, SAMPLING FOUR NEIGHBORHOODS
(N = 164. 33 extreme values excluded)

A finer histogram of the raw data points from the original sample suggests that the cut off point might lie between 2.0 and 2.8 L.E. This histogram is labeled H5. However, one must keep in mind that the original sample merely drew from adjacent property units and that these were grouped together as belonging to one owner only when directly adjacent. Our larger set of 2,414 data points reclassified tax on properties by owner, even if the properties were in distant areas of the city. Therefore the histogram above, H5, underestimates the concentration of property holding. The cut off point setting off the lowest range of owners is probably much closer to the 3.5 level predicted above.

A second problem that could vitiate this picture of social groups is the question of occupation. Property owners were included in our urban elite either because they paid taxes of about four pounds on property (X 12 X 100/6) or because of their political or social role. Perhaps the inclusion of lower level government employees in the urban elite, based as it is on a non-economic factor, has skewed the lower range of the elite and is hiding the existence of peaks that do not lie near 1.5 or six L.E. as in the larger group of 2,414 owners. The histogram below, labeled H6, demonstates that this is not true and that government employees seem to follow the same pattern of urban property holding as the larger groups.

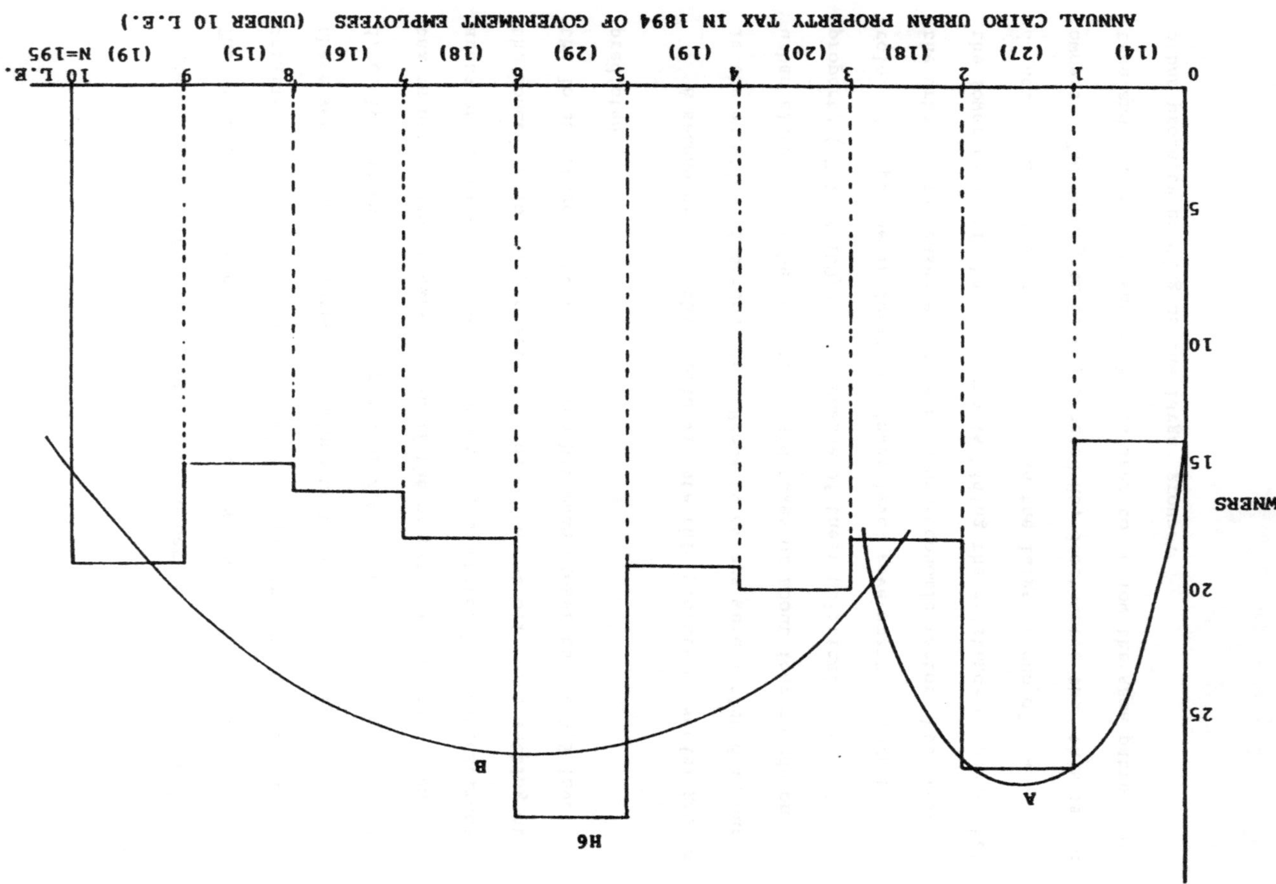

OWNERS
25
20
15
10
5
0
H6
A
B
ANNUAL CAIRO URBAN PROPERTY TAX IN 1894 OF GOVERNMENT EMPLOYEES (UNDER 10 L.E.)
(14) 1 (27) 2 (18) 3 (20) 4 (19) 5 (29) 6 (18) 7 (16) 8 (15) 9 (19) 10 L.E.
N=195
100

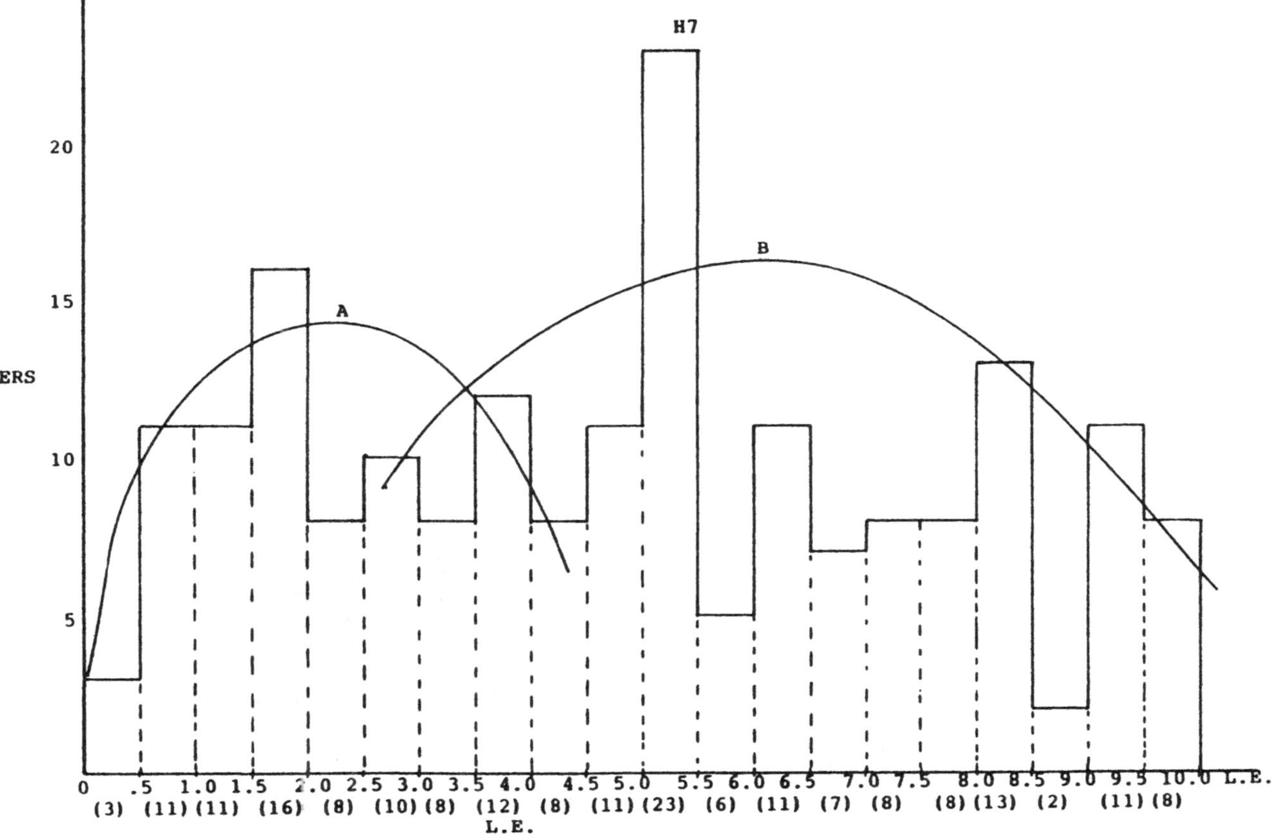

URBAN PROPERTY TAXES IN CAIRO PAID BY GOVERNMENT EMPLOYEES UNDER 10 L.E.

A finer histogram above, H7, confirms the observation that there was a tightly grouped social class of small urban property holders, paying from .1 to 3.5 L.E. tax per year and a second wealthier group whose taxes were clustered around a peak near 5.5 L.E. This is true for both the old and new urban elites, the 732 owners in the first twelve years of the occupation but dead by 1894 and the new urban elite of 1,682 property holders still alive in 1894.

The mortgage records of the Mixed Courts of Cairo for the period from 1876 to 1883 offer further evidence that confirms this picture of social stratification in Cairo at the start of the occupation. These courts recorded 3,566 acts of mortagage between January 1, 1876 and November 14, 1883, of which ninety-nine were on houses in Cairo.[3]

The average mortage was 2321.16 L.E. for these 99 urban property owners. Since the mortage usually represented sixty percent of its assessed value, the average value of the property was 3868.60 L.E. The average rental value was six percent of this, or 232.12 L.E. The annual tax was one-twelfth of that, or 19.34 L.E. The average tax paid by the 732 members of the old urban elite was 20.52 L.E. Thus these two samples confirm our impression of the old urban elite so far. The distribution of urban property among the ninety-nine owners who mortgaged their houses is pictured in the histogram below, H8.

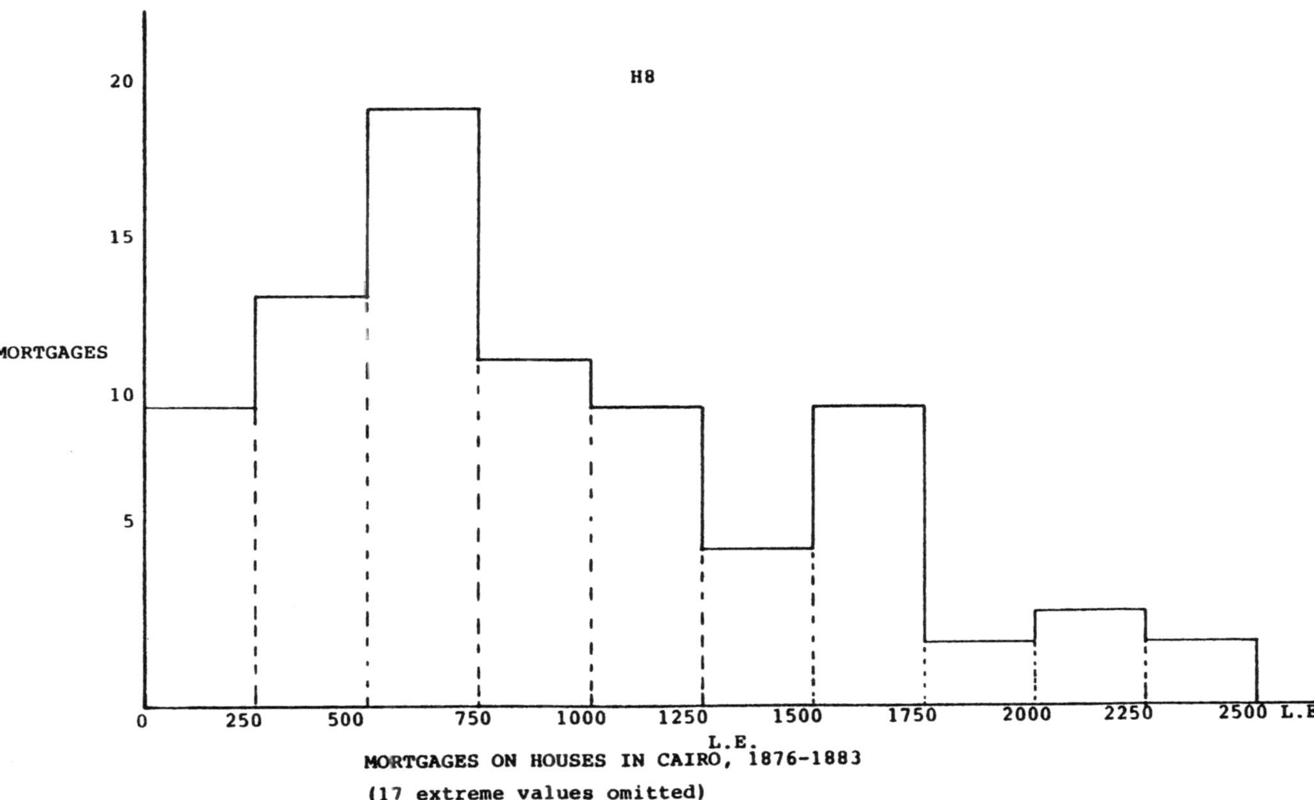

MORTGAGES ON HOUSES IN CAIRO, 1876-1883

(17 extreme values omitted)

The curve of this histogram is remarkably similar to that for the old urban elite, H1. There is a first peak at 625 L.E. and a second at 1,625 L.E. Seventeen extreme values have been omitted so the curve of the distribution can be seen more easily. The peak at 625 L.E. corresponds to the second peak for the old urban elite.

Since houses were mortaged for only 60% of their value, the peak at 625 L.E. should be multiplied by 1/60%= 1.67 to equal 1,041.67 L.E. This should be divided by twelve and then multiplied by .06 to produce the annual tax of 5.21 L.E. This peak at 5.21 L.E. is near the second peak for taxes in the old urban elite that lies between five and seven pounds evident in H1. The second peak for the ninety-nine landowners who mortgaged their property, at 1,625 L.E., produces an annual tax of 13.54 L.E. when the same operations are performed. This corresponds very roughly to a possible third peak for the old urban elite, at around eighteen pounds.

The first peak for the old urban elite at 1.5 L.E., which also appeared in the sample in H4, does not appear in H8, which suggests that small holders did not often mortgage urban property at the start of the occupation because of the novelty of the practive, or that such mortgages were not commonly registered with the Mixed Courts. If we accept Eid's assertion that urban property was undervalued about 25% for tax purposes, then the peak in H8 would translate into 6.51 L.E. and 16.93 L.E., which would correspond even more closely to the second and third peaks in H1.

We can conclude that detailed analysis of mortgages on houses in Cairo from 1876 to 1883 confirms our picture of the structure of urban society with a basic division into small property holders and a second wealthier group whose holders were clustered around 6.0 L.E. annual urban property tax.

If we examine the old urban elite more closely, it appears to contain three sub-groups. As in the larger population, there was a compact group of small property holders, here numbering 103 who paid taxes from .1 to 3.5 L.E. per year. Looking again at the histogram labeled H1 of the old urban elite, the second curve reaches a peak near six pounds and seems to end at about twenty pounds. Beyond this point only extreme values are located and the curve loses any resemblance to normality. See the dotted line on H1. The middle segment of the old elite included 471 property owners who paid from 3.6 to 20 L.E. in taxes with an average of 9.049 L.E. Though the most common tax was about six pounds, larger values to the right raised the average to over nine. The upper segment of the old urban elite contained 158 owners who paid over twenty pounds, with an average of 124.9 L.E. These three components groups of the old urban elite may be labeled small, middle and large property holders. In the tables that follow they will be abbreviated SPH, MPH and LPH. The table below summarizes the average and collective taxes paid by members of these three groups.

Old Urban Elite

	SPH	MPH	LPH	Total Cairo
Owners	103	471	158	17,867
Average Tax	1.898	9.049	66.855	4.558
Group Total Tax	195.5	4262	10563.099	81440.879
% Cairo Tax	.240	5.233	12.970	100.00

All three groups of the old urban elite had a large percentage of members who possessed titles, far more frequently than among the general population. Moreover, the proportion of Effendis, Beys and Pashas was almost constant in all three groups.

Old Urban Elite

	SPH		MPH		LPH	
	N	%	N	%	N	%
No Title	47	45.63	294	62.55	95	60.13
Effendi	29	28.16	52	11.06	17	10.76
Bey	14	13.59	66	14.04	21	13.29
Pasha	13	12.62	58	12.34	25	15.82

The proportion of those without any title declined rapidly above 3.5 L.E., but the percentage of Beys and Pashas does not increase greatly past this level. Some of this is due to the selection of government officials with the title of Bey or above who had relatively little property. It appears that there was little correlation during this period between the social status recognized in a title such as Bey or Pasha and the possession of urban real estate. This could have

a number of causes. At the onset of the occupation, many important
figures in Egyptian society did not live in the major cities or
maintain residences there. Secondly, the old urban elite perhaps was
not easily able to pass on its property or transfer its titles to the
younger generation during the 1870's. Finally, a close study of the
Official Journal, in both its European and Arabic editions shows
that relatively few titles of Bey and above were awarded from 1880 to
the late 1890's, when they became much more common.

A breakdown of the old urban elite by religion shows that
Christians had penetrated the upper ranks of urban society at the
start of the occupation far beyond their frequency in the general
population.

Old Urban Elite

	SPH		MPH		LPH	
	N	%	N	%	N	%
Muslim	97	97.0	396	88.20	130	84.42
Christian	3	3.0	52	11.58	22	14.29
Jewish	0	0	1	.22	2	1.30

It is important to note that the small property holders,
representing the great majority of taxpayers on real estate in Cairo,
were almost entirely Muslim. The Jewish minority constituted an
insignificant percentage of the old urban elite, though when Jews
appear in our sample they are found in the upper strata of the social
structure. The lowest stratum of small shopkeepers and lower level

funtionaries was pentrated by a large minority populus in the
following two decades.

This lowest level of the urban elite had a very small
non-Egyptian presence at the onset of the occupation, less in fact
than their percentage in the population of Cairo as a whole. However,
foreigners and proteges had become an important part of the wealthiest
segment of the urban elite, significantly larger than their proportion
of the general population.

Old Urban Elite

	SPH		MPH		LPH	
	N	%	N	%	N	%
Proteges	1	.98	9	1.95	11	7.28
Foreigners	0	0.0	10	2.16	6	3.97
Egyptian Subjects[4]	101	99.02	438	94.81	131	86.75
Royal Family	0	0	5	1.08	3	1.99

Though foreigners began to play an important role in Egypt's
economic life under Sa'id and during the cotton boom of the 1860's,
their presence was significant only in Alexandria during this period.
Their economic role centered on the export sector in the 1860's but by
the start of the occupation they constituted 4.67% of the population
of Cairo and had begun to penetrate the middle and upper levels of the
propertied elite. There they were joined by an even greater number of
proteges who shared their legal privileges under the occupation. Both
proteges and foreigners were classified as foreigners in the 1882

census. These two groups were represented among the middle level
property holders (4.11%) on about the same level as their presence in
the broader population of Cairo (4.67%). Yet foreigners and proteges
constituted a much greater percentage, 11.25%, of the large property
owners. Though these two groups formed a block with far greater
wealth in Cairo than its numbers at the start of the occupation, their
wealth and power went on to expand much more in the first decades of
the British occupation.

Egyptian society continued to be dominated by men at the start of
the occupation. If the only obstacles to property holding by women
derived from the Islamic laws of inheritance, women should have held a
bit more than a third of Cairo's taxable property. Taking into
account the non-Muslim minorities and the fact that women constitued a
little less than half the population of the capital in 1882, women
would have owned about 40% of Cairo's taxable property if male
domination were not a factor.

Old Urban Elite

	SPH		MPH		LPH	
	N	%	N	%	N	%
Men	93	91.18	397	86.12	138	92.0
Women	9	8.82	64	13.88	12	8.0

These figures seem to indicate that women in the middle segment
of the old urban elite were dominated somewhat less by men than the
women in both higher and lower social strata at the start of the

occupation.

Because of the manner in which the old urban elite was selected,
one would expect a high percentage of employment in the public sector
among small property holders, as is the case.

Old Urban Elite

	SPH		MPH		LPH	
	N	%	N	%	N	%
Public Sector	17	16.50	48	10.19	21	13.29
Private Sector	86	83.50	423	89.81	137	86.71

The percentage of employment by the government here is greater
than in Cairo as a whole for all but perhaps the middle stratum. The
breakdown of occupations in the 1882 census is very inexact.
Government employees fell under the rubrics of
Militaire(armée,police,etc.) and Fontionnaire, employé. Because
employé included white collar workers in the private sector, the
percentage of government employment calculated in this manner, 10.5%,
is certainly inflated. All three levels of the urban elite, then,
contained more than their share of government employees. This is
perhaps a byproduct of the sampling process for the group with taxes
below 3.6 L.E. and the middle group most likely had close to its
share of employees in the public sector. Yet the high percentage of
government employees among the large property holders is too great to
be a coincidence. We can conclude that government empoloyment
provided a path of social mobility for a number of urban families at

the start of the occupation.

The following section will describe the composition of the new urban elite and compare it with the older elite described above. For purposes of comparison both elites were separated into three sub-groups along the natural breaks within the new urban elite. The small property holders paid from .1 to 3.5 L.E. a year in Cairo property taxes, the middle group paid from 3.6 to 8.2 L.E. and the large property holders paid more than 8.2 L.E. The new urban elite contained 1,682 members whose taxes are compared with the previous elite below.

	SPH		MPH		LPH	
	Old	New	Old	New	Old	New
Mean	1.898	1.826	5.787	5.785	35.694	37.694
Stand.						
Dev.[5]	.837	.907	1.150	1.226	85.338	164.858
N	103	314	255	666	374	702
Sum	195.5	573.3	1475.7	3852.5	13349.398	26461.497

In both periods the small and middle level property holders formed tight groups whose taxes clustered around a mean. The form of the distributions has been illustrated in histograms and described above. Unlike the large property holders, the two lower groups had small standard deviations, which is a reflection of the fact that the curves were close to normal. The 417 owners who paid under 3.6 L.E. per year represent a sample of all Cairo property owners who paid taxed in this range, numbering approximately 16,000. On the other hand, because of the way in which the raw data was gathered, the 1997 owners who paid above 3.5 L.E. comprise virtually the entire group who paid taxes in this range. In other words, the small property holders formed a normal group. Large property holders constituted the entire group in question but did not form a normally distributed set. Thus, somewhat different statistical approaches will be necessary in dealing with the three groups.

Titles became more common in the lower ranks of the urban elite by 1894. The greatest increase was in Effendis who were small and middle property holders. Unlike those who held the official titles of Bey and Pasha, anyone who identified with urban commerce or the central government could encourage his neighbors to call him Effendi. Hardly a title, it showed that a man did not wish to identify with the <u>fallahin</u> of the countryside.

	SPH			
	Old		New	
	N	%	N	%
No Title	47	45.63	101	32.17
Effendi	29	28.16	106	33.76
Bey	14	13.59	83	26.43
Pasha	13	12.62	24	6.74

Beys became much more common among small and middle land property holders in the mid 1890's when the government began to give the title

to almost all bureau chiefs in the administration and to wealthy men
in both the towns and countryside.

MPH

	OLD		NEW	
	N	%	N	%
No Title	175	68.90	368	55.26
Effendi	27	10.63	141	21.17
Bey	30	11.81	106	15.92
Pasha	22	8.66	51	7.66

The mix of titles at the wealthiest level of the urban elite
changed little from 1882 to 1894. The majority had no title, but we
should not be misled into thinking that the compositon of the group
was stable.

LPH

	Old		New	
	N	%	N	%
No Title	214	57.22	398	56.78
Effendi	42	11.23	90	12.84
Bey	57	15.24	117	16.69
Pasha	61	16.31	96	13.69

The most fundamental changes in the composition of the urban
elite took place in religion and nationality. Muslim Egyptians in
Cairo were elbowed out by Christians on all levels of the elite during
the first decades of the occupation.

SPH

	Old		New	
	N	%	N	%
Muslim	97	97.0	272	88.47
Christian	3	3.0	31	10.20
Jewish	0	0.0	1	.33[6]

The increase in minority representation was also dramatic among middle level property owners.

MPH

	Old		New	
	N	%	N	%
Muslim	213	88.75	477	77.06
Christian	26	10.83	133	21.49
Jewish	1	.33	9	1.45

The percentage of non-Muslims in the middle level of the urban elite more than doubled between 1882 and 1894.[7] Non-Muslims also swept into the upper echelons of the urban elite between 1882 and 1884, drastically changing its character.

LPH

| | Old | | New | |
	N	%	N	%
Muslim	313	86.23	399	61.10
Christian	48	13.22	234	35.84
Jewish	2	.55	20	3.06

Christians already constitued a larger proportion of the upper elite in 1882 than their percentage of the population. Yet by 1894 non-Muslims had almost tripled their representation at the apex of the urban elite. This shift is significant statistically and forms one of the most crucial changes in Egyptian urban society during the occupation. The only other transformation of comparable importance was the rise to wealth of proteges and foreigners in the highest stratum of the urban elite.

SPH

| | Old | | New | |
	N	%	N	%
Proteges	1	.98	3	.96
Foreigners	0	0	3	.96
Egyptians*	101	99:02	306	97.76
Royal Family	0	0	1	.32

Among small property holders in the urban elite, non-Egyptians were under represented in both 1882 and 1894. At The start of the

occupation they constituted 4.67% of Cairo's population, but only .98%
of the lowest elite stratum. By 1897 they accounted for 6.21% of the
city's population, but only 1.92% of the small property holders in the
elite. These figures may be less reliable than the preceding and
following statistics, because they represent merely a sample of the
general population. It would probably be correct, however, to retain
the impression that Cairo's small elite property holders were
overwhelmingly Muslim and Egyptian.

Middle level property holders mirrored the general
population of Cairo in nationality.

	MPH			
	Old		New	
	N	%	N	%
Protege	5	1.99	24	3.61
Foreign	4	1.59	26	3.91
Egyptian	242	96.41	614	92.33
Royal Family	0	0	1	.15

During the first twelve years of the occupation, the foreign
community grew from 4.67% to 6.21% of Cairo's population. Within the
middle level of the urban elite they increased from 3.58% to 7.52%.
The most dramatic shift in nationality occurred in the highest level
of Cairo's property holders.

LPH

	Old		New	
	N	%	N	%
Protege	15	4.14	64	9.34
Foreign	12	3.31	93	13.58
Egyptian	327	90.33	512	74.74
Royal Family	8	2.21	16	2.34

Egyptian nationals who constituted 95.33% of Cairo's population and 92.54% of the top level of the urban elite in about 1882, were invaded by a host of foreigners and proteges who tripled their representation by 1894, making up almost 23% of Cairo's elite property owners who paid more than 8.2 L.E. in property tax.[9]

During the first decade of the occupation, male domination may have increased a little at the lowest level of the urban elite and probably decreased among middle and large proerty holders. The shift for small property holders was not significant statistically.

SPH

	Old		New	
	N	%	N	%
Men	93	91.18	278	89.10
Women	9	8.82	34	10.90

This small change may well be due to sampling error because the Chi square test indicates that the change is not significant.[10]

Women made the most progress within middle level property holders.

MPH

	Old		New	
	N	%	N	%
Men	212	84.80	527	79.37
Women	38	15.20	137	20.63

Although this shift is only marginally significant statistically, the evidence points to the conclusion that a real shift in favor of women took place within the group of middle property holders.[11] In the top stratum of the urban elite women definitely made progress.

LPH

	Old		New	
	N	%	N	%
Men	323	89.47	570	83.82
Women	38	10.53	110	16.18

Though the percentage change is not much greater than in the middle group, here at the apex of urban society male domination decreased in a statistically significant manner.[12] Large numbers of the urban elite worked for the Egyptian government both in 1882 and 1894. At the lowest level, the upward shift was small and not statistically significant.[13]

The increase in government employment among the middle property holders was large and statistically significant.[14] This shift is

mirrorred in the increase in the titles of Effendi and Bey in this
group, as described above.

MPH

	Old		New	
	N	%	N	%
Public Sector	23	9.02	103	15.47
Private Sector	326	87.17	566	83.24

Government employment was high in the wealthiest group of the new
urban elite, probably twice as frequent as in the total population of
Cairo.

LPH

	Old		New	
	N	%	N	%
Public Sector	48	12.83	114	16.76
Private Sector	326	87.17	566	83.24

The shift, however, was only marginally significant.[15] We can
conclude that government employment remained high at the apex of tho
urban elite, but will have wait for a fuller analysis of government
cadres in chapter seven to see the patterns.

Up to this point, the discussion has centered on changes form
1882 to 1894 for the three groups of property holders when compared
with one another. The discussion will now focus on the internal
dynamics of the various groups of urban property holders.

Small property holders in Cairo at the start of the occupation
formed an extremely homogeneous group. Neither religion nor
nationality divided this group into different levels of wealth.
Muslims paid an average of 1.9072 L.E. in urban property taxes and
Christians paid 2.000 L.E. Egyptian nationals paid an average of
1.9109 L.E. and one protege paid an average of 2.0625 L.E., while 86
persons in the private sector paid an average of 1.8786 L.E. in tax.
Members of this group lived in every district of Cairo except
al-Muski, as can be seen in Appendix 19.

Small property holders tended to live in the popular quarters
like al-Darb al-Ahmar, Gamaliyya, and Sayeda more than the general
population, but was less frequently in both neighborhoods where there
were wealthy residents like al-Azbakiyya and poorer ones like Old
Cairo and al-Muski. Like those in the private sector, government
employees were scattered all over the city. Two members of this group
bought Domains land and one bought Daira Saniyya land. All of these
purchasers were government employees. In general, the 103 small
property holders at the bottom of the elite in 1882 formed a very
homogeneous group.

By 1894 this group had changed considerably. Not only had its
non-Muslim population more than tripled in proportion to the group and
the non-Egyptian population doubled as shown above, but part of its
homogeneity disappeared as well.[16]

We can conclude that government employment and minority religion

alone did not have a statistically significant impact on wealth, but
that they both have a positive effect and that taken together, they
are significant. The characteristics of nationality, sex, and
employment in the public or private sector, however, had no
significant impact on wealth. Small property holders lived in all the
districts of Cairo, as can be seen Appendix 20.

Again, this group was scattered throughout the city though it
continued to be under represented in Old Cairo compared with the total
male population. Its presence increased most in Bab al-Sha'riyya,
Shubra and 'Abdin. It continued to have a disproportionately large
number of members in Sayeda, though somewhat less than in 1882. At
this level of the urban elite, there seems to be little concentration
in any set of neighborhoods. The group's three foreigners lived in
Gamaliyya, Khalifa, and Shubra. The proteges lived in Azbakiyya,
Muski, and Shubra. Of the twenty-one Christians, there was a large
concentration only in Azbakiyya, where sixteen lived. Of the total
312, occupation could be determined for only one hundred. Of these,
six out of seven Christians were employed by the government and the
one Jewish property owner lived in Shubra and was in trade. To
summarize, the group of small property holders lost some of its
homogeneity and Christians began to acquire greater wealth when
compared with Muslims. Among middle property holders, Muslims lost
their former dominant position and the group became more homogeneous.

Middle level property holders, paying between 3.6 and 8.2 L.E.
per year, were dominated at the start of the occupation by

Muslims.[17] Sex, nationality, and employment in the public or private
sectors had no impact on wealth within this group. A large majority
of this group, 72.44%, was concentrated in five of the neighborhoods
of Cairo: 'Abdin, al-Darb al-Ahmar, Azbakiyya, Gamaliyya, and Sayeda.
In 1882 these five districts contained only 47.36% of the total
population of Cairo. Of the nine proteges and foreigners, four lived
in Azbakiyya, the prestigious area where large private houses were
given tax benefits under Isma'il.[18]

Unfortunately, occupation can be determined for only 54 of the
255 members of this group. Of these, the majority, 61.11%, were
employed by the government (23) or worked in trade (10). This
suggests that we are dealing with a lower middle class whose wealth
depended on commerce and public employment.

By 1894 Muslims had lost their comparative advantage within the
group of middle property holders. The average property tax paid by
Muslims was 5.784 L.E., less than the 5.927 L.E. paid by non-Muslims.
Considered as isolated factors, neither religion, nationality, sex nor
employment had much impact on wealth within this group. However,
within the Christian community of middle property holders, proteges
paid considerably higher average taxes (6.760 L.E.) than did foreign
Christians (5.665) or Egyptian Christians (5.902). If both
nationality and religion are considered, the wealthiest subgroups were
Jewish proteges (4) who paid 7.350 L.E. and one member of the royal
family who paid 8.1 L.E. We can conclude that within the minority
religious communities, proteges held considerably more urban property

than their coreligionists.

By 1894 middle property holders were a little more spread out in
Cairo than at the start of the occupation, though 65.86% lived in the
five districts of 'Abdin, Bab al-Sha'riyya, al-Darb al-Ahmar,
Azbakiyya and Sayeda. Al-Darb al-Ahmar had lost its relative
popularity to the advantage of 'Abdin and al-Azbakiyya which continued
to draw wealthy residents during the early decades of the occupation.
Christians were heavily concentrated in al-Azbakiyya, where 39.85%
lived and four of the group's nine Jews lived in al-Muski. Of the 26
foreigners, twelve lived in al-Muski and five in al-Azbakiyya. Muslim
residence tended to follow the pattern for the group as a whole, as
can be seen in Appendix 21.

Occupation can be examined in detail for middle level property
owners because profession could be determined for 259 members of the
group, or 38.89 percent of the total. Compared with the distribution
of occupations within Cairo as a whole, middle property holders were
concentrated in government, trade, the liberal arts and manufacturing.
The classification scheme of the census of 1907 was used because it
broke down job categories in finer detail than those of 1882 or 1897.
Then occupations were reclassified into fourteen groups, which can be
seen in Appendix 22 where middle property owners are compared with the
male working population of Cairo in 1897.

Although less than half of Cairo's active male population worked
in government, trade, the liberal arts or manufacturing, nearly

three-quarters of the middle level property holders, 72.97%, were
employed in these four areas. The importance of government employment
for this group cannot be overemphasized, encompassing as it did over
forty percent of all those whose occupation could be determined. If
we combine all the other professions which are traditionally
associated with the middle class, finance, architecture,
manufacturing, trade and the liberal arts, the percentage is still
less than that for government employment among this group. These
middle class professionals total 39.77%, while government employment
stood at 40.15%. It is interesting to note that by 1894 the 'ulama
or traditional Muslim religious notables and their non-Muslim
counterparts had all but disapperared from the urban elite. Compared
with the active male population, activity in manufacturing,
transportation, building, hotels, restaurants, and domestic labor was
under represented and government employment was pervasive and
dominant.

The religious composition of the group as a whole is closely
parallelled within the subset of its members who were employed by
government, except for Jews.

	MPH		MPH in Government	
	N	%	N	%
Muslim	477	77.06	80	80.81
Christian	133	21.49	19	19.19
Jewish	9	1.45	0	0

Government employment was obviously an important vehicle for
Christian entry into the middle level of the urban elite. The pattern
of employment for Muslims and Christians was very similar, except for
trade, where Muslims dominated. See Appendix 23.

Jews, on the other hand, tended to gravitate toward the more
capital-intensive professions of manufacturing and finance. In
general non-Muslims were over represented in the occupations of
finance, manufacturing and government, when compared to the general
population of Cairo.

Large property holders at the beginning of the British occupation
formed a stratified group that pointed to the direction in which the
urban elite would evolve in the following decades. Muslims were not
only under represented within the group, but held less property on the
average then Christians or Jews. Average property taxes are ranked by
religion and national status as shown in Appendix 24.

We can conclude that urban property was distributed in a
relatively even way among members of the major religious communities
taken as a whole at the top of the old urban elite, despite the
presence of a few extremely rich Christian and Jewish property owners.

Nationality, on the other hand, divided the group of large
property owners at the start of the occupation into different strata.
Foreigners and proteges were significantly wealthier than
Egyptians.[19] However, sex and employment in the public or private
sectors seemed to have little impact on property holding in this

group.

A large proportion of the top level of the old urban elite was concentrated in 'Abdin, al-Darb al-Ahmar, Azbakiyya, Gamaliyya, and Sayeda, as was the case for the old middle property holders. In terms of residence and titles, two major indications of life style, these two groups were remarkably similar. See Appendix 25.

Although the group's fifteen proteges were scattered through the districts favored by the large property holders of the old elite, nine of its twelve foreigners were concentrated in al-Azbakiyya, foreshadowing the neighborhood's growing popularity for wealthy residents of Cairo during the entire period under study. Information on occupation was available for only 85 of the group's 361 members. Forty-eight worked for the government, constituting 13.30% of the persons in the group and 56.47% of those whose occupation was known. Employment in government (48), the liberal arts (12), manufacturing (7), and trade (4) accounted for 83.53% of known occupations in this group, compared to 72.97% for middle property holders in 1894. All Christians at the apex of the old urban elite for whom occupation could be determined worked for the government, in trade and in the liberal arts.

Large property holders formed a group that was stratified both by religion and by nationality by 1894. As at the beginning of the occupation, proteges and foreigners were generally wealthier than their co-religionists. Muslims sometimes held less urban property

than Christians, who in turn held less than Jews. The breakdown of
group means is shown in Appendix 26.

Foreigners of all three religions had little capital invested in
urban property, compared with the average tax paid by the entire group
of 37.69 L.E. As outlined in the section above covering demography,
most incoming foreigners were Greeks who often had little capital. It
appears that foreign Jews and Catholic or Protestant foreigners began
buying urban real estate in large quantities only after the boom began
in 1897.

Although Muslims were included in only one of the top seven
groups by rank, the fact that Egyptian Muslims held a bit more
property on the average than Egyptian Christians makes religion only
marginally significant for the entire group.[20]

Muslims did well compared to other religious groups at this level
as did a handful at the apex of the urban elite. It is significant to
note that at the top, Muslims improved their relative position a bit
from 1882 to 1907, despite the fact that they constituted a
considerably smaller percentage of this stratum, 61.10%, than at the
start of the occupation, 86.23%.

Nationality, however, was a very significant indicator of wealth
at the apex of the urban elite in 1894.[21] Proteges were those who
most improved their status during the early years of the occupation.
Though women and employees in the private sector generally paid less
taxes than men or government functionaries, the differences were not

significant. The gap between men and women increased slightly over that of 1882. Where wealth was almost perfectly balanced between the private and public sectors in 1882, a small gap developed by 1894 in favor of public officials.

The pattern of residence changed considerably for property holders at the apex of the urban elite in the first twelve years of the occupation. Azbakiyya, Shubra, and Muski became more popular for the wealthy, while Gamaliyya, Sayeda and al-Darb al-Ahmar became much less desirable as elite residences. See Appendix 27. In the first decades of the occupation, Cairo was becoming a city where residence patterns increasingly indicated social status. For a detailed breakdown of ranking changes in the pattern of elite residence by neighborhood, see Appendix 28.

The pattern of occupations for large property holders in 1894 was similar to that for middle property holders at that time. See Appendix 29. Most large property holders were employed in government, manufacturing, the liberal arts and trade in 1894. These four fields occupied 71.77% of this group where profession could be determined (281), compared with 72.97% for middle property holders. Compared with the entire population of active men in Cairo in 1897, the same fields were generally favored by both elite groups, with some minor discrepancies. Trade was a less common occupation for large property holders, while architecture, engineering and especially manufacturing were more frequent. The farther one moves up the scale of urban wealth, the more often one encounters proteges, members of the royal

family, Christian foreigners, government officials and captial
oriented sources of wealth like manufacturing. Minority groups played
a major role in some of the key professions favored by large property
holders. For purposes of comparison in the following table, the
percentage of non-Muslims among the large property holders as a whole
was 38.9% and the percentage of foreigners was 22.92%.

Large Property Holders in Cairo, 1894

Occupation	% Non-Muslim	% Foreign
Government	23.68	4.24
Manufacturing	37.93	15.63
Liberal Arts	26.92	14.29
Trade	47.62	36.36
Finance	69.23	61.54
Architecture, Engineering	54.55	30.77

Though non-Muslims, foreigners and proteges constituted a much
greater percentage in all occupations favored by large property
holders than their proportion of the Cairo population, minority groups
also outweighed local Egyptian Muslims in finance, architecture,
engineering, and trade within the context of large property holders.
Christians and Jews also outweighed Muslims witin the liberal arts at
the top of the new urban elite. Muslims retained an advantage in
government and held their own in manufacturing. We shall see in the

following sections that local power within the Egyptian government remained purely numerical. The preceding description of joint stock companies engaged in manufacturing showed that control of the modern sector of Egyptian industry was almost totally in the hands of proteges, Christians and foreigners.

Detailed analysis of property holding has thus shown that non-Muslims and foreigners were penetrating all levels of the urban elite in Cairo at the start of the British occupation and that they were increasing their share of property at each of the three upper levels of society: (1) small scale merchants and lower level civil servants, (2) middle ranking functionaries, professionals and employees, and (3) high government officials, merchants, industrialists, financiers and successful professionals in the liberal arts.

There appear to have been major obstacles limiting social mobility out of the bottom level where urban property taxes reached a maximum of 3.5 L.E. per year. Movement into the two upper sectors where 1,997 owners held 55.43% of Cairo's taxable property in 1894 was becoming more and more difficult for Muslim Egyptians, though government employment opened doors for a few. Most were elbowed aside by proteges and non-Muslims who became increasingly over represented in those occupations that were to prove the greatest sources of wealth and power in modern Egyptian society: government, manufacturing and finance. At the apex of the elite, foreign status under the Capitulations, membership in the royal family and access to foreign

capital helped families to acquire far greater wealth than mere
government employment. The upper levels of the urban elite became
more statified by religion and nationality from 1882 to 1894. Muslim
Egyptians were being forced out of neighborhoods like al-Muski and
Cairo was becoming a city where residence followed patterns of social
stratification. Women improved their relative position at some
levels, but only marginally. Cairo remained a city where men
dominated property holding.

Footnotes: Chapter Four

1. Note: Personal property endowed as waqf by a donor who was
alive in 1894 was classified as personal property, not waqf.

2. Owen, "The Cairo Building Industry...", p.339.

3. Dar al-Mahfuzat, Storehouse 42, Shelf 24, Volume 608, Etat
des inscriptions hypothécaires à partir de l'année 1876 jusqu'au 14
novembe, 1888.

4. Sudanese and Ottoman subjects were classified as Egyptians
because they did not benefit from the capitulatory privileges that set
other foreigners off from the general populus, as explained in the
preceding section on demography.

5. Standard deviation is abbreviated as Stand.Dev. in this
table.

6. Here it is pertinent to recall that below the level of 3.6
L.E. tax, we have two samples rather than the total groups of
property owners. There is a statistical test called Chi square which
can indicate whether this increase in the percentage of Christians is
probably a result of sampling rather than a real change in religious
composition among the larger groups in the population. The
calculation of the Chi square statistic is somewhat tedious, so the
operation will not be detailed here. The result is that chances are
less than five in one hundred that the increase in the number of
Christians is merely due to sampling. Chi square equals 5.0891106.

In statistical terms, the difference is significant.

7. The middle stratum of the new elite is here in entirely but
the older group is merely a sample of a larger population, so a test
of significance is called for. As might be expected, the Chi square
test indicates that this increase is highly significant. Chi square
equals 13.464856. The test excluded the Jewish group to facilitate
calculation. Chances are less than one in a thousand that the
increase in the proportion of Christians is due to the sampling
process.

8. This category excludes members of the royal family in this
and the following two tables.

9. This shift is statistically insignificant. Chi square equals
39.084133. Chances are less than one in ten thousand that the shift
is due to sampling error for the old urban elite.

10. Chi square equals .3552148.

11. Chances are a little above five in one hundred that the
change is merely due to error in sampling among the old urban elite.
Chi square equals 3.4623908. Since this test assumes that both groups
were sampled, as is not the case here because we have all members of
the middle stratum of the new urban elite, it is probably safe to
conclude that a real shift took place. In the top stratum of the
urban elite women definitely made progress.

12. Chi square equals 6.1726885. Chances are just a bit over

one hundred that the shift was due to sampling among the old urban elite.

13. Chi square equals .43454502 for the following two by two table.

SPH

	Old		New	
	N	%	N	%
Public Sector	17	16.50	61	19.43
Private Sector	86	83.50	253	80.57

14. Chi square equals 6.4878049.

15. Chi square equals 2.8657132. Chances were a little less than ten in a hundred that the increase was merely due to the process of sampling the old urban elite.

16. By 1894 Christian small property holders paid an average of 2.2419 L.E. in urban property taxes, while Muslims paid only 1.7746. The difference is statiscally significant. Chi square equals 6.0013764. However, when the 62 property owners who worked for the government are excluded, the Chi square test reveals that religion is a less significant factor.

When property owners in the private sector are classed by religion and tax paid, above or below 1.75 L.E., the following distribution results.

134

                    Tax (L.E.)

        <u>Low</u>   <u>0-1.7</u>   <u>High</u>   <u>1.8-3.5</u>

Muslim   106   114

Non-Muslim   10   22

    Here Chi square equals 3.2239143. Religion is only
marginally significant in determining tax as an indicator
of urban property. Chances are about seven in one hundred
that the correlation is due to chance.

    17. Muslims paid an average tax of 5.845 L.E. per year.
Non-Muslims paid an average of 5.559 L.E. per year. The Chi square
test indicates that the difference is statistically significant. Chi
square equals 5.20016; that is, chances were less than three in one
hundred that the difference was due to chance.

    18. Owen, <u>Cotton</u>, p.156, citing Clerget, <u>Le Caire</u>, v.1,
p.198.

    19. When the same test is applied to Egyptian subjects versus
foreigners or proteges of foreign powers, the Chi square test
indicates that differences in the group means are statistically
significant. The distribution of urban property by nationality among
this group was as follows.

                    <u>Low</u> (<u>8</u>.3-37.<u>7</u>)   <u>High</u> (<u>37</u>.8-Top)

Egyptian   268   67

Foreigner or Protege 25   14

Chi square equals 4.30857; that is, chances are less than four in
a hundred that the differences in group means are not representative
of differences in a two-by-two table.

20. The breakdown of religion and taxes by sector was as
follows.

            Large Property Holders (1894)

        <u>Low</u> (<u>8</u>.3-37.<u>7</u>)   <u>High</u> (<u>37</u>.8-Top)
Muslim   333   66

Non-Muslim   200   57

The Chi square test reveals that here religion was only
marginally significant as a determinant of wealth. Chi square equals
3.261155; i.e., chances are a little better than five in one hundred
that the difference is not important.

21. Property taxes and nationality were broken down as follows.

Large Property Holders (1894)

            <u>Low</u> (<u>8</u>.3-37.<u>7</u>)   <u>High</u> (<u>37</u>.8-Top)
Egyptians   442   86

Foreigners and Proteges 123   151

136

Because Chi square equals 14.13987, chances are less than one in a thousand that the correlation is not sigificant. This same split by national status was present in 1882 but had expanded by 1984.

Chapter Five

Agriculture and Rural Society

This chapter will demonstrate that a massive shift took place in
the distribution of agricultural land and the balance of power among
social groups in the Egyptian countryside. The predominance
established by non-Muslims in large scale commerce was transferred
into the rural sector during the first twenty-five years of the
British occupation. As land became fully alienable and the 'ezbah
became the dominant form of labor organization in the countryside,
non-Muslims in the private sector and government employees took
advantage of rising opportunities in agriculture and of the sales of
the former royal estates to establish positions of power in rural
society that were not successfully challanged until after the
revolution of 1952. The ranks of landless peasants began to swell
during the same period. They became dependent wage laborers or were
absorbed into the 'ezbah-s. In general, rural society became less
homogeneous and more stratified by religion while the opportunities
for upward social mobility decreased sharply. In describing shifts in
rural society, this chapter will stress both the ownership of land and
the organization of agricultural production. The latter was dominated
by the 'ezbah.

The development of Egyptian agriculture from 1882 to 1907 has
been investigated in considerable detail. This chpater will commence
with a brief summary of the evolution of agricultural output so as to

sketch in a background for economic and social transformations in the countryside from 1876 to 1907. The basic studies of agriculture for this period were done by A. E. Crouchley, Patrick O'Brien, Roger Owen, Samir Radwan and 'Ali Barakat.[1]

The British rulers of Egypt realized that the key to productivity in the country had been cotton cultivation since the middle of the century. To increase productivity, and therefore taxes, they gave the highest priority to the repair and extension of Egypt's irrigation system. The Delta barrage was completed in 1891 and transformed irrigation in much of the delta from seasonal to perennial. The water level was raised, eliminating the need for pumps or primitive systems to lift the water from the channels to the fields. This also permitted more crops to be grown each year on fully irrigated fields and so encouraged Egyptian cultivators to abandon triennial for a biennial system of crop rotation. In 1894 only 17% of the area under cotton followed the system of biennial rotation, whereas this had increased to 56% by 1907.[2] The system of perennial irrigation was extended to Upper Egypt with the construction of the Aswan barrage in 1902, the Assyut barrage in 1902, the Zifta barrage in 1903 and the Isna barrage in 1908.[3]

The investment in irrigation was massive, increasing the capital stock in irrigation and drainage by 135.85% from 1882 to 1907. Expressed in 1960 constant Egyptian pounds, this capital stock rose from 49.1 million L.E. in 1882 to 115.8 million in 1907.[4] The cultivated area therefore expanded as well, moving from 4,742,000 feddans in 1877 to 5,327,000 in the season for 1907-1908, up 12.34%, while the cropped area rose from 4,742,000 feddans to 7,598,000 at the same time, up 60.23%.[5] Increased irrigation and greater credit facilities, especially after 1900, enabled cultivators to invest in rural dwellings and farm buildings, which increased in value from 16.10 million L.E. in 1882 to 31.32 in 1907, up 94.53%. The capital ivested in livestock likewise rose from 31.22 million L.E. in 1882 to 56.17 in 1907, up 79.94%. Traditional agricultural machinery rose from 1.5 million L.E. in 1882 to 2.3 million in 1905, up 53.33%.

Total net fixed capital stock in agriculture thus increased from 97.9 million L.E. in 1882 to 211.9 million in 1907, up 116.45%. The greatest share of the increase was in irrigation and drainage, whose percentage of net fixed capital stock rose from 50.14% in 1882 to 54.65% in 1907.[6]

The first impact of the massive irrigation program was increased output, which rose almost 100% from the period 1872-8 to 1905-9.[7] Not all of the effects of the irrigation program were beneficial. Though output per unit of land continued to rise, up 60% from 1872-8 to 1895-9 and again up 3% by 1905-9, the output per capita rose only 13% from 1872-8 to 1895-9. Then output per worker rose only another two percent to 1900-4 and next moved back down four percent by 1905-9 when compared to 1895-9. The British agricultural experts who carried out the expansion of the irrigation underestimated drainage requirements. Salt and other deposits built up. Crop pests thrived on the plants

and though cotton yield per feddan rose up to 1895, it declined in the
period 1895-9 from 5.47 cantars to 4.67 in 1900-4 and sank to 3.13 by
1909.[8]

Egypt became increasingly dependent on cotton monoculture in the
first decades of the occupation, as was explained in the chapter above
treating commerce. Because Egyptian cotton output was far smaller
than that of the United States or India, cotton prices were set in a
world market over which Egyptians had no control. Revenues were
therefore hurt badly when prices declined from 3.271 L.E. per cantar
in 1882 to 1.597 in 1897. As yield declined in the 1890's, only
greatly increased production saved Egptian agriculture from a major
crisis.

When cotton prices began to rise at the turn of the century,
rents and the price of land entered a period of frenetic speculation
that ended in the crash of 1907. Whereas good land was offered for
sale at prices of from 25 to 50 L. E. per feddan in 1881, some delta
fields were sold for 160 L.E. per feddan in 1905.[9] Rent was as low
as 1.4 L.E. per feddan at the beginning of the 1890's but reachod the
range of twelve to eighteen pounds by 1912. This rapid rise in rents
led to the decline of the sharecropping system or direct cultivation
by middle proprietors and encouraged a cash rental system called
fermage "in which the land was taken over by the tenant for a
certain period of time for a fixed sum." The landnowners supervised
cultivation less and less, which led to the spread of crop pests and
further decline in yield. In general the flood of Eurpoean capital

into Egyptian agriculture and the inflation in prices and rents increased the advantage landlords had over renters and provoked the speculative boom that burst in 1907.

The rapid rise in land prices was partly based on rapidly rising agricultural income after 1900. The value of Egyptian cotton and cotton seed exports rose from 11,925,000 L.E. in 1898-9 to 27,000,000 in 1907-8, up 126.58%.[10] The rise was also dependent on a massive influx of speculative European capital which was abruptly halted in 1907 when world wide crop failures cut the demand for Eurpoean manufactured goods, speculation slackened and prices fell. In the ensuing restriction of credit, debts were recalled from Egypt and the bottom fell out of the markets in Egyptian stocks, urban land and agricultural land. These basic transformations in the rural sector of Egyptian society benefitted some groups and hurt many at the bottom who were unable to adapt to changing conditions.

Agricultural output and its value in real terms onthe world market thus grew rapidly in Egypt from 1882 to 1907, though this growth was not without deleterious sideeffects such as the decline in soil fertility and inflated and values after the turn of the century. Hundreds of thousands of families lost their land or their traditional rights to work the land where they had been born, as willbecome clear in the following sections.

The Distribution of Agricultural Land in Egypt, 1876-1885

Analysis of agricultural land mortgages recorded by the Mixed Courts of Cairo from 1876 to 1883 will show that large rural properties were concentrated in the hands of a stratified elite group at the beginning of the occupation. A line at about 32.5 feddans divided wealthier landholders into a homogeneous middle level and a stratified upper level dominated by town dwellers and government employees. Both groups parallelled the national population in religion and nationality and women were under represented at all levels, though mortgage laws tended to bias the sample to the detriment of women.

The Mixed Courts of Cairo recorded 3,566 acts of mortgage from 1876 to November 14,1883. On the basis of a sample of every twenty-fifth mortgage, ninety-six of the total 143 loans in the sample were made on agricultural land, or 67.13%. Twenty-eight were made on houses alone, or 19.58%, and nineteen or 13.28% on a combination of houses and farm land. Of the total inscribed in the register, 887 acts of mortgage involved over 500 L.E. or forty feddans or concered members of the political or economic elites. These 887 mortgages were made by 730 property holders. These mortgage records confirm the general impession that most landholders held small plots but that Egypt's large landholders possessed a majority of the country's good farm land.

The histogram below labeled H9 plots the number of feddans in 93 mortgages in the sample of every twenty-fifth mortgage before the Cairo Mixed Courts from 1876 to Novermber 14, 1883. Twenty extreme values over 64.9 feddans were omitted so the shape of the distribution would be obvious. As expected, the curve descends sharply from a peak at its lowest interval. Most owners who mortgaged their property in this sample held little land, while a few wealthy landowners held most of the land. The owners in the first three intervals, from one to fifteen feddans, made 61.3% of all the mortgages but held only 24.18% of the property mortgaged in the historgram. Including the twenty extreme values, the poorest landowners in the first three intervals held only 7.48% of the total 4,773.27 feddans mortgaged in the sample. In other words, landholding was extremely concentrated.

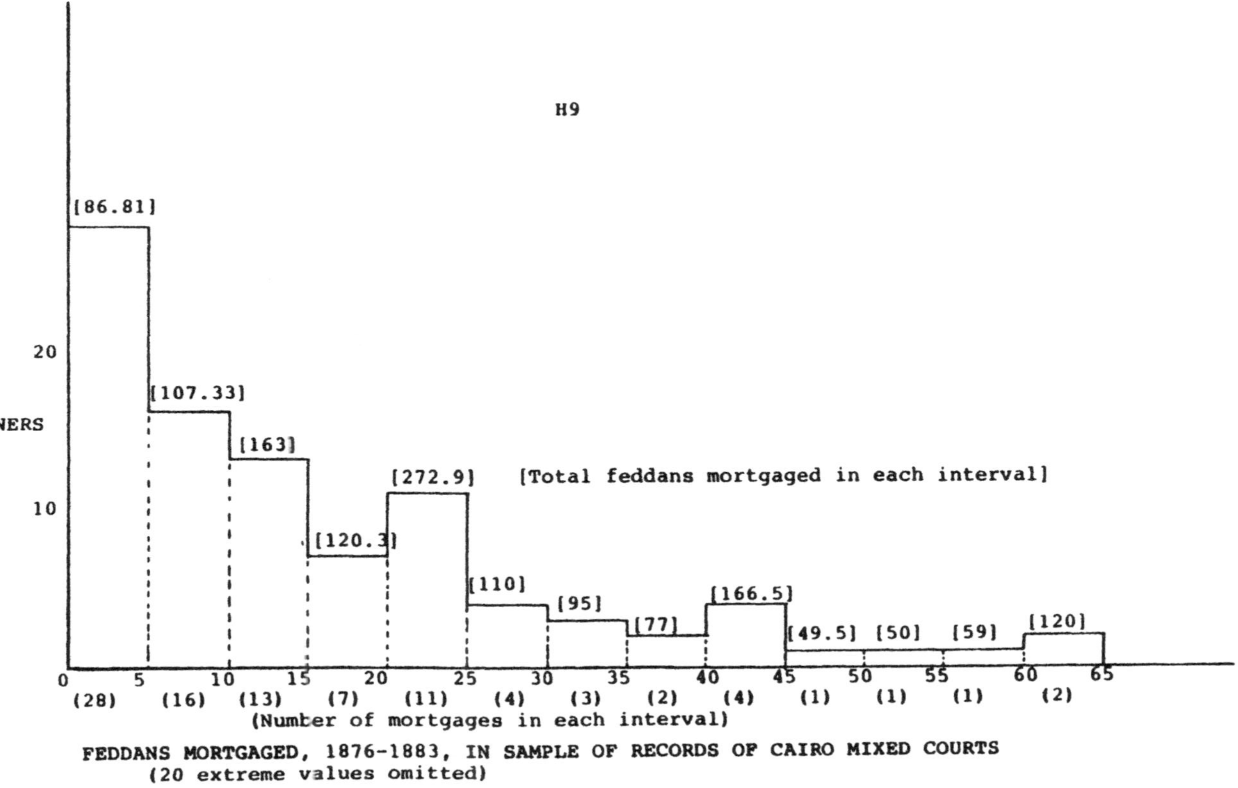

FEDDANS MORTGAGED, 1876-1883, IN SAMPLE OF RECORDS OF CAIRO MIXED COURTS
(20 extreme values omitted)

An efficient way to measure concentration of property holding is the Gini index. Computation of this statistic is extremely tedious and it should be sufficient to explain that the index varies from zero to one. Zero indicates absolute equality and one indicates that a small percentage of the population holds all the property. The above sample of land mortgages can be divided into six intervals as follows.

Interval (feddans)	Mortgages	Total Feddans
0 - 4.9	28	86.81
5 - 9.9	16	107.33
10-19.9	20	283.25
20-29.9	15	382.88
30-49.9	10	388.00
50 and Above	24	3525.00

The Gini index for this sample of land mortgages before the Cairo Mixed Courts from 1876 to 1883 is .6180356. It is relatively high and its utility will become obvious in comparision with later indexes.[11]

Several words of caution are necessary here. Firstly, one must remember that the data in H9 form a sample of a sample. The 113 land mortgages in the sample represent merely every twenty-fifth mortgage in the dossier, minus the twenty-eight mortgages on houses alone. Secondly, these mortgages are not necessarily representative of all types of rural landholding. The European type land mortgage became an important economic institution in Egypt only with the establishment of

the Mixed Courts in 1876. Furthermore, the cost and trouble involved
in registering acts of mortgage meant that large mortgages would
appear far more often than smaller ones. Finally, almost all lenders
in the 887 mortgages before these courts had foreign status, either
under the Capitulations or by birth, and almost all borrowers were
Egyptians. This would again tend to over represent large blocks of
land. With these remarks in mind about the statistical bias of the
data, we can continue to analyze the data in H9.

The curve in H9 is not a smooth line of descent from the numerous
small plots at the left of the scale. There is perhaps a significant
gap in the interval between twenty-five and forty feddans. The small
number of mortgages between fifteen and twenty feddans is probably due
to the fact that larger mortgages are over represented in the sample,
but the gap from twenty-five to forty suggests that we may be dealing
with two different social groups, with the dividing line close to 32.5
feddans. The larger sample of mortgages will be discussed in detail.

The Cairo Mixed Courts recorded a total of 887 mortgages made by
730 property owners as described above. Excluding ninety-nine owners
who mortgaged only houses, 586 landowners mortgaged a combination of
land and houses for a total of 1,704,944.1 L.E. Thus the average
mortgage involving agricultural land was 2,321.71 L.E. The amount of
mortgage varied from 21 L.E. to 165.005 L.E. The land mortgaged
varied from one feddan to 9,027 feddans. The vast majority of the
land mortgages, 83.2%, were for less than two hundred feddans and are
represented in the histogram labeled H10. There appears to be a peak

147

at fifty feddans and then the curve tapers off slowly to the right, as
is common when land is highly concentrated. Yet a finer histogram of
land mortgages on less than one hundred feddans reveals that the curve
is not smooth and perhaps represents two groups, as is shown in H11.
When the same data is re-drawn in a still finer histogram, H12, it
becomes clear that we are dealing with two distinct social groups,
with a dividing line at about 32.5 L.E. The following paragraphs will
describe these two elite groups of rural land owners.

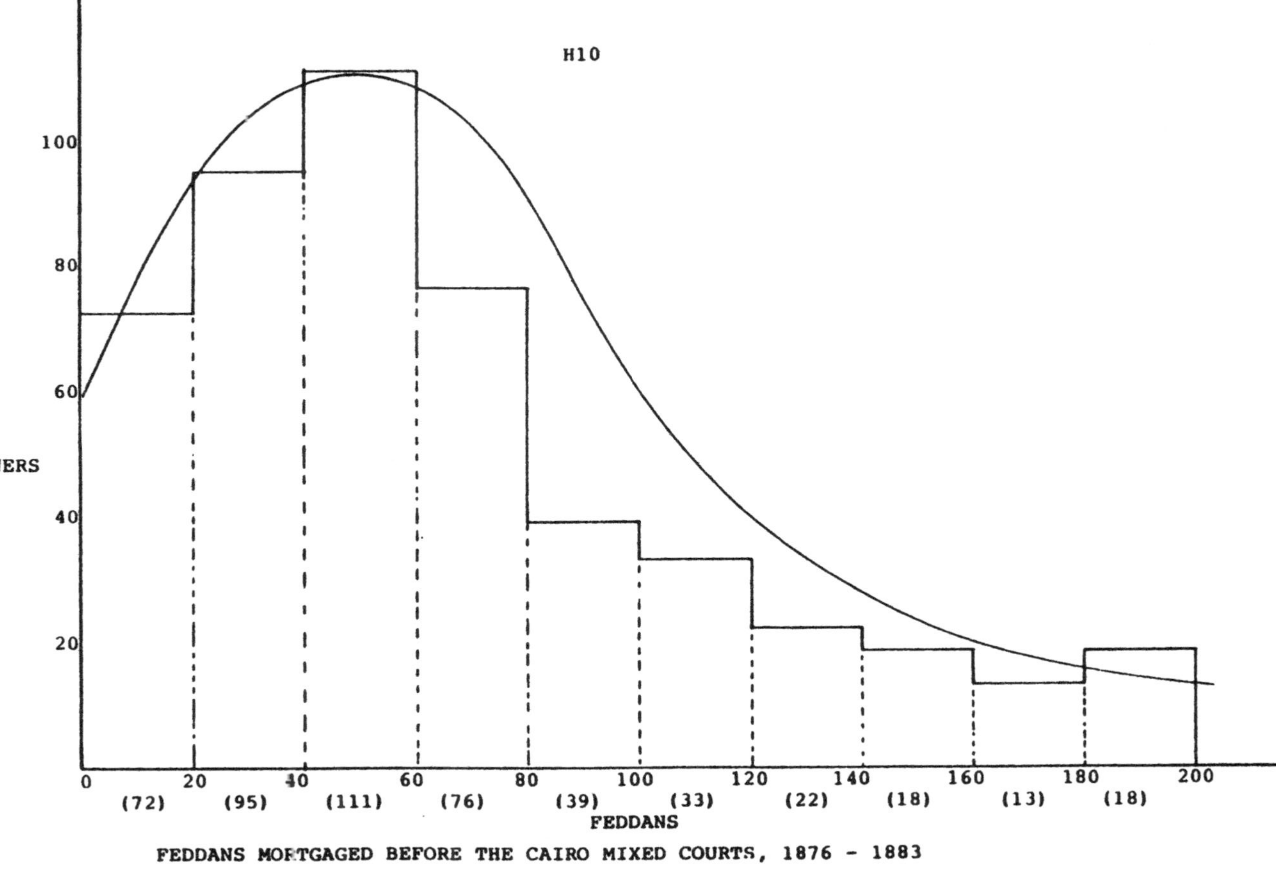

FEDDANS MORTGAGED BEFORE THE CAIRO MIXED COURTS, 1876 - 1883

149

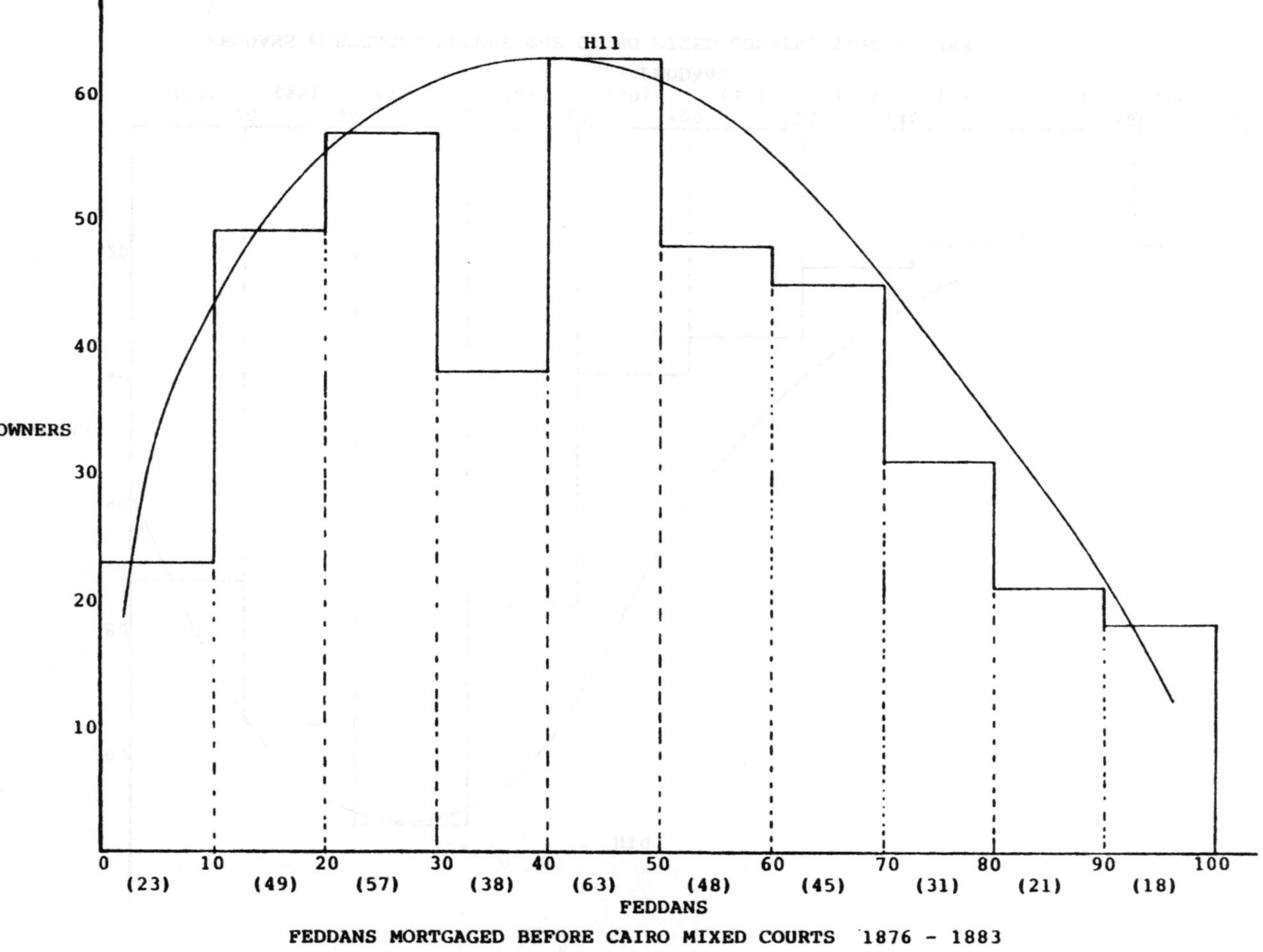

FEDDANS MORTGAGED BEFORE CAIRO MIXED COURTS 1876 – 1883

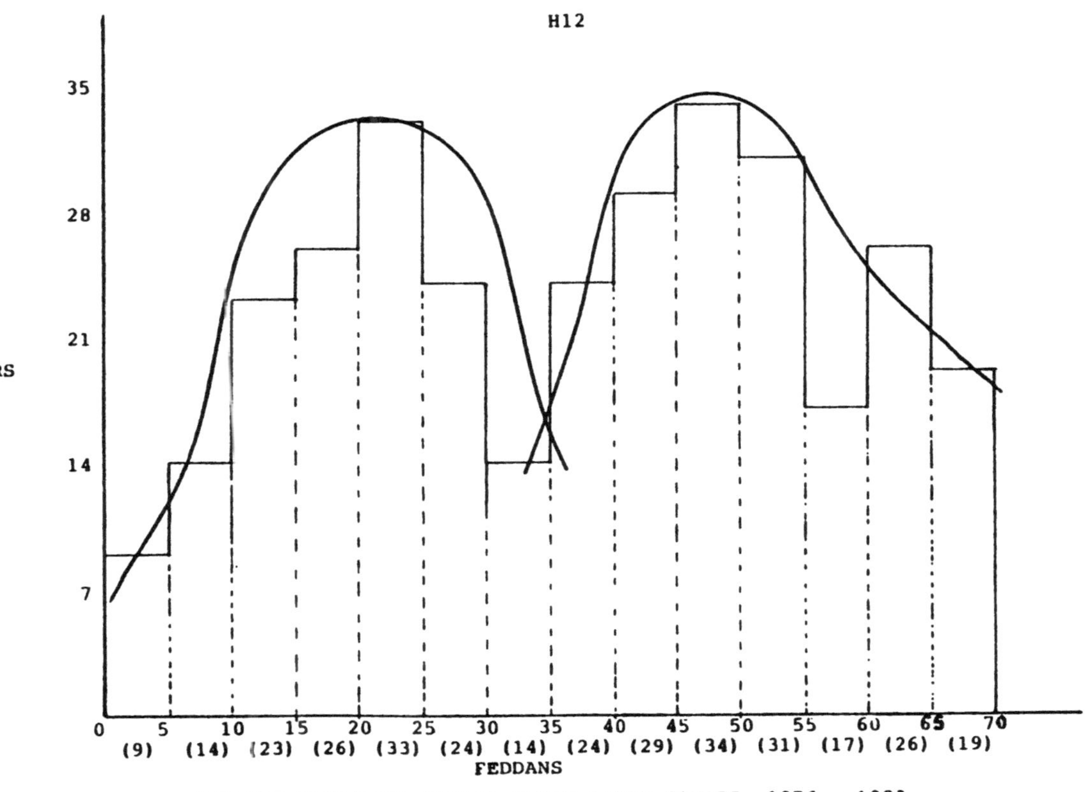

FEDDANS MORTGAGED BEFORE CAIRO MIXED COURTS 1876 - 1883

These elite landholders will be called large landholders (LLH)
and middle landholders (MLH). Only nine of those who held under 32.5
feddans owned less than five feddans, the usual ine between small and
middle landholders. As we shall see later, most rural property
holders in Egypt owned less than the four or five feddans necessary to
sustain a family without going into excessive debt.

Of the 139 middle landholders, few had a title while 28.10% of
their richer neighbors had titles.

	MLH		LLH	
	$\underline{N}$	$\underline{\%}$	$\underline{N}$	$\underline{\%}$
No Title	123	88.49	325	71.90
Effendi	10	7.19	69	15.27
Bey	5	3.60	45	9.96
Pasha	1	.72	13	2.88

Both groups resembled the national population in religion.[12]
Comparing Muslims with all others, the middle landholders were 92.14%
Muslim while the large landholders were 92.25% Muslim. All middle
landholders were Egyptian nationals and 99.66% of the large
landholders were Egyptians, though there are two reasons to believe
that this sample is not representative. Firstly, only Egyptian
borrowers seemed to have had mortgages recorded before these courts
and secondly, secondary material and archival data indicate foreigners
owned a bit less than ten percent of rural land early in the

occupation.

Both groups were overwhelmingly male, 92.67% and 96.38%
respectively. The mortgage documents systematically under represent
property held by women because of local requirements discussed above.
Only 4.94% of the large landholders worked for the Egyptian
government, while none of the small landholders was employed in the
public sector. Of the 31 large landholders in government, thirteen
were 'umda-s. In both groups, residents of Lower Egypt and the
governorates were over represented. The registration of land
mortgages before the Mixed Courts was not a common practice in Upper
Egypt in the period from 1876 to 1883 for middle landholders.

	MLH		LLH	
	N	%	N	%
Governorates	22	16.30	119	27.74
Lower Egypt	108	80.00	186	43.36
Upper Egypt	5	3.70	124	28.90

Large landholders were also more likely to be absentee landlords
than those who held less land and they more often lived in
governorates. A larger proportion of the large landholders lived in
towns than the middle landholders.[13]

	MLH		LLH	
	N	%	N	%
Villages	100	78.13	259	64.43
Towns	28	21.87	143	35.57

Large landholders were also more likely to own land far from their residence.

Location of Land Mortgaged

	MLH		LLH	
	N	%	N	%
Governorates	6	4.35	14	3.20
Lower Egypt	122	88.41	259	59.13
Upper Egypt	10	7.25	165	37.67

All land mortgaged outside the governorates by middle landholders was in the six provinces of Minufiya (56), Qalyubiya (29), Beni-Suef (1), Assyut (2) and Giza (5), i.e., those closest to Cairo except for Assyut. The types of mortgage documents signed were similar for the two groups.

Types of Mortgage Documents

	MLH		LLH	
	N	%	N	%
Jugement de contrat	17	12.41	71	16.14
Acte de prêt	105	76.64	317	72.05
Jugement de défaut	15	10.95	52	11.82

The types of lenders were different, partly because the Credit
Foncier Egyptien preferred to make only large loans.

Lender Types

	MLH		LLH	
	<u>N</u>	<u>%</u>	<u>N</u>	<u>%</u>
Credit Foncier	17	12.23	154	35.08
Individuals	102	73.38	218	49.66
Partnerships	14	10.07	27	6.15
Banks	0	0	3	.68
Companies	6	4.32	34	7.74
Egyptian Government	0	0	3	.68

The expanded role of the Credit Foncier Egyptien limited the
opportunities for Greek and Syrian money lenders among the large
landholders. These two types of lenders, the Credit Foncier and
individual Greeks, made about two-thirds of the loans to both groups.

Nationality of Lenders[14]

	MLH		LLH	
	N	%	N	%
Credit Foncier	17	12.32	154	36.49
Greek	77	55.80	108	25.59
French	7	5.07	30	7.11
British	3	2.17	10	2.37
Egyptian	9	6.52	21	4.98
Russian	3	2.17	10	2.37
German	1	.72	11	2.61
Persian	1	.72	3	.71
Other	20	14.49	70	16.59

An internal analysis of the middle landholders indicates that the group was relatively homogeneous, as was the lowest level of Cairo's old urban elite. Neither religion, sex nor type of occupation appears to stratify the middle landholders into different groups by wealth.

If we look at the breakdown of total land mortgaged or loans received by Muslims and Christians, the percentages follow the national breakdown very closely. Excluding only 5.77% of all mortgages of fifty feddans or more, where religion was unknown, Muslims held 93.13% and Christians 6.87% of the land mortgaged between 1876 and 1883.

Religion	Owners	Mean Land (feddans)	Sum	Total
Muslim	318	230.87	73,416	93.13
Chrisitan	25	216.76	5,419	6.87

The breakdown for mortgage loans also mirrorred the national population.

Religion	Owners	Mean Mort.(L.E.)	Sum	% Total
Muslim	316	3,231.99	1,021,309	92.03
Christian	25	3,539.36	88,484	7.97

Residence however, is marginally significant as an indicator of landholdings.[15] Large landholders at the start of the occupation formed a much less homogeneous group, one that was stratified by both residence and sector of employment.[16]

Employment in the public or private sector at the start of the occupation was a significant indicator of both land and the size of mortgage for large landholders.[17]

Among the 259 large landholders who lived in villages, fifteen government officials mortgaged an average of 227.8 feddans while owners in the private sector mortgaged an average of only 122 feddans. Among the 143 who lived in towns, 128 landowners mortgaged 263.8 feddans on the average, while fifteen government officials mortgaged 965.5 feddans.

From this examination of land mortgages before the Cairo Mixed Courts we can conclude that rural landholding was extremely concentrated at the beginning of the occupation. A line at about 32.5

feddans divided wealthier landholders into a homogeneous middle level

and a stratified upper level dominated by town dwellers and government

employees. Both groups parallelled the national population in

religion and nationality, and women were under represented at all

levels.

It is possible to extend our knowledge of the wealthiest stratum

of rural landholders at the start of the occupation by examining the

records of tax delinquincies for 1884 and 1885. In each of these

years the Egyptian Ministry of Finance compiled a list of all property

owners with over 200 L.E. back taxes on a minimum of 200 feddans.[18]

Combining the lists of November, 1884, and February, 1885,

produces a group of 255 owners of rural property in excess of two

hundred feddans. The distribution of back taxes is illustrated in the

histogram labeled H13. This group is not far from representative of

Egypt as a whole in religion and nationality, but differs markedly

from the majority of the population in title, sex, occupation and

residence. Of the 255 large landowners, 70.06% (185) were Muslim,

20.09% (47) were Christian and .85% (2) were Jewish. Ninety point six

percent (231) were Egyptian nationals, .4% (1) protected by foreign

status under the Capitulations, 6.3% (16) were foreign and seven

others were actually private institutions. Eighty-five percent were

male and thirteen percent female.[19]

158

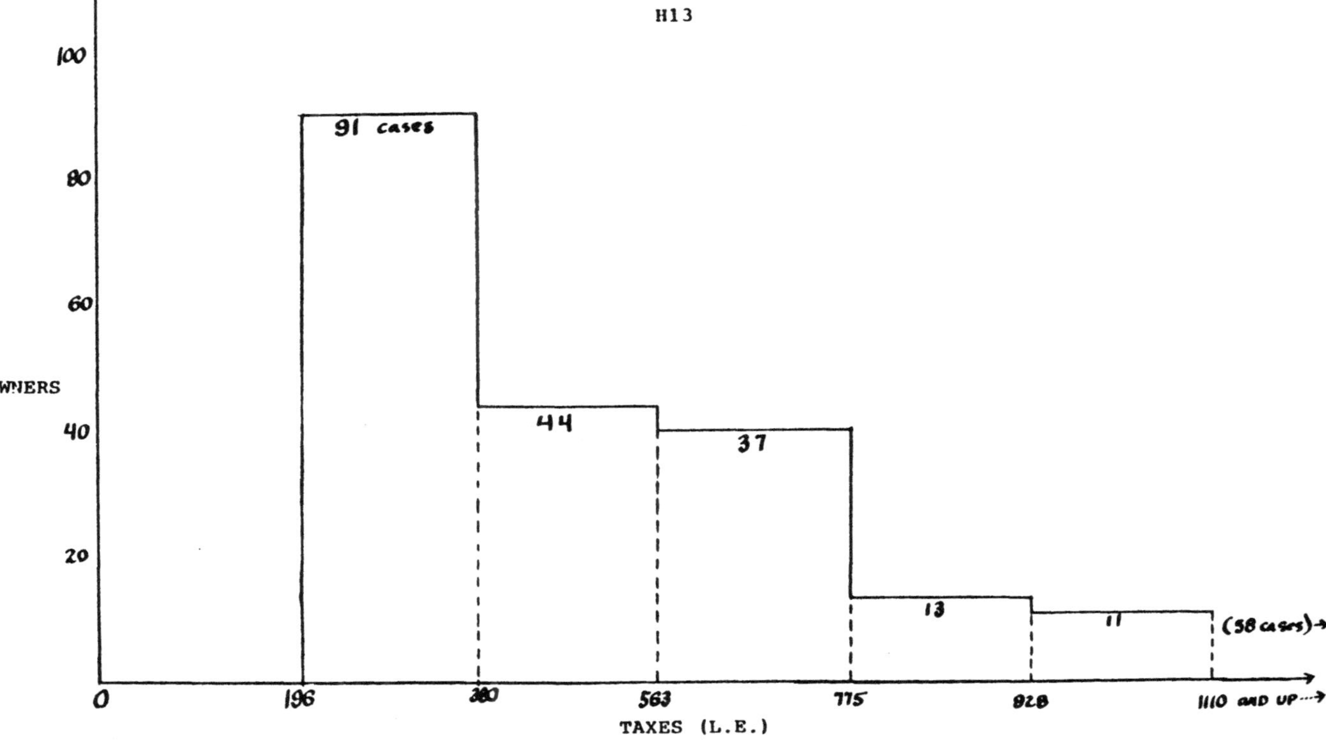

BACK TAXES ON OVER 200 FEDDANS OWED IN 1884 AND 1885 EXCEEDING 195 L.E.

Approximately half bore titles: 12.2% were Effendis (31), 14.9% were Beys (38) and twenty-two percent were Pashas (57). Twenty-five percent lived in towns, most of them (59) in Cairo. A suprisingly large number (46 or 18%) of the "owners" were in fact the estates of deceased persons and adminisitered for the collectivity of the heirs. Fifty owners also paid urban taxes on real property in Cairo in 1894. The tax ranged from seventy piasters to two hundred and ninety-eight pounds. The mean tax was 33.8 L.E., representing as calculated above real property valued at 8,112 L.E. The distribution is extremely skewed. The most popular quarters of residence in Cairo were Sayeda Zaynab (15), 'Abdin (7), al-Azbakiyya (6) and Shubra (6). The rural property on which the back taxes were owed was concentrated in the commercialized provinces of the Delta: Buhaira (74), Gharbiyya (58), Daqahliya (40), Qalyubiya (21) and Sharqiya (15).

A significant percentage of the total, 15.3%, were employed by the government, of which nine were 'umda-s. Only eight of the owners were waqfs. Of those whose residence can be determined (90), 73.3% living in the provinces lived in Lower Egypt. Six property owners sat as members of the Maglis al-Nuwwab from 1881 to 1882 and four were members of the Maglis Shura al-Qawanin or General Assembly from 1885 to 1889. Four bought from 42 to 21,157 feddans of Daira Saniyya land. The price varied from 924 L.E. to 13,200 L.E. Nine bought from three to 4,092 feddans of Domains land, varying in price from 88 to 192,478 L.E.

Of those owing back taxes, twelve also mortgaged two hundred feddans or more and six mortgaged a total of six houses. The amount of mortgage varied from 2,925 to 165.005 L.E. This sub-group of twelve included two Effendis, two Beys and four Pashas. Seventy-five percent were Muslims, 16.7% Christian and 8.3% Jewish. One was a member of the royal family. One was female. They paid from 15 to 298 pounds of urban property taxes in Cairo in 1894, thus holding property valued at from 3,600 L.E. to 71,520 L.E. Seventeen percent worked for the government. None bought Domains land but one bought 389 feddans of Daira Saniyya land for 13,200 L.E. All twelve were Egyptian nationals. Seven resided in Cairo, three in Lower Egypt and two in Upper Egypt. Two-thirds lived in towns, the rest in villages. Of the twelve, eight borrowed from the Credit Foncier Egyptien. Of the land mortgaged, 83% was in Lower Egypt. Three-quarters of this group signed more than one act of mortgage; the total was thirty. One of the twelve was President of the Legislative Assembly from 1885 to 1889. Again, in religion and nationality, this elite group resembles the nation as a whole, but is markedly different in occupation, sex, residence and title.

Of the large landowners who registered their mortgages before the Cairo Mixed Courts, 98 mortgaged two hundred feddans or more. Thus we have information about two similar elite groups which can be compared to enhance our description of elite landholders at the srart of the occupation. These two groups were (1) those who mortgaged over 200 feddans and (2) those who owed back taxes on over 200 feddans.

Elite Landholding, 1876-1883 [20]

	MORT		B TAX	
	N	%	N	%
No Title	53	54.64	128	50.39
Effendi	13	13.40	31	12.20
Bey	23	23.71	38	14.96
Pasha	8	8.25	57	22.44

Though both elite groups had more than their share of titles, it appears that Egyptian public figures used their status to delay payment payment of taxes. As was mentioned above, titles began to proliferate in the 1890's but were less common at the start of the occupation. Those mortgaging two hundred feddans or more resembled the national population in religion, while those owing back taxes had a heavy representation of the minority religions. It was especially Christians who were over represented.

Elite Landholding, 1876-1883

	MORT		B TAX	
	N	%	N	%
Muslim	85	91.40	185	79.06
Chrisitan	7	7.53	47	20.09
Jewish	1	1.08	2	.85

The disparity in religious composition is striking. The mortgage documents indicate that Christians owned a share of Egypt's largest

agricultural estates in proportion to their numbers in the overall
national society. The list of back taxes seems to indicate that
Christians constituted a disproportionately large percentage of the
landholding elite. This may be a reflection of a greater delinquency
rate for Christians. Muslims, on the other hand, owed average back
taxes of 1,379 L.E., while Christians owed only 963 L.E.

It seems much more likely, however, that non-Muslims held a is
disproportionately large share of big rural properties in certain
specific areas. If we assume that back taxes are a reliable indicator
of landholdings, we see that Christians held as much as 16.6% of the
large estates concentrated in lower Egypt.

Elite Landholding, 1876-1883

Religion	Owners	Total Back Taxes (L.E.)	% Total
Muslim	185	244,923	85.52
Christian	47	45,258	16.60
Jewish	2	2,384	.87

It appears as if Christians had begun to penetrate, and to
penetrate out of proportion to their numbers, the very highest strata
of both urban and rural property holders at the start of the
occupation. The relationship will become more clear as we consider
the areas of large landholdings.

Once Christians had established a powerful presence in the top
strata of urban and rural society, they began to move into the middle
groups in large numbers following the first years of the occupation.

Non-Egyptians followed the same pattern, first entering the political
elite at the apex, then penetrating the middle strata of the urban and
rural elites.

Although foreigners made up only 1.34% of the population of Egypt
in 1882, they constituted 6.27% of the elite landowners owing over 200
L.E. in back taxes, but perhaps mortgaged their land before consular
courts rather than the Mixed Courts or chose not to mortgage their
land.[21] Because the group that mortgaged over 200 feddans is so
small, it would probably be safer to follow the tax figures and
conclude that foreigners held a disproportionate share of the
country's great agricultural estates as early as 1885.

Men dominated both groups. Far more than mortgage conventions
was responsible for such a degree of male domination.

Elite Landholding, 1876-1883

	MORT		B TAX	
	N	%	N	%
Men	86	88.66	217	87.50
Women	11	11.34	31	12.50

Information about residence is unfortunately available for few of
those who owed back taxes.

Elite Landholding, 1876-1883

	MORT		B TAX	
	N	%	N	%
Governorates	42	43.30	60	23.62
Lower Egypt	22	22.68	22	8.66
Upper Egypt	27	27.84	8	3.15
Unknown	6	6.19	164	64.57

Absentee landownership is a fundamental characteristic of the top of the landholding elite at the start of the occupation, with Cairo the prefered residence. The landholdings of the two groups differed markedly.

Elite Landholding, 1876-1883

	MORT		B-TAX	
	N	%	N	%
Governorates	8	8.89	0	0
Lower Egypt	38	42.22	225	88.24
Upper Egypt	44	48.89	30	11.76

The distribution of landholdings indicates that our sample of mortgages is representative of all areas of Egypt but that most back taxes were owed on the commercial areas of the delta. It is no coincidence that these two elite groups differ in religious composition and in the areas where holdings were concentrated. The most progressive sector of the agricultural elite had the highest percentage of Christians, Jews and foreigners and they placed their

capital in the area then best suited to cotton production for export,
the delta.

For example, in the district of Kafr al-Shaykh in Gharbiyya,
larger proprietors owned 37,000 feddans or 25.5% of the total
cultivable area of 145,000 feddans. As late as the 1885-1886 cotton
season, only 48,351 feddans in Upper Egypt produced cotton, or 5.53%
of the total, compared with 826,114 feddans in Lower Egypt.[22]

Cotton was a summer crop dependent on abundant water. It became
possible to produce large quantities of cotton in Upper Egypt only
after the Assyut, Zifta and Isna barrages had been completed, starting
in 1903. Because minority groups and foreigners had greater access to
Eurpoean capital, we should expect their representation in the
agricultural elite of Upper Egypt to increase only after the turn of
the century, which was exactly what happened.

Neither of these elite groups of landowners holding over 200
feddans was internally stratified by religion, nationality or sex.
For those ninety landholders who owed back taxes and whose residence
can be identified, residence appears to be a significant indicator of
taxes owed but not of the amount of mortgage.[23]

Beyond any statistical tests, there is considerable background
evidence that these two groups were representative of the landholding
elites from which they were drawn. Those owing over 200 L.E. back
taxes on more than 200 feddans in 1884 and 1885 were characteristic of
the most progressive agricultural entrepreneurs for the following

reasons. On the date of October 31, 1884, back taxes owed on
agricultural land in all of Egypt totalled 592,061 L.E.[24] Of this
total, the categories of "notables and foreigners" owed 282,387 L.E.
Landowners in our elite group owed 130,387 L,E. of this total on
Novermber 14, 1884, or 46%. It appears highly unlikely that if those
who owed over 200 L.E. on over 200 feddans accounted for forty-six
percent of all back taxes of "notables and foreigners," that they
would be unrepresentative of all owners of two hundred feddans or
more. If anything, this elite group of 255 property owners is biased
toward the top of the elite, i.e., its most progressive elements,
those who used their status to withhold taxes until the last minute to
maximize profits and pay only after the most advantageous sales of
crops had been made. Up to 1880 large landowners could legally pay
taxes at the end of the tax year and at the location of their choice,
whether the Caisse of the <u>mudiriyya</u>, the Caisse de la Dette Publique
or the Caisse of the Ministry of Finances. After February 28, 1880,
they were supposed to pay them according to monthly tax schedules and
to the <u>Sarraf</u> of their commune. It appears that the ruling was not
tightly enforced and that large landowners delayed payment to maximise
profits.[25] Secondly, in 1885 "notables and Europeans" acounted for
30.54% (1,420,789/4,651,986 L.E.) of all land taxes due, and 47.7% of
all taxes on land overdue on October 31, 1884, (282,387/592,061).[26]
It seems that the highest status taxpayers were the most likely to owe
back taxes, and for all the reasons cited above our groups of back
taxpayers was extremely likely to be representative of the
entrepreneurial rural elite. On the other hand, the elite group which

mortgaged over two hundred feddans seems to be representative of a
more traditional landholding elite.

Thus far a pattern has emerged in the transformation of urban and
rural elite groups at the start of the occupation. The lower levels
of property holders were relatively homogeneous and representative of
the national population, women excepted. Minority religious
communities and non-Egyptians first penetrated the top levels of the
urban elite groups out of proportion to their numbers and then these
groups began to lose some of their homogeneity. By 1885 our data show
that non-Egyptians and non-Muslims were establishing a large presence
in the middle elite groups in Cairo and setting up the beginnings of
social stratification at the apex of the rural elite, especially in
the cotton producing areas of the delta. We shall now examine the
continuing transformation of elite groups of agricultural landowners
down to 1907 on the basis aggregate statistics on land holding
collected by the Egyptian government.

Aggregate Statistics on Rural Land Distribution from 1894 to 1907

Statistics are available for the distribution of private agricultural land in Egypt from 1894 when they were drawn from the village land tax registers and published in a government report. Two years later a modern cadastral survey was begun which was able to cover two provinces per year. By 1907 data were available for all of Egypt with a relative degree of statistical accuracy. This section will analyze these data so as to make some general statements about the evolution of property distribution in the countryside.

The distribution of land by size of plot and number of owners was published for all of Egypt in the Statistical Yearbook for Egypt for 1909. Five basic observations about the validity of the data in this table appear in Appendix 30.

The raw data from 1896 can be summarized as follows.

Size of Plot

(feddans)	Owners	% All Owners	Area	% All Area
0 - 5	611,074	79.64	993,843	19.87
5 - 30	135,014	17.60	1,457,235	29.14
0 - Top	21,172	2.76	2,549,923	50.99
Total	767,260	100.00	5,001,001	100.00

Making use of the available inforlmation we can correct this table by increasing the number of owners of plots in the category 0 - 5 feddans by (1) 77.55 to compensate for the under registration of shared plots and (2) by 10% of the number in the category 5 - 30

feddans to allow for the shared plots in this category that were

actually in the lowest range. Next, the number of owners in the

middle category can be reduced by a similar ten percent and again by a

like amount to compensate first for the above operation and secondly

to compensate for owners holding land in more than one village.

Finally, the category of 30 feddans and above can be reduced by 40% as

a crude approximation of the number of plots in more than one village

actually held by a single proprietor. In the column for area, the

amount in the range 0 - 5 can be increased by 10% of the area held in

the range 5 - 30 feddans and the figure for this range reduced by the

same area. These modifications result in the following corrected

table for land distribution in 1896.

Size of Plot

feddans	Owners	%All Owners	Area	% All Area
0 - 5	1,098,157	90.10	1,139,566	22.79
5 - 30	108,011	8.86	1,311,512	26.22
30 - Top	12,703	1.04	2,549,923	50.99
Total	1,218,871	100.00	5,001,001	100.00

The table below shows the raw data for 1907.

Size of Plot

Feddans	Owners	%All Owners	Area	% All Area
0 - 5	1,120,791	88.43	1,323,313	24.34
5 - 30	125,401	9.89	1,328,509	24.44
30 - Top	21,211	1.67	2,783,967	51.22
Total	1,267,403	100.00	5,435,789	100.00

The final table in this series illustrates corrected data for
1909 where (1) the number of owners in the range 5 - 30 feddans has
been reduced by 10% to compensate for holdings in more than one
village and (2) the number of owners in the category over 30 feddans
has been reduced 40% for the same reason.

Size of Plot

feddans	Owners	%All Owners	Area	% All Area
0 - 5	1,120,791	89.92	1,323,313	24.34
5 - 30	112,861	9.06	1,328,509	24.44
30 - Top	12,727	1.02	2,783,967	51.22
Total	1,246,379	100.00	5,435,789	100.00

The corrected percentages are almost identical for land
distribution in 1897 and 1907. The only difference seems to be a
slight increase in the percentage of land held by the owners of under
five feddans, up 1.55% to 24.34% at the expense of owners in the
category directly above. These hypothetical tables confirm the

impression that the distribution of land by the size of holdings
changed little from 1896 to 1907.

This picture, however, must be placed in the context of rapid
growth in the rural population. The number of landholders as a
percentage of rural inhabitants shrank from 1896 to 1907 as can be
seen in the table below.

Owners Placed by Holdings in Feddans[27]

Year	0 - 5	5 - 30	Over 30	All Owners	Rural Pop.	%
1896	1,098,157	108,011	12,703	1,218,871	8,361,540	14.58
1907	1,120,791	112,861	12,727	1,246,379	9,777,985	12.75

Considering the fact of increasing absentee ownership among
owners of thirty feddans and above, this percentage decline was
probably greater than the 1.83% observed here. Looking at the figures
from another angle, the number of landless peasants probably increased
from 7,142,669 (8,361,540 - 1,218,871) to 8,531,606 (9,777,985 -
1,246,379), up 19.45%. Though these figures are hypothetical and very
approximate, they establish the impression of an important
transformation of the rural population, an increasing body of landless
peasants, and secondly of a real increase in the effective
concentration of landholding in light of rural population growth. We
should also not overlook the fact of one fundamental element of
continuity: the presence of a large population of small peasant
proprietors whose average holdings were little above one feddan, using
the corrected statistics, in both 1897 and 1907. The acreage per

family was close to the level of bare subsistence on the average.
Royal land sales will next help us extend our description of
transformations in the rural sector.

Agricultural Land Distribution, 1879-1907: Royal Land Sales

The coded Daira Saniyya and Domains sales analyzed in this study
total 557,621 feddans, or 10.32% of Egypt's entire cultivated area for
the 1906-1907 season. [28] The records of this massive land transfer
will therefore provide an excellent picture of the changing
distribution of land in Egypt under Cromer and thus of the balance of
power among different groups competing for productive land. Because
some sales below forty feddans were coded and all those above were
treated, four types of sales records will be analyzed simultaneously:
(1) Daira Saniyya sales under forty feddans, (2) Daira Saniyya sales
over that amount, (3) Domains sales under forty feddans and (4)
Domains sales over that amount.

Christians and Jews constituted a disproportionately large share
of the elite groups that purchased Daira Saniyya land and non-Muslims
bought an astounding 53.87% of the total acreage.

Daira Saniyya Sales

| | Less than 40 Feddans | | | | More than 40 Feddans | | | |
Religion	N	%Owners	%Cost	%Fedans	N	%Owners	%Cost	%Fedans
Muslim	54	72.97	77.59	76.84	370	64.12	57.13	45.98
Christn	19	25.68	22.41	21.27	194	33.62	39.28	50.10
Jewish	1	1.35	Unk.	1.89	13	2.25	3.59	3.91
Non-Mus.	21	28.00	22.87	23.20	209	36.10	42.96	54.07

Of the total 313,047 feddans coded here that were taken from the
royal family, 168,652 feddans were purchased by non-Muslims. These

land sales constituted the greatest single shift in the balance of
rural power from the deposition of Isma'il to the revolution of 1952.
Domains land sales show an important, but less disproportionate,
transfer of large rural properties into the hands of non-Muslims.

Domains Land Sales

	Less than 40 Feddans			More than 40 Feddans			
Religion	N	%Owners	%Cost	%Fedans	N	%Owners	%Cost	%Fedans
---	---	---	---	---	---	---	---	---
Muslim	107	86.29	84.45	84.75	534	79.82	77.72	72.05
Christn	16	12.90	13.89	14.64	125	18.68	18.70	21.84
Jewish	1	.81	.65	.57	10	1.49	3.59	6.11
Non-Mus.	17	13.71	14.55	15.25	140	20.77	22.50	28.14

Of the 212,845 feddans of Domains land coded here, non-Muslims
purchased 59,461 feddans, or 27,94%. In 1907 non-Muslims constituted
only 8.23% of the national population. For both Daira Saniyya and
Domains sales, Christians and Jews constituted a disproportionately
large share of buyers and for sales over forty feddans, bought an even
greater percentage of former royal lands. As was the case for the
lower strata of urban property owners and the old rural elite, the
groups that bought less than forty feddans were relatively
homogeneous. That is, within these groups religion was not highly
correlated with the size or cost of land purchased. On the other
hand, Domains land buyers who purchased over forty feddans formed a
group that was stratified by religion.[29] The group of Daira Saniyya
purchasers was not divided into more and less wealthy segments by

religion.

These observed advantages for non-Muslim buyers of Domains land were statistically significant. Considering Muslims versus non-Muslims, chi square equals 5.60990 for the cost and 10.99529 for the feddans purchased. Religion was not a significant indicator of land or cost however, for the Domains sales. Again rating Muslims versus non-Muslims, chi square was 2.76234 for cost and 2.38327 for feddans purchased in the Domains sales.

Nonetheless, non-Muslims purchased 228,113 feddans or 43.38% of the total 525,892 feddans transferred from the royal family to private holders in the coded Daira Saniyya and Domains sales from 1879 to 1907. These were private holders for whom religion could be determined. Since religion was unknown for several multi-national land companies conrolled by Europeans that purchased 29,050 feddans, non-Muslims actually bought 257,163 of the 555,032 feddans where religion can be inferred, or 46.34% of the total. Foreign individuals or European controlled companies made few small purchases and bought about fourteen percent of the large estates sold.[30]

The royal family did very badly in the Daira Saniyya land transfers, considering the fact that it owned and operated all of this land before the Law of Liquidation of 1880. It retained by purchase only 1.90% or 6,138 of the total 323,855 feddans sold. Proteges, foreigners or private institutions used the Daira Saniyya sales to acquire 46,226 feddans, or 14.27% of the land. Proteges and foreign nationals constituted only 1.34% of the residents of Egypt in 1907. Non-Egyptians used the Domains sales to even greater advantage.[31]

The royal family was able to buy back 30,959 feddans, or 13.38% of the Domains lands sold where information on nationality is available. Proteges, foreigners and private institutions dominated by Europeans used the Domains sales to acquire 39,204 feddans, or 16.95% of the Domains lands sold. These non-Egyptian groups thus acquired a total of 85,430 feddans of Domains and Daira Saniyya land, most of it among the best farm land in Egypt, or 15.33% of the land transferred. This land represented approximately one and non-half percent of the total cultivable land in Egypt in 1907. These land sales show that absentee landownership was on the increase during the first twenty-five years of the British occupation.[32]

The Daira Saniyya sales show an inreasing trend to absentee landownership during the first decades of the British occupation. Though nearly all of the Daira Saniyya lands were located in Upper Egypt, 117,522 feddans or 46.45% of the total were purchased by residents of the governorates, mostly living in Cairo. Residents of the capital purchased 101,071 feddans of Daira Saniyya lands. Absentee ownership was most widespread among buyers who purchased over forty feddans, 48.74%, than for those buying less than that amount, 26.79%. The area of residence, classified as governorates, Lower Egypt or Upper Egypt, was the same as the general area of purchase for 265 of the 493 buyers where both the location of residence and of purchase was known.

Resdience could be determined for very few buyers of Domains
land, only 151 of the total 885, or 17.06%. Well over half of these
buyers lived in Cairo, though the total proportion of buyers in the
capital was probably lower. It proved much easier to locate the
residence of those in Cairo than for others outside. On the basis of
information available, buyers living in Cairo paid 4,274,682 L.E. for
Domains and Daira Saniyya land, or 30.62% of the total 13,959,186 L.E.
They also bought 142,586 feddans, or 25.57% of the total 557,621
feddans sold. Both actual percentages were probably greater than
those stated, because residence could not be determined for many
buyers probably living in the capital. For Daira Saniyya sales above
forty feddans, residence was a significant indicator of the size and
cost of purchase; residents of the governorates bought more land on
the average and at greater cost than those in the provinces. For all
sales, residents of towns consistently purchased more land and paid
more for it than villagers. The differences were greatest among
groups that bought over 40 feddans of both Daira Saniyya and Domains
land. On the other hand, before the land transfers, all these royal
lands were held by a small group that spent most of its time in the
governorates. The sales thus added to the area held by villagers,
even if the best land was purchased in large lots by urban
entrepreneurs.

Government employees bought a large share of the Daira Saniyya
lands, especially among owners who purchased more than forty feddans,

paying 31.35% of the total laid out in this category for 47.88% of the
acerage.[33]

From 1887 to 1898 Daira Saniyya lands were given to veterans and
pensioned civil servants in lieu of monthly pensions. Thus many
functionaries were able to use public service to become landowners,
purchasing a total of 120,677 feddans for 2,056,764 L.E. from the
Daira Saniyya Administration. Most of these functionaries were
Muslim: ten out of twelve who bought land under forty feddans and 108
out of 136 who purchased more than that amount.

A large percentage of Domains sales went to government employees
following a decision made in October of 1886 to sell land to retired
functionaries in return for their pension rights in order to speed up
the transfer of former royal lands. Between October 23, 1886 and the
end of that year, 519 pensioners applied to buy the following types of
lands.

Land Type	Feddans	Value (L.E.)
Domains	23,395	448,104
Daira Saniyya	9,632	102,112
Biens Libres[34]	18,028	74,955

Within two years the lands were exchanged, Domains sales
accounting for 71.68% of the value of these exchanges. Government
employees eventually paid 31.39% of the price of the coded Domains
lands sold.[35]

Government service appears to have offered a path of social
mobility for the largely Muslim functionaries who bought Domains land.
Most of the Christians who purchased Domains land were in the private
sector.

Thus both the Daira Saniyya and the Domains sales brought about a
massive transfer of farm land to non-Muslims and non-Egyptians in the
private sector and also to Muslims in the government service. Public
employees acquired a total of 189,674 feddans or 34.01% of the total
for 3,605,592 L.E., or 25.83% of the total price for all coded Daira
Saniyya and Domains sales. Because of the fact that almost all
government employees were men, any breakdown of these sales by sex
would be misleading. The final category of information that can bear
on the continuing transformations of wealth and power in the rural
sector centers on the division of labor.

The Organization of Production in Agriculture

There is little statistical evidence about the organization of
production in Egyptian agriculture before the agricultural census of
1929. For this reason the following discussion must remain
speculative and rather inconclusive until further data become
available from the Shari'a court archives throughout Egypt.
Agriculture under Cromer was in the latter stages of a long transition
from pre-modern to modern commercial relations of production. As
such, different forms of organization coexisted along a varied
spectrum from forced labor to wage labor at the beginning of the
occupation: (1) corvee or forced labor, (2) the 'ezbah system (3)
share cropping, (4) cash rental, (5) direct cultivation by the owner
on small plots and (6) wage labor.

Muhammad 'Ali's system of agricultural monopolies subordinated
rural elite groups and attempted to force them to act as mere
supervisors of peasant labor from which the state reaped most of the
benefits. To the extent that this system worked, rural families with
great local power under the Mamluks lost their autonomy and other
families controlling peasant labor on ten to thirty feddans probably
suffered as well. By the late eighteen thirties this system was
abandoned and an elite of Turko-Circassian and Muslim civil servants
emerged in charge of large agricultural estates. As certain
categories of land became partially alienable, enterprising peasants
and village shaykhs emerged as middle estate holders. Parallel with
the slow emergence of private property in land, the coercive nature of

rural labor relations began to diminish. As cotton production for export came to dominate the rural economy, a slow transition to cash labor relations began to occur and compulsory labor diminished both on private estates and state public works projects such as canal cleaning.[36]

From 1885 to 1889 the Egyptian government eliminated the compulsory nature of corvee work on state irrigation projects. After 1889, these were carried out with wage labor. The change occurred partly for humanitarian reasons but also because forced labor was inefficient and because large landowners objected to the loss of peasant labor from their estates.[37] Ra'uf 'Abbas Hamid argues that the government began to pay corvee laborers because it was able to gather only 83,346 peasants out of the 116,607 it summoned in 1885.[38] The annual budget for corvee works began at 24,243 L.E. in 1885 and rapidly rose to about 400,000 L.E. where it remained until it disappeared as a category in state accounting in 1905.[39]

After the 1850's all these forms of corvee coexisted with the dominant form of agricultural organization, the 'ezbah system. This system does not form a category that is mutually exclusive from the other five in the list above, but will be treated separately because of its unique character and dominance after 1850. In the 'ezbah system, resident peasants were granted rotating plots to grow subsistence crops such as corn and beans. The use of this land rent free provided an important benefit to the peasants. In return, they probably provided labor at a fraction of the prevailing wage on the

lands of the 'ezbah owner where production centered on cash crops
like cotton for the export market. These resident tamaliyya
laborers were supplemented by migrant laborers called tarahil. We
can conclude that most uncompensated labor was eliminated from
Egyptian agriculture by the beginning of the twentieth century, but
that the coercive aspects of the 'ezbah system continued in full
force long after 1907. Its continuing coercive aspects included debt
peonage and the estate owner's privilege of settling local
disputes.[40]

The 'ezbah system flourished throughout the first twenty-five
years of the British occupation as well as later because it combined a
flexible mixture of different types of labor relations well suited to
Egypt's main crops. By allowing tamaliyya laborers to cultivate
their subsistence crops on rent free land, the 'ezbah owner could
command their labor on cash crops at a fraction of its true cost.
Thus another coercive trait entered into this system of labor
relations, beyond the modern spectrum of commercial or cash relations.
For example, the tamaliyya laborers who worked on Riaz Pasha's lands
at Mahallet Ruh in Gharbiyya formed about one hundred families or six
hundred fallahin. Each family received three-quarters of a feddan
for subsistence crops and free housing and worked Riaz's lands for
annual wages of two hundred piasters.[41] Tamaliyya laborers
generally worked the owner's land twenty-five days a month during
harvest season.[42] These tamaliyya laborers therefore received
wages of about 2/3 of a piaster per day.[43] One hundred and fifty

183

migrant laborers joined them at harvest time when they were paid wages
between 1 1/2 and 2 1/2 piasters per day.[44] Thus migrant laborers
were paid more than twice as much per day than the resident
tamaliyya peasants. Chelu reported that tarahil workers earned an
average of 2 1/2 piasters per day in the delta but that wages were
twenty-five percent lower in Upper Egypt where labor was
plentiful.[45]

The 'ezbah system worked because it encouraged peasants to
carefully cultivate their subsistence plots from which they benefitted
directly and it allowed close supervision of the fallahin for labor
intensive, cash crops like cotton.[46] The largest farms were called
taftish, plural, tafatish, and were administered by a director
general or mufattish who supervised section leaders, called
nazir-s in charge of qism-s. Each nazir or mufattish was
assisted by foremen known as kholi-s.[47] This hierarchy of
supervisors permitted the relatively efficient running of large
agricultural estates. Depending on the fluctuation in the prices of
different crops, the availability of tarahil labor and the level of
the prevailing rents, the 'ezbah owner could rent out or permit
sharecropping on a varying percentage of his land, working the rest
with kholi-s and tamaliyya labor most of the year. Although there
are no conclusive statistics for Egypt as a whole, contemporary
sources agree that 'ezbah-s were especially common in the delta.
This impression is supported by village names listed in the censuses
of the period. For example, in the markaz of Quwaisna in

al-Minufiyya there were eighty-one 'ezbah-s with an area of fifty
feddans in 1900.[48]

Egypt had a wide variety of sharecropping arrangements in the
early decades of the British occupation. The mukhamis worked land
in return for one-fifth of the crop after the landowner had deducted a
previous fifth for his expenses. The munasif supplied seed,
fertilizer and labor, caring for the crop until harvest, when he took
half as his share. The munasif assumed part of the risks of crop
failure and any debts he contracted with the landlord diminished his
share of the harvest. The murabi' cultivated summer corn in return
for a quarter of his crop. The cultivator bi-l-mithal worked an
area of the owner's land on which he received none of the crop in
return for full right to the harvest on an equal area for which he
paid rent.[49] The exact type of sharecropping arrangement varied
according to local traditions, the bargaining power of each party and
the overall evolution of relations of production in agriculture as a
whole.

Cash rental was most common in the commercialized areas of the
delta at the beginning of the occupation, but spread to upper Egypt
with perennial irrigation after the turn of the century. The great
majority of smallholders cultivated their small plots themselves,
mobilizing all members of the family. In 1894, the first year for
which statistics are available, the great majority of landowners,
512,160 or 77.6% of the total, owned less than five feddans. These
five hundred and twelve thousand families owned 930,000 feddans, or

19.8% of the cultivated area.[50] Since the average holding in this category was only 1.8 feddans, these small holders could barely maintain their existence, were in constant danger of losing their land through debt, and naturally were unable to hire extra labor. The poorest cultivators practiced self cultivation or perhaps rented out their small plots which were too little to justify cultivation alone.

Wage labor was probably used by only the larger estate owners and usually in combination with other labor arrangements such as the 'ezbah system or cash rental. The balance between these six forms of labor organization shifted in the first twenty-five years of the occupation, away from forced labor and probably toward greater cash rental. Alan Richards in the above quoted articles argues that sharecropping and the 'ezbah system continued to dominate and Roger Owen argues that cash rental became more common.[51] I will offer evidence which supports the hypothesis that cash rental became more common from 1882 to 1907.

With the exception of some large estates where close supervision of production was maintained in an effort to increase productivity, the general trend among estates of over thirty feddans was toward increased cash rental within the framework of the 'ezbah system. This interpretation is consistent with the major trends observed in Egyptian agriculture during this period. Firstly, biennial crop rotation on cotton land in Lower Egypt increased from 17% of the acerage in 1894 to 56% in 1907.[52] Because the smallholders owned less than a third of all cultivable land, it is not likely that the switch from the three year to the two year cycle occurred only on the lands of smallholders. The biennial pattern is consistent with increasing cash rental and the lack of close supervision it normally implies.[53] Secondly, the steadily declining output per feddan on cotton land in this period is consistent with increasing cash rental. The British official James I. Craig documented the declining productivity which he argued would be partly accounted for by (1) the difference in fertility in Upper and Lower Egypt, (2) the extension of cotton cultivation into poorer land in Lower Egypt and (3) the switch from three year to two year crop rotation.[54] Renters tended to over crop the soil more than others. Thirdly, land owners derived a steadier income from renting land than from cultivating it themselves at this time.[55] Fourthly, cash rental is consistent with the pattern of increasing absentee ownership observed in both middle and large agricultural estates as demonstrated above. On the other hand, "Tenants who paid their rents in cash were not in a position to obtain more than a small share of the rise in agricultural profits" that occurred after the turn of the century.[56] Finally, there was an increase in the number of small 'ezbah-s between thirty and fifty feddans and the 'ezbah was quickly capable of responding to shifting conditions by allocating larger areas to cash rental. The increase in small 'ezbah-s is documented in a law passed in 1889 that declared the formation of new 'ezbah-s under fifty feddans to be illegal.[57]

During the first twenty-five years of the British occupation massive investment in irrigation and in the national transport

infrastructure increased agricultural output, which became more and
more dominated by cotton. These shifts increased the total wealth in
the agricultural sector, but mismanagement by Anglo-Egyptian
irrigation advisers led to a sharp decline in yield per feddan at the
same time as Egypt became more dangerously dependent on fluctuating
world market prices for its dominant cash crop.

On the eve of the occupation, most rural dwellers owned no land
or less than five feddans. Those elite landowners holding more than
five feddans were divided into two groups, those holding more and
those holding less than about thirty-two feddans. The lower group,
middle landholders, was relatively homogeneous and representative of
the national population. The wealthier group of large landholders was
stratified by occupation and residence. By 1885 non-Egyptians and
non-Muslims had established a large presence among middle elite groups
in the commericalized areas of the delta and were beginning to gain a
disproportionate share of large agricultural estates. The apex of the
rural elite was beginning to lose its homogeneity by 1885.

Aggregate statistics on land distribution from 1896 to 1907 show
that the overall spread of holdings by size of plot changed little.
However, the social consequences of this seeming stability were great.
The increase in the cultivated area lagged behind the growth in rural
population so that the ranks of landless peasants greatly increased.
Placed against the background of growing absentee ownership,
competition for land increased considerably during the first quarter
century of the British occupation. This competition was exacerbated

by the sharp inflation in land prices and rent after 1900.

Sales records of the Domains and Daira Saniyya estates indicate that the processes of social differentiation within the elite, competition for land, and the shift away from continued dominance by the Turko-Circassian and Muslim rural elite families all accelerated through 1907. These sales show wealth and power flowing out of the hands of the royal family and the old rural elite families and into the hands of a new spectrum of elite groups dominated by urban dwellers, Muslim government employees, non-Muslims and non-Egyptians.

Agricultural relations of production shifted simultaneously in the following ways from 1882 to 1907: (1) forced labor without compensation was almost completely eliminated by 1889, (2) the 'ezbah system remained dominant and the pattern spread to many estates between thirty and fifty feddans, (3) cash rental, by itself or within the 'ezbah system, bacame more common, (4) sharecropping remained important but may have decreased slightly in order to permit the rise of cash rental and (5) small plots under five feddans continued to be cultivated by their owners though there wore cases of rental here as well.

These simultaneous shifts in output, land distribution and the organization of agricultural production had tremendous social consequences. The swelling population of landless peasants was absorbed partly by the prosperous 'ezbah plantations while other segments of this displaced group became wage laborers for middle

estate owners. Demographic statistics cited in chapter one show that
Egypt's urban areas absorbed few peasants up to 1907 though they
opened their doors to a great flood of foreigners. Because all land
became alienable by 1896 and forced labor almost completely
disappeared, farm laborers became increasingly mobile. Here the trend
was for excess labor in Upper Egypt to migrate to the delta during the
cotton season. In general rural society became much more stratified
and opportunities for upward mobility diminished. The elite group of
large landowners which developed under Cromer was able to maintain its
dominant position in rural society down to the revolution of 1952.[55]

Footnotes: Chapter Five

1. (1) A. E. Crouchley, <u>The</u> <u>Economic</u> <u>Development</u> <u>of</u> <u>Modern</u>
<u>Egypt</u>, (2) Patrick O'Brien, "The Long-Term Growth of Agricultural
Productivity in Egypt: 1821-1962," in P. M. Holt, ed., <u>Political</u>
and Social Change in Modern Egypt, <u>pp.162-195</u>, (<u>3</u>) <u>Roger</u> <u>Owen</u>,
<u>Cotton</u> <u>and</u> <u>the</u> <u>Egyptian</u> <u>Economy</u>, (4) Samir Radwan, <u>Capital</u>
<u>Formation</u> <u>in</u> <u>Egyptian</u> <u>Industry</u> <u>and</u> <u>Agriculture</u>, <u>1882-1967</u>, and (5)
'Ali Barakat, <u>The</u> <u>Development</u> <u>of</u> <u>Large</u> <u>Agricultural</u> <u>Property</u>
<u>Holding</u> (Arabic).

2. James I. Craig, "Notes on Cotton Statistics in Egypt,"
<u>Egypte</u> <u>Contemporaine</u>, No.6, March, 1911, p.177.

3. Radwan, <u>Capital</u> <u>Formation</u>, pp.22-25; Crouchley, <u>Economic</u>
<u>Development</u>, pp.147-151.

4. Radwan, <u>Capital</u> <u>Formation</u>, p.32.

5. O'Brien, "Long-Term Growth," p.172 and <u>Statistical</u>
<u>Yearbook</u> <u>for</u> <u>Egypt</u> <u>for</u> <u>1909</u>, p.270. All prices here and in the next
paragraph are expressed in 1960 constant Egyptian pounds.

6. All figures below the last citation are from Radwan,
<u>Capital</u> <u>Formation</u>, p.118. Egyptian pounds will be expressed in
contemporary prices from this point on unless indicated otherwise.

7. O'Brien, "Long Term Growth," pp.185-189.

8. Crouchley, <u>Economic</u> <u>Development</u>, p.155.

9. Owen, <u>Cotton</u>, pp.241-243.

10. <u>Ibid</u>.,p.197; Crouchley, <u>Investment of Capital</u>,
pp.64-65.

11. Computation of the Gini index is described in detail in
<u>Historian's Guide to Statistics: Quantitative Analysis and
Historical Research</u>, by Charles Dollar and Richard Jensen, New York,
Holt, Rinehart and Winston,Inc., 1971, pp. 124-125.

12. Elite Landholding, 1876-1883

| | MLH | | LLH | |
	<u>N</u>	<u>%</u>	<u>N</u>	<u>%</u>
Muslim	119	85.61	397	87.83
Christian	10	7.19	30	6.64
Jewish	0	0	2	.44
Not Muslim	0	0	2	.44
Not Jewish	7	5.04	11	2.43
No Info.	3	2.16	10	2.21

Names that could be either Muslim or Christian like 'Issa were
classified as "Not Jewish" while others that could be either Christian
or Jewish were labeled "Not Muslim."

13. Towns here were defined to include governorates and
provincial capitals. The difference is statistically significant; chi

square equals 8.3345293.

14. A number of "other" nationals, especially those accorded Italian nationality, had obviously Egytian Coptic names, such as Girgis Awad.

15. Chi square equals 3.09892 for the following two by two table.

Residence for MLH

Land (feddans)	Villages	Towns
1 - 17.5	83	19
17.5 - 32	17	9

Chances are almost eight in one hundred that the difference is due to the process of sampling. There are so few town dwellers that we can come to no firm conclusion.

16.   Residence for LLH

Land (feddans)	Villages	Towns
33 - 200	216	100
200 and above	43	43

Residence was sigificant as an indicator of land holdings for large landholders. Chi square equals 9.93707; i.e., chances were less than two in one thousand that the differences were due to the process of sampling. Residence was also significant as an indicator of the size of mortgage made; chi square equals 4.85431.

17. Employment   for   LLH

Land (feddans)	Government	Non-government
1 - 200	15	342
Over 200	16	79

Chi square equals 18.76762.

Mortgage (L.E.)	Government	Non-government
1 - 2,500	12	339
Over 2,500	19	82

Chi square equals 29.09201.

18.   Ministere des Finances, <u>Direction des Contribuables qui possèdent deux cent feddans et au-dessus et qui sont en retard pour le paiement de l'Impôt foncier à fin Novembre, 1884, non compris ceux dont la dette n'excèdent pas Lst. 200</u>, Dar al-Mahfuzat Library, 54/12/1 646, eight pages; Idara al-Amwal al-Muqarrara, <u>Kashf 'an al-Matlub min al-Mumawallin al-Lathina 'Atyanuhum Tablaghu Ma'tani Faddan fa'fuqu wa Muta'akhar 'Alihim min al-Amwal li-Ghayat Shahar Fibrayar Sanat 1885 min Mablagh Ma'tani Gunih fa ma fawqa ma'ada al-Lathina Muta'akhar 'Alihim Aqal min Hadha al-Mablagh</u>, Dar al-Mafuzat Library, 33/3149/326, eight pages. The title of this second work is exactly the same as the previous title in French.

19.   The disparity between the percentage of males who mortgaged land, 90%, and those who owed back taxes, 85%, can be explained in part by Egyptian mortgage law. Women whose husbands were alive could

not conclude a valid act of mortgage. "La loi egyptienne ignore les

hypotheques legales du mineur et de la femme mariee." Gabriel Guemard,

Le Régime Hypothécaire Egyptien, Aix, B.Niel, 1914, p.92.

20. MORT signifies group one above and B-TAX group two.

21.   MORT   B TAX

            N   %   N   %

Proteges   1   1.02   1   .39

Foreigners 0   0.00   16   6.27

Egyptians 96   97.96   231   90.59

Private

  Institutions 1   1.02   7   2.75

22. Baring to Granville, Note for the Council of Ministers,

Enclosed in No.47, PRO,FO, 407/64, Cairo, January 19, 1885; Owen,

Cotton, p.184.

23. Back Taxes (L.E.)   Governorates   Provinces

    196 - 653   27   20

    654 - Top   33   10

Chi square equals 3.7629886, i.e., chances are just a little

under the desired 95% confidence level that the two variables are

significantly correlated.Residence was not a significant indicator of

the amount of mortgage, but was for the number of feddans mortgaged,

where chi square equals 5.9635544. With a dividing line at 408 feddans between high and low feddans mortgaged, sixteen in the Governorates fell into the low group and twenty-seven were high. For those in the provinces, thirty-three were low and twenty high.

24. Table No.1 enclosed in a Report by Sir E. Baring of December 8, 1884, British Sessional Papers, 1884-1885, v.87, p.712, cited by Owen, Cotton, p.239.

25. Gelat Bey, Répertoire Général, v.3, pp.23-24.

26. Report of Sir E. Baring, cited above, p.712.

27. The population figures for 1896 are those from the 1897 census. All ownership data are from the corrected tables directly above. The final % category represents landowners as a percentage of rural dwellers.

28. See Appendices 31 and 32.

29.   Sales of over Forty Feddans

	Daira Saniyya			Domains		
Religion	N	Avg.Fdns.	Avg.Cost	N	Avg.Fdns.	Avg.Cost
Muslim	368	386.19	12,926	534	281.92	6,356
Christn	193	802.54	16,947	125	634.99	6,520
Jewish	13	935.31	23,008	10	1277.20	15,636

Note: As in some other tables, the category "non-Muslims" is not always equal to the sum of "Christians" plus "Jews" because of the addition of other categories such as "non-Muslim" where the owner could be either Christian or Jewish, but not Muslim. The original categories used in coding, it will be recalled, were (1) Muslim, (2) Chrisitan, (3) Jewish, (4) Non-Muslim, (5) Non-Jewish and (6) No Information or Unknown.

30. National Status of Daira Saniyya Purchasers

Religion	N	%Owners	%Cost	%Fedans	N	%Owners	%Cost	%Fedans
Protege	0	-	-	-	6	.96	2.36	3.58
Foreign	0	-	-	-	24	3.85	9.83	6.30
Local	85	97.70	99.35	99.91	581	93.26	78.53	82.68
Royal Fm.	0	-	-	-	8	1.28	2.31	1.90
Pub.Ist.	1	1.15	.13	.05	1	.16	2.69	1.16
Priv.Ist.	1	1.15	.52	.05	3	.48	4.27	4.39

The categories Public Institutions and Private Institutions are the last two listed. Free land transfers to government agencies and exchanges were not coded.

31. National Status of Domains Purchasers

| | Less than 40 Feddans | | | More than 40 Feddans | | | |
Status	N	%Owners	%Cost	%Fedans	N	%Owners	%Cost	%Fedans
Protege	0	-	-	-	6	.81	2.67	2.86
Foreign	5	3.57	3.23	3.90	26	3.49	4.90	7.79
Local	128	91.43	92.56	93.42	691	92.88	66.65	69.28
Royal Fm.	2	1.43	.17	.46	14	1.88	19.22	13.59
Pub.Ist.	0	-	-	-	0	-	-	-
Pri.Ist.	5	3.57	4.05	2.22	7	.94	6.56	6.48

32. Residence of Daira Saniyya Purchasers

| | Less than 40 Feddans | | | More than 40 Feddans | | | |
Resid.	N	%Owners	%Cost	%Fedans	N	%Owners	%Cost	%Fedans
Govnts.	16	25.81	31.20	26.66	182	39.14	58.57	46.58
Lower E.	4	6.45	8.02	7.21	36	7.74	8.40	5.30
Upper E.	42	67.74	60.78	66.12	247	53.12	33.03	48.13

Location of Daira Saniyya Sales

| | Less than 40 Feddans | | | More than 40 Feddans | | | |
Locat.	N	%Owners	%Cost	%Fedans	N	%Owners	%Cost	%Fedans
Govnts.	0	-	-	-	1	.20	.03	.03
Lower E.	1	1.39	.68	1.32	15	3.02	2.04	4.22
Upper E.	71	98.61	99.32	98.68	480	96.78	97.93	95.75

A few of these sales transferred land in more than one
mudiriyya, in which case the mudiriyya containing the largest

acreage was chosen as the location.

33. Occupation of Daira Saniyya Purchasers

Less than 40 Feddans   More than 40 Feddans

Occup.   N %Owners %Cost %Fedans N %Owners %Cost %Fedans

Govt.   11 17.74 20.56 18.95 128 27.59 31.35 47.88

Non-Govt.51 82.26 79.44 81.05 336 72.41 68.65 52.12

34. This was publically held land resulting from earlier
inaccuracies in cadastral surveys, often land without easy access to
water. Rapport addresse a son Excellence le President du Conseil (des
Ministres) par la Commission chargee, par Decret du 23 Octobre, 1886,
d'echanger les Pensions contre des Terres, Supplement of the Journal
Officiel, January 15, 1887.

35. Occupation of Domains Purchasers, 1879-1906

         N Price (L.E.) % Total   Feddans   % Total

Govt.   300 1,548,828   31.39   68,997   29.81

Others   584 3,386,062   68.61   162,485   70.19

36. Muhammad 'Ali had moved to change the compulsory naturo of
work on state irrigation projects but the corvée was reinstated
under Sa'id and Isma'il. Conversation with Afaf Marsot, May 2, 1981.

37. Cromer, Modern Egypt, v.2, p.409, cited in Barakat,
p.337.

38. Hamid, Al-Nizam, p.144.

39. Statistical Yearbook for Egypt for 1909, p.51.

40. Alan Richards, "The Political Economy of Gutwirtschaft, Comparative Studies in Society and History, v.21, no.4, October, 1979, p.501.

41. Hamid, Nizam, p.177.

42. Alan Richards, "Land and Labor on Egyptian Cotton Farms, 1882-1940," Agricultural History, v.52, No.3, July, 1978, p. 505, citing Report by His Majesty's Agent and Consul-General on the Finances, Administration, and Condition of Egypt and the Soudan, 1903, London, HMSO, 1904, p.71.

43. 200 divided by (25 x 12) = 2/3.

44. Hamid, Nizam, p.177.

45. Chélu, Le Nil, p.209.

46. Richards, "Land and Labor," p.507.

47. Hamid, Nizam, p.175.

48. Barakat, p.135.

49. Hamid, Nizam, pp.179-180.

50. Statistical Yearbook for 1909, as corrected above.

51. It should be noted that the observations by Richards and Owen are not necessarily contradictory or mutually exclusive.

52. Alan Richards has pointed out that landowners recognized the
deleterious impact of the two year rotation system and may have been
disinclined to lease their land to renters who employed it. Letter to
the author, August 25, 1980. However, the statistics analyzed by
Craig indicate owners allowed this to happen. For a discussion of the
ambiguities of cash rental, see Richards, "Land and Labor on Egyptian
Cotton Farms," pp.508-513.

53. James I. Craig, "Notes on Cotton Statistics in Egypt,"
Egypte Contemporaine, No.6, March, 1911, p.197.

54. Ibid., pp.195-198.

55. Owen, Cotton, p.233-235.

56. Ibid., pp.266-267.

57. Gelat Bey, Repertoire, v.2, p.664.

58. Further studies will enable us to add significant
qualifications to this observation. See 'Asim Dasuqi, Kubar mulak
al-iradi al-zira'i wa duruhum fi al-mujtam' al-misri 1914-1952
(Large Agricultural Landowners and their Role in Egyptian Soceity,
1914-1952), (Cairo, 1975), pp.21-61.

Chapter Six

The Khedivate and Representative Institutions

Analysis of the changing organization of the Egyptian government
under Cromer should help us to answer the following basic questions
about politics. How was the state organized and what was the pattern
of authority? Were these relatively stable or did major changes occur
from 1882 to 1907. To what extent were the nominal heads of state its
real rulers? What kinds of individuals were recruited into the
government at each level and to what extent did the makeup of
officials in each department change? Were the changing size and
economic roles of different groups in Egyptian society reflected
inside the government as a whole or within various parts of it? This
chapter will show how the British established full control over the
Khedives. It will also explain how the national representative
institutions designed by the British created a legitimizing "native
screen" for foreign rule that worked smoothly until 1892 but with some
friction toward the end of Cromer's rule. Chapter seven will respond
to the questions above on the levels of government ministers and
subordinate civil servants.

The Khedivate

The royal family was the great loser in the 'Urabi revolution and
the British occupation, both economically and politically. The
occupation reaffirmed the Law of Liquidation of 1880, by which the
family of Khedive Isma'il lost title to 934,637 feddans, retaining

approximately 150,000 feddans of 'ushuriyya land.[1]

Politically, the blow to royal power was just as devastating. During the revolution, a broad spectrum of the Egyptian population probably agreed with 'Urabi that Tawfiq had betrayed his country. His loss of legitimacy was clearly expressed in the Official Journal of July 25,1882.

> Every native knows the Khedive has brought ruin upon his country, first, by listening to the advice of the English Representative, and, secondly, by bringing the fleet, which opened fire on the forts of Alexandria.... The Khedive, (after the British occupied Alexandria,) instead of returning to Cairo to complete the military preparations and to encourage his troops by his presence, took refuge on board the enemy's fleet with his household.... the Khedive, who sold the nation and the country to our bitterest foe.[2]

Tawfiq returned to his throne in Cairo in 1882 in the baggage of a foreign army, much like Louis XVIII after the defeat of Napoleon. British attempts to calm the situation by showing clemency to the rebels only weakened Tawfiq further.

> In spite of its avowed intentions, every step the British government was to take in the direction of reaffirming the Khedive's power was to have the opposite effect - to weaken it, thereby giving England a firmer hold over Egypt. For example, in its handling of the court martial of the insurgents, the British government made the Khedive look like "a man of straw" to the Egyptians.[3]

Despite his weakness, the Khedive had some room to maneuver and intrigue because of the ambiguity of England's position in Egypt. The occupation was not sanctioned by international law. Egypt was definitely not a British colony. So the British needed the collaboration of the Khedive and other Egyptian figureheads through

whom they administered the country. Had no suitable Egyptians been
found to cooperate, England would have had to withdraw or declare
Egypt a protectorare at the risk of collision with France, which
became reconciled to British control of Egypt only after the Entente
Cordiale of 1904. Britain's indirect government of Egypt through
Egyptian pawns came to be known as the Veiled Protectorate.[4]

This arrangement worked smoothly until Tawfiq's death in 1892.
When 'Abbas Hilmi became Khedive at the age of eighteen in the winter
of 1892, he made a good impression on Cromer and relied upon the older
man to straighten out the terms of his firman of investiture from the
Turkish Sultan. The Consul-General wrote to London on January
11,1892, "I am endeavouring to arrange that directly he arrives, the
Khedive should reappoint his present Ministers without any personal
intervention on my part."[5] 'Abbas cooperated fully and Baring was
able to reply five days later that the desired reappointments had been
made.[6]

However, 'Abbas began a brief and unsuccessful campaign of overt
rebellion against British authority that summer. In January of 1893
'Abbas dismissed Musfafa Fahmi and appointed Fakhri Pasha as Prime
Minister. Before the appointment could be announced, Cromer received
authority from the Foreign Office to take any steps necessary short of
increasing the British garrison in order to thwart the appointment.
'Abbas was forced to back down but had gained in popularity by his
opposition.[7]

After a series of jabs at British authority, the young Khedive discovered that his own government would not back him against Cromer. In January of 1894 the Prime Minister, Riaz Pasha, pleaded with him to apologize for disparaging remarks the Khedive had made about British officers of the Egyptian army. After this lesson 'Abbas adopted a covert policy of oppositon through third parties. From 1894 until the summer of 1895, the Khedive directed opposition to approval of the government budget in the General Assembly and Legislative Council. Then in the summer of 1895 the Turkish Sultan sided with the British against him, so 'Abbas felt compelled to turn back for some time toward the British for support. He secretly helped to finance the career of the nationalist orator Mustafa Kamil from 1895 to 1904 though he could not overtly block the sale of the Khedival Steam Navigation Company to a British firm in January of 1898.[8]

The Khedive lent his financial support to several of the political parties that developed around Mustafa Kamil such as the Nationalist Party (al-Hizb al-Watani) and the Society for the Revival of the Nation.[9] The Khedive also helped finance the popular newspaper, al-Mu'ayyid, of Shaykh 'Ali Yusuf.[10]

Although 'Abbas Hilmi lost all overt contests for power with the British rulers of Egypt, he played a major role in reviving the Egyptian national movement from 1895 until the Anglo-French Entente Cordiale of 1904. He covertly encouraged such Egyptian financial elite members as 'Umar Bey Sultan and Prince Gamil Toussoun to back Nationalist Party publications like Mustafa Kamil's Egyptian

<u>Standard</u>.[11]

Realizing that no major European power would back him against the British after the Entente, 'Abbas moved away from the nationalists and bowed to British authority on November 9,1904, when he first attended the British parade in Abdin Square on the occasion of Queen Victoria's birthday.[12]

Like Tawfiq before him, 'Abbas was part of the "native screen" behind which the British ruled Egypt. Cromer described this most eloquently.

> Broadly speaking,the system of government which now prevails in Egypt involves the interposition of a native screen between the English Governemnt and the Anglo-Egyptian officials on the one hand, and the native population on the other hand. Whether this is in itself a good form of government may be open to question .... But so long as this system lasts, it is essential that our native screen should be effective, and that it should fulfill the main objective for which it is intended, that is to say, that it should truly serve to hide from the native population that they are in great degree governed by foreigners.[13]

The Khedivate was an institution with little power under the British occupation down through 1907. Tawfiq accepted his role as part of the "native screen" and 'Abbas Hilmi rapidly learned that he could play no other role without the support of his own ministers. Egypt's representative institutions served as a forum for the country's large landowners to add their presence to this screen.

Representative Institutions

Egypt's pseudo-parliamentary institutions under the occupation
were designed by the British to have a powerless advisory role.
Parliamentary government in general offers a vehicle for stable rule
of the middle class. In a semi-colonial context such as that of Egypt
at the end of the nineteenth century, the indigenous middle class was
too weak to provide stable government and prevent foreign invasion.
In an unstable political environment, many elements of the Egyptian
political and economic elites welcomed the foreign invasion. Once
British troops had defeated organized resistance, the occupying power
naturally emasculated local parliamentary institutions and made them
into a legitimizing screen for foreign rule. There can be no
mistaking the fact that Egypt's pseudo-parliamentary institutions were
a purely British creation. After drawing them up, Lord Dufferin wrote
to "my dear Dilke" on January 11,1883, "I have fabricated for you a
general Representative Assembly of some seventy members, which I hope
you will consider satisfactory."[14]

The structure of Egypt's representative institutions is summed up
in a table drawn up by a British official in Cairo. This is located
in Appendix 33.

The provincial councils grouped together the most respected large
landowners in each _mudiriyya_ and were thus useful to the British
administrators as a conduit to local elites, though these councils had

no real power under Cromer. In 1886 it was decided

> to utilize the Provicial Councils instituted by Lord
> Dufferin by submitting to them the proposals for Public Works.
> It is thought by this means local opinion will be elicited, an
> friction avoided between the population and the engineers of
> irrigation.[15]

All members of the Provincial Councils were large landowners because of the qualifications for office set up by Dufferin in the *loi organique* that created them. All members had to be thirty years old or more, pay fifty pounds land tax anually in the *mudiriyya* and be on the local electoral list for five years.[16]

The Provincial Councils, like all other representative institutions under Cromer, had mere advisory capacity. They met at the discretion of the provincial governor and could spontaneously offer advice only about innocuous subjects such as educational affairs. When they did proffer such advice, it was usually ignored. The Minufiyya provincial council suggested an education tax of five milliemes per feddan, but the idea was not approved.[17]

The Legislative Councils and General Assemblies (*Maglis Shura al-Qawanin wal-Gam'iyya al-'Umumiyya*) changed somewhat in role from 1883 to 1907. Up to the accession of 'Abbas Hilmi in 1892 they were so quiescent that they were sometimes forgotten. Although the General Assembly was supposed to convene at a specific date every two years, this was forgotten in 1885 and then it met two months late.[18]

Even when minor objections were made to British policy during this period, they had little impact. Cromer commented in 1884 that

> The Report on the Budget has just been sent in by the
> Legislative Council. Its criticisms appear to be mainly based on
> those of the local Anglophobe press, and are conceived in a
> spirit hostile to the Government. The Report of last year
> contained many of the points to which allusion is again made. I
> do not consider that much importance need be attached to the
> action of the Council. Things are going very quietly here.[19]

It is perhaps overstating the case to say that "the Legislative

Council was powerless after the occupation and left no trace on the

development of Egypt during the next generation."[20] As a club for

large landowners, the Council regularly requested that land taxes be

reduced.[21]

From 1892 to 1904 the Legislative Council and General Assembly

regularly offered a forum for orderly and non-violent criticism of the

occupation and of specific government decisions such as the

Anglo-Egyptian condominium over the Sudan.[22]

For example, on December 20, 1892, the Legislative Council voted

down the proposed national budget for 1893 drawn up by Sir Elwin

Palmer on the grounds that it was not submitted in time for full

study. This first refusal was followed by non-approval of the budget

for military expenditures for 1894, set at 85,000 L.E. and this was

understood as a clear sign of protest against the occupation. The

criticism by the Council in April of 1896 of the government's

expenditure of 500,000 L.E. for the battle of Donqala was directed

against British policy in the Sudan. After the Egyptian government

had agreed to the creation of the Anglo-Egyptian condominium for the

Sudan in January of 1899, the Council looked into the budget for 1900

and found a deficit of 417,000 L.E. It voted to investigate this

deficit, stating that "...the Sudan is an integral part of Egypt, not

separate from it in any way."[23]

From 1900 to 1904, criticism centered on government educational

policy. After the Anglo-French entente of 1904, the Legislative

Council returned to its former policy of submission. Late in 1904,

for example, it agreed to the proposed budget for the following year.

In January of 1906 several Council members offered their blessings

upon the new situation in the Sudan by attending celebrations led by

Cromer for the inauguration of Port Sudan.[24]

From 1904 to 1906 the Council returned to its former policy of

submission until the Dinshwai incident of 1906 in which British

officers were beaten and a _fallah_ was killed. The severe

punishments meted out to villagers served as a catalyst for emotional

nationalism and resistance to the occupation.After this the

Legislative Council and General Assembly followed the lead of Mustafa

Kamil in asking for a speedy end to the occupation and in March of

1907 the General Assembly requested "the introduction, with as little

delay as possible, of full Parliamentary institutions."[25]

Egypt's parliamentary institutions thus provided a "native

screen" for local leaders to collaborate with the British rulers of

Egypt from 1882 to 1907. The Legislative Council and General Assembly

followed the lead of the Khedive or Mustafa Kamil in offering harmless

criticism of some aspects of the occupation and the tone of discussion
changed significantly during this period from (1)
submission,1883-1892, to (2) criticism, 1892-1904, to (3)
acquiescence,1904-1906 and finally to (4) strong criticism, 1907.
These institutions were designed by Lord Dufferin to have no real
power and their advice, at most, reflected the growing nationalism of
the period but did not initiate it. A detailed examination of the
composition of parliamentary bodies from their appearance in 1866 will
now follow. This examination should help to understand why their
members acted to provide a legitimizing "native screen" for British
rule after 1882. From 1866 to 1913, approximately 500 men sat in
Egypt's national representative bodies. The first four
proto-parliaments met during the rule of the Khedives Isma'il and
Tawfiq, before the occupation. Five Legislative Councils and five
General Assemblies met from 1884 to 1893. The basic composition of
these fourteen bodies is summarized in Appendix 34.

All these proto-parliamentary institutions were dominated by
'umda-s before the occupation, especially up to the deposition of
Isma'il in 1879. Because of the preponderence of 'umda-s, 77.66% of
all members were employees of the Egyptian government before 1883.
All members were Egyptian nationals by law and 96.97% were Muslim
before the occupation. Again because of the large percentage of
'umda-s, only 16.15% were residents of muhafza-s or provincial
capitals before 1883.

All these characteristics changed significantly after the

occupation. Thus the Btitish occupation had a profound impact on the
membership of Egyptian parliamentary institutions. After 1882, the
percentage of umdas rapidly stabilized at about ten percent for the
Legislative Council and between fifteen and twenty percent of the
General Assembly. The percentage of Muslims remained steady at about
90% under Cromer; the percentage of Chritstians increased from 3.53%
to 5.85%. No Jews were elected or appointed before 1913. The
apparent discrepancy is due to the fact that religion could not be
determined for a small percentage of members. It has been shown above
that non-Muslims acquired much greater wealth under the occupation;
here it is clear that they also acquired greater political power at
the national level, though Muslims retained a preponderance in the
assemblies. Residents of towns acquired much greater power during
this period, more than doubling their parliamentary representation to
42.93%. This accords with the observation above that absentee
ownership of large estates increased rapidly after 1883.

Appendix 35 shows that government employees in Egypt's national
representative institutions were more likely to hold high office after
1882 than before the occupation. We can conclude that families
holding large agricultural estates had a more pronounced tendency to
send leading family members into the cities, into high government
positions and into the nation's parliamentary bodies after 1882. With
tighter central control, the post of 'umda became less desirable.

Before the occupation, national representatives tended to cluster
in the Ministry of the Interior, mostly as 'umda. After 1882 the

212

spread of employment in government was broader as is shown in Appendix
36.

This data probably does not indicate a rise to power of families
from the private sector, but merely the loss of influence by 'umda-s
under the British. If 'umda-s are eliminated, government employees
totalled 42 before 1882, or 14.43% of the 291 representatives. After
the occupation, they diminished to 31, or 12.76% of the 243
representatives.

Members of the Legislative Council held more land than those in
the General Assembly; they were also more frequently government
employees and residents of the larger towns. Our very incomplete
records of landholding from 1876 to 1907 reveal that the 496
representatives held an average of at least 262 feddans. This average
is based solely on (1) records of mortgages before the Cairo Mixed
Courts from 1876 to 1883, (2) back tax records for delinquencies over
200 L.E. on 200 feddans or over, (3) Domains or Dairiyya Saniyya
sales records and (4) a few scattered estimates of landholdings from
secondary sources. These records document a small percentage of
property holding by individuals in Egypt during this period, but
reinforce the observation above that members of Egypt's national
representative institutions were large landholders.

Of the total 496 representatives, 45 bought Domains and/or Daira
Saniyya land, making an average purchase of 729 feddans for 21,863
L.E. Of the 43 whose religion could be determined, 38 or 88.37% were

Muslim and the other 11.63% were Christian. This can be taken as
another indication of the rise to greater wealth and power of Egypt's
minority religious groups after 1882. The reader may recall that
Christians constituted only 7.51% of the resident population in 1897,
and 6.62% of the national population.[26]

Members who sat in more than one assembly from 1866 to 1907 were
more often residents of the larger towns, 54 out of 133 or 40.60%,
than those who were members of only one assembly, 68 out of 333 or
20.42%. Again we see a broad movement of the powerful and wealthy
into Egypt's largest cities. Repeaters were, however, somewhat less
likely to be employees of the government, 67 out of 133 or 50.38%,
than those elected or appointed only once, 209 out of 333 or 62.76%.
Taking only the national assemblies from 1882 to 1907, these
percentages increased to 35.88% urban for one time members and 45.78%
for repeaters. This is one more indication of the increasing movement
of the powerful and wealthy into the larger cities after the
occupation. Again after 1882, repeaters also held somewhat higher
government offices.[27] Members who sat more frequently in national
assemblies during this period also generally held more land.[28]

Members of the <u>Maglis Shura al-Nuwwab</u> of 1881-1882 who opposed
the British takeover did not reappear in Egypt's national
parliamentary bodies. Muhammad Galal, for example, was a rich
cultivator and the <u>'umda</u> of the village of al-Qis in al-Minya. He
was one of the few members present at the meeting in Sultan Pasha's
house on May 27,1882, who agreed to the suggestion that Tawfiq be

deposed. He told the peasants that the <u>dhawat</u>, high officials, who

sided with the English should leave the country. He reportedly

shouted, "the Khedive has sold the country to the English."[29]

After the occupation he was placed under house arrest and asked

to pay a fine of 3.000 L.E. or go into exile at Cosseir for three

years. He was stripped of all rank and titles by Khedival decree on

December 24, 1882.[30] He does not even appear in <u>Tarikh al-Hiyyat</u>

<u>al-Niyabiyya</u> in the list of <u>Maglis al-Nuwwab</u> members.

This detailed examination of Egypt's national assemblies helps to

understand why members were likely to collaborate with their British

rulers in the first years of the occupation: (1) they were large

landowners; (2) they were also often government employees whose rank

increased after 1882; (3) those who sat in more than one assembly were

wealthier and held higher offices ; (4) they were increasingly

Christian and Christians were happy to cooperate with their foreign

co-religionists and (5) they were increasingly residents in the large

urban centers whose elite members flourished under the occupation. In

other words, they were well rewarded for their collaboration.

After 1892 however, and especially in 1906 and 1907, the national

representative institutions provided a focal point for moderate

nationalist criticism of the occupation. This growing agitation at

the end of Cromer's period of rule resulted in the re-emergence of

indigenous political parties whose major goal was greater power for

local elites.

Footnotes: Chapter Six

1. For a detailed breakdown of the 934,637 feddans, see chapter
five. The royal family retained 147,477 feddans of 'ushriyya land
at the end of Isma'il's reign if we include three female slaves as
part of the extended family. Barakat, p.162.

2. Extract from the official journal, Al-Waqa'ia
al-Misriyya, July 25, 1882, English translation enclosed in No.
229, Sir E.Malet to Earl Granville, Alexandria, September 9, 1882,
PRO,FO, 407/23/2879, pp.101-102.

3. Lutfi al-Sayyid, Egypt and Cromer, p.29.

4. Op.Cit, p.66.

5. Baring to Salisbury, PRO,FO, 407/113, No. 28, Cairo, January
11, 1892.

6. Baring to Salisbury, Loc. Cit., No. 48, Cairo, January
11, 1892.

7. Al-Sayyid, Egypt and Cromer, pp.109-112.

8. Mohammad Gamal El-Din El-Messady, "The Relations between
'Abbas Hilmi and Lord Cromer", Ph.D. thesis, University of London,
SOAS, 1966, pp.119-200, 252. It is unnecessary to expand upon the
much studied career of Mustafa Kamil Pasha. See 'Abd al-Rahman
al-Ra'fi'i, Mustafa Kamil, Ba'ith al-Haraka al-Wataniyya (Leader of

the Nationalist Movement), Cairo, Maktaba al-Nahda al-Misriyya, 1962;
Juliette Adam, <u>Angleterre en Egypte</u>, Paris, 1922 and the works by
al-Sayyid and El-Messady cited above.

9. <u>Gam'iyya li-Ihya' al-Watan</u>. Arthur Goldschmidt, "The
Egyptian Nationalist Party," in <u>Political and Social Change in
Modern Egypt</u>, ed. P.M.Holt, p.313.

10. Al-Sayyid, <u>Egypt and Cromer</u>, pp.96-97; <u>El-Messady</u>,
p.218.

11. Ibrahim Ghali, <u>L'Egypte nationaliste et libérale</u>, p.57.

12. Al-Rafi'i, <u>Musfafa Kamil</u>, pp.183,249.

13. Cromer to Salisbury, PRO,FO, No. 138, Cairo, 26
February,1889.

14. PRO,FO, 78/3565, Private Correspondence.

15. Wolff to Iddesleigh, PRO,FO, 407/68, No.261, Cairo, October
21, 1886.

16. Gelat Bey, <u>Répétoire</u>, v.3, p.346. From 1882 to 1907 the
average tax per feddan varied from .798 L.E. in 1900 to a maximum of
1.046 in 1884. The average tax over the entire period per feddan was
.933 L.E. Thus an annual tax of 50 L.E. implied ownership of
probably more than 53.6 feddans, placing members of the Provincial
Councils and the national representative institutions securely in the
top 1.52% of all landowners who in 1897 for example, had title to

44.01% of the country's privately owned agricultural land. The top
12,184 owners of over fifty feddans held 2,227,740 of the total
5,062,071 feddans held by 800,782 private land owners in 1897.
Statistical Abstract for 1909, p.44.

17. El-Messady, pp.313-314, citing Al-Muayyad of January 2,
1900 and June 25, 1901.

18. Alexandre Holynski, Nubar-Pasha devant l'Histoire,
Paris, E. Dentu, Editeur, Librarie de la Societe des Gens des
Lettres, 1885, p.41.

19. PRO,FO, 407/127, No.182, 21 December 1884.

20. Ahmad Abd al-Rahim Mustafa, Misr wal-Masala al-Misriyya,
min 1876 ila 1882 (Egypt and the Egyptian Question, from 1876 to
1882), Cairo, Dar al-Ma'arif, 1965, p.283.

21. See the minutes of the Council proceedings of December
11,1893, August 28, 1893 and February 11, 1896, cited in Hamid,
Nizam, p.134.

22. Al-Rafi'i, Mustafa Kamil, pp.370-374.

23. Loc.Cit., pp.371-372.

24. El-Messady, p.308, citing Wingate Papers, Box 278/1,
Owen to Wingate, 3 January, 1906.

25. Cromer to Grey, PRO,FO, 407/170, No.27, Cairo, March 4,1907.

26. <u>Census</u> <u>of</u> <u>1897</u>; see chapter one above.

27. Rank of Government Employment for Members of
National Representative Institutions, 1883-1907

| | <u>One-time</u> <u>Members</u> | | | <u>Repeaters</u> | |
<u>Rank</u>	<u>N</u>	<u>%</u>		<u>N</u>	<u>%</u>
Minister	5	11.90%		5	14.71%
Wakil Minister	2	4.76%		1	2.94%
Head Division	3	7.14%		4	11.76%
Nazir Qism	7	16.67%		5	14.71%
Ma'mur	7	16.67%		4	11.76%
Mufattish	1	2.38%		2	5.88%
Umda,Skilled					
Employee	17	40.48%		13	38.24%
Total	42	100.00%		34	100.00%

28. Landholdings of Members of Egypt's National
Assemblies by Frequency in Assemblies, 1882-1907

		<u>Average</u> <u>Landholdings</u> (feddans)	<u>Standard</u> <u>Deviation</u> (feddans)
<u>Times</u> <u>in</u> Assemblies	<u>N</u>		
1	131	123.97	486.57
2	48	353.42	1896.67
3	26	383.42	694.72
4	8	150.75	284.41
5	1	2525.00	---

29. <u>Barakat</u>, pp.258, 405, 409-410.

30. <u>Moniteur</u> <u>Egyptien</u>, December 26, 1882.

Chapter Seven

The Egyptian Bureaucracy

This chapter will examine the ministers at the top of the
government, offer collective descriptions of the seven cabinets that
sat from 1882 to 1908, describe the structure of the Egyptian
bureaucracy, document its growth in size and in level of expenditures,
describe the increasing British control over all levels of activity
and examine the changing composition of employees in each major
subdivision. Within the framework of growing British control of the
Egyptian government, power shifted to an expanding cadre of foreigners
and to non-Muslims at the expense of Turko-Circassians and Muslims.
British fiscal and personnel policies under Cromer both illustrate
their reluctance to cut short the occupation.

Egyptian ministers from 1882 to 1907 were in a position of
weakness and ambivalence with respect the British rulers of Egypt.
When the English occupied Cairo in 1882 they reinstated the
Turko-Circassian ministers who had been ousted by the 'Urabi
revolution. Like the Khedive, the ministers depended upon foreign
troops to stay in power. To understand the role of cabinets during
this period, it is necessary first to dwell on the limits of their
powers and secondly, within this context, to examine the varying
patterns of behavior followed by important ministers.

As an alien elite propped up by yet another foreign group, the
Turko-Circassian ministers were in a difficult position. They

constituted the overwhelming majority of ministers during the entire
period, though their numbers diminished from 89% of acting cabinet
ministers in 1882 to 57% in 1906. The problems of the
Turko-Circassians were most obvious in the army, which had rebelled
under 'Urabi against their monopoly of top ranks. For this reason
Cromer had some doubts about Sir Francis Grenfell's recommendation of
Yusuf Shuhdi as Minister of War in 1891, yet offered no objections
because of the man's popularity.

> I did not, therefore, offer any objections to it, but I have
> begged Sir Francis Gernfell to watch very carefully that Shuhdi
> Pasha does not manipulate promotions in the army in a manner
> calculated to give rise to any renewal of jealousy between the
> Turkish and Egyptian elements. I do not doubt that a sufficient
> watch will be kept to avert any danger of this sort.[1]

It is significant that the British understood the discontent felt
by Egyptian officers toward the Turko-Circassians who led both the
army and the ministries and that the British felt they could manage
the problem by close control of the Turko-Circassians. It was made
clear that any major policy decisions made by cabinet members had to
be approved by the British. In case there was any doubt of this,
Grenville asserted Cromer's right to control in a message of January,
1884.

> It is essential that, in important questions affecting
> administration and safety of Egypt, advice of Her Majesty's
> Government should be followed as long as provisional occupation
> continues. Ministers and Governors must carry out this advice,
> or forfeit offices. Appointment of English ministers would be
> most objectionable, but it would, no doubt, be possible to find
> natives who would execute the Khedive's orders under English
> advice. Cabinet will give you full support.[2]

Understanding their ambivalent position in the Egyptian population, the British chose mostly Turko-Circassian collaborators to sit as figure-heads over the ministries. The exceptions to this rule were three Muslim Egytians and three minority sect officials of the total twenty-five ministers who held office from 1882 to 1908.[3]

'Ali Murarak was the first Muslim Egyptian who held cabinet office under Cromer. He left the 'Urabi forces to join the Khedive in Alexandria before the battle of Tall al-Kabir where the revolutionaries were defeated by General Wolsey's forces. He was rewarded with the Ministry of Public Works unti January 10, 1884. He was not renominated as head of Public Works because the English advisor, Scott-Moncrieff, could not tolerate a competent and independent rival for power in the ministry.[4] He was, however, Minister of Public Instruction in Riyad's first cabinet of 1888-1891.

Muhammad 'Abani was the second Muslim Egyptian to hold a cabinet post under Cromer and acted as Minister of War in Mustafa Fahmy's long cabinet from 1895 to 1908. The only other Muslim Egyptian minister was Sa'd Zaghlul, who was appointed Minister of Public Instruction four months after Dinshwai to deflate the growing nationalism the incident had aroused. Cromer wrote to the British Foreign Minister on October 27,1906, that "I had an audience with the Khedive yesterday and arranged with His Highness that Saad Zaghlul, now a judge in the Native Court of Appeal, should be appointed Minister to the Department of Public Instruction." The wording makes it clear that the decision was not made by Abbas Hilmi and that the British Agent and

Consul-General could appoint whichever cabinet members he chose,
whether or not they had experience in the ministry. In the same
message Cromer described Zaghlul as

> a competent man from Muhammad 'Abduh's gradualist school
> whose members could be safely be put into positions of power to
> replace "dummies or figure-heads."[5]

Other than these three Muslim Egyptians, ministers from 1882 to
1908 were Turko-Circassians whom Cromer described as "dummies" or they
were minority sect Egytpians. The three Christians were the Copt
Butrus Ghali and the Armenians Tigrane and Nubar. The British thus
used foreigners or minority group residents to provide a "native
screen" in a common variant on the old tool of "divide and conquer."
British and local opinion of the Turko-Circassian ministers was very
low when expressed in private. One British official wrote of Ahmad
Mazlum that he

> knows Turkish and is a good French scholar. Rich landowner.
> Remarkably frank and bluff way of expressing himself; a man of
> character and good private life. Idle, selfish, cynical, lazy
> and good-tempered. A grasping miser. No diplomat, and has a
> scantily veiled comtempt for Egytians, reckoning himself a
> Turk.[6]

Speaking of two other Turko-Circassian ministers, Cromer stated

> Both Abder Rahman and Zeki are weak and inoffensive men.
> They are honest enough, and will do no harm, but cannot be
> expected to show any vigour or power of initiation. They are
> representative of a small class, who neither belong to the old
> Turkish party nor to any party of reforms, but who represent with
> great accuracy the time-honoured principles of the Vicar of
> Bray.[7]

Cromer chose weak, inoffensive men to act as figureheads and did
not believe that Egyptians were capable of governing their own
country. He wrote after leaving Egypt in 1907 that

> Personally, I do not believe that such education as can be
> imparted in the schools and colleges will ever render the
> Egyptians capable of self-government without some transformation
> of the national character, which must necessarily be a slow
> process.[8]

Yet despite the weakness of their positions, not all Egyptian
ministers acted out a role of complete submission. Their conduct
varied from the active resistance of Sharif and the passive, limited
resistance of Nubar to outright submission by Musfafa Fahmi. Sharif
actively resisted British policy when he felt it ran counter to
Egyptian interests. He resigned office in 1884 to protest the
abandonment of the Sudan and threatened to expose the veiled
protectorate. Nubar accepted to form a ministry directly afterwards,
but moved to limit the sphere of British influence. He forced
Clifford Lloyd's resignation as Adviser to the Ministry of the
Interior, where provincial governors retained great freedom of action
and control of local police until 1893. Though as a Christian in a
Muslim country Nubar looked to the British for protection and
privileges over the Muslim majority, he did not accept total British
control. Mustafa Fahmi's position represents the other end of the
spectrum. Louis Brehier, a contemporary, described him as "un
Algérien des plus dociles."[9] Cromer himself wrote that "Mustafa Fahmy
has the reputation of being a weak man...."[10] His docility and his
"well-known sympathy with English policy " mentioned in the same

message kept him in office as Prime Minister for exactly thirteen years without a break.

Now that characterizations have been drawn for the different types of ministers, we will turn to collective descriptions of the seven cabinets that sat from 1882 to 1908. With the addition of Sa'd Zaghlul in 1906, the last two years of the long cabinet of Mustafa Fahmi can be considered an eighth cabinet. The social composition of these cabinets is succinctly summarized in Appendix 37.

After the 'Urabi revolution, the traditional Turko-Circassian elite lost its monopoly of top positions. Under the British a more subservient elite was allowed to hold cabinet posts, but under foreign tutelage it was, somewhat less able to translate political position into vast urban and rural properties.

The cabinet members from 1882 to 1907 were clearly near the apex of the urban and rural property holding elites. Large landowners formed the overwhelming majority in all eight ministries. The high average holdings of the first ministry are due to Sharif Pasha, who owned 23,013 feddans at the time of his death. The uneven decline in agerage holdings is due to (1) the inclusion of ministers like Sa'd Zaghlul not from the great landowning families and (2) the fragmentary nature of our sources, which are more representative in the early years of the occupation. It is also significant that new government officials under the British were not as richly rewarded with land grants as were those who reached top rank under Isma'il. Ministers after 1894 were also less likely to hold extensive property in Cairo than their predecessors, for the same reason. Most new appointees like Sa'd Zaghlul were not of the wealthiest urban families and did not use their posts to acquire urban property as quickly as their predecessors.

The Egyptian bureaucracy was, briefly, a complex and changing mechanism for the execution of state policy determined by the British and legitimized by the presence of Egyptian figureheads at the minister-ial level. The stated plan of the English was to wield control with as little European manpower as possible, but this plan was not followed. The Egyptian bureaucracy became an employer of last resort for Europeans who were unwilling or unable to find satisfactory employment at home. It also provided comfortable employment for a disproportionately large number of minority group families.

There were sixty-three cohesive governmental subdivisions as seen in Appendix 38. These can be regrouped into sixteen departments as follows:

1.Khedivate

2.Council of Ministers

3.Foreign Affairs

4.Finances

5.Interior

6.Public Works

7.Justice

8.War

9.Health

10.Public Instruction

11.Mixed (Explicitly European Controlled) Administrations

12.Miscellaneous Administrations

13.Awqaf

14.Sudan Administration

15.Towns

16.Churches

The structure of authority theoretically ran from the Khedive, to the Council of Ministers appointed by him, and thus down through the various ministries. There are two important qualifications to this description. Many critical administrative units were not under the authority of any minister, e.g., the Health Department. The Khedive theoretically appointed the Director General of the Health Department but certain departments known as Mixed Administrations were structured by international agreements which set up boards of directors. The Caisse de la Dette, or Public Debt Office offers a good example. The Khedive appointed an Egyptian Director to the Caisse board of directors, but his advice could be ignored if the other two directors, named by the governments of England and France, were able to agree on policy. Moreover, the Caisse de la Dette was the creditor of perference of the Egyptian treasury according to the Law of

Liquidationof 1880 and thus exercised great control in setting the

national budget. Hence, Egpytian authority was again circumscribed.

The Egyptian civil service was viewed as inefficient and

excessively large in 1882, so the British reduced it from around

20,000 to a little over twelve thousand n 1897. Including the armed

forces, Lord Dufferin estimated that there were about 53,000 "natives"

in the Egyptian service in 1883 and reported that

> If one-third of these men were dismissed to-morrow, the work
> of the Ministries they encumber would be all the more efficiently
> performed.[11]

The size of the bureaucracy has been studied by Morroe Berger and

Robert Tignor, who cite the above source and agree that employment

statistics during this period are unreliable and difficult to

interpret. They also agree that the Egyptian civil service became

progressively European in the upper ranks toward the end of the

century and down to World War I.[12] The British were able to bring

about such a drastic reduction firstly by retiring or imprisoning all

the important officials who sided with 'Urabi. Secodly, they cut

annual hiring down from 600 for the period from 1880 to 1882 to 200

for the period from 1882 to 1886.[13] Lord Dufferin advised in 1883

that "it is very desirable that the European staff should be

considerably reduced...."[14]

However, just the opposite occurred until World War I.[15] It

appears that the British rulers of Egypt wanted to reduce the size of

the bureaucracy immediately after the occupation. The civil service
will be treated first, followed by the army. Although conclusive
statistics are not yet available, it seems that the civil service was
reduced from "about 20,000" employees in 1882[16] to perhaps fewer
than thirteen thousand at the time of the 1897 census.[17] In any
case, the early intention to cut back the bureaucracy was clear.
However, the size of the civil service expanded greatly from 1897 to
1907, if we are to trust the figures of the censeses for these years,
rising from 12,085 to 28,896 male employees.[18]

Thus it appears that that the British cut back the Egyptian civil
service during the first fifteen years of the occupation while they
established control, balanced the national budget and reorganized the
civil service. Then they allowed it to expand as state revenues
increased near the turn of the century.

The 'Urabist army was the single most important threat to British
domination of Egypt, so it was disbanded in 1882. At the time of the
revolution, it had a nominal strength of 11,000 or 12,000 men and
effective strength of 8,769, down drastically from 57,000 in 1878.[19]
Contemporary observers estimated the army's strength at 12,000 during
the revolution.[20]

After the defeat of Hick's army in the Sudan, a new Egyptian army
was organized by Sir Evelyn Wood. This stood at 6,700 men in April of
1884.[21] This force expanded to about 12,000 until it was cut back to
9,000 in 1887 in an effort to balance the budget. After the budget

crisis of 1887 had passed and nationalism in the new army appeared under control, its strength was increased to 13,765 men in 1891.[22] For the British conquest of the Sudan in 1897 and 1898, the army was increased to its limit of 18,000 set by the Ottoman Sultan, and then increased further. Lord Cromer wrote to Salisbury,

> Present strength of Egyptian army 23,000, that is, 5,000 above number fixed by the Sultan's firman. If Kassala is to be occupied, its strength will be up to 25,000. If questions are asked, 2 battalions, about 2,700 strong, are called "railway battalions."[23]

With the Sudan comfortably administered by Britain, the Egyptian army was reduced to 6,953 in 1907. [24] Following the occupation, the size of the gendarmerie and police probably stabilized at six to seven thousand men until the turn of the century and then increased to over ten thousand in 1907.[25]

We can conclude that the civil service, the army, the police and the gendarmerie changed size under Cromer according to British estimates of financial possibilites and according to British capacity for control. In the early period the armed forces were reduced because they constituted a potential threat to foreign domination. After they had been reorganized under English officers and their loyalty had been tested, they were allowed to expand to carry our British policies in Egypt and the Sudan.

The pattern of government expenditures shifted from a medium level for the early period of 1882-1891, to a low level until 1901, and then to a high level of expenditure down through 1907. Appendix

39 details Egyptian government expenditures under Cromer. If we
exclude 1885 because of the unusual indemnities paid, the mean index
for the period up to 1901 is 111, while that for the following period
is 116. Investment in irrigation was responsible for the medium level
of expenses in the period from 1882 to 1891, despite low government
revenues. The middle period was stable at a low level because income
from cotton exports was low, and the increasing expenditures in the
final period were made possible by the cotton boom that began near the
end of the century. It is important to note that the only period
where there was a tendency for expenditures to outstrip revenuses was
the earliest, when the British had to take strong measures to assert
control. The financial crisis brought on by this policy came in 1887,
when final salaries were not paid until the following year.
Government priorities become more apparent when expenditures are
broken down into the major areas as in Appendix 40.

The following section will describe the process by which the
British gained direct control over the different departments of the
Egyptian government. Immediately following the occupation, the
British took steps to assert control over the Ministry of War, the
Ministry of Finances and the Ministry of Public Works. After the
battle of Tall al-Kabir, the English disbanded the Egyptian army and
organized a new one which remained a docile instrument of foreign
power through 1907. The Egyptian army did not foster the fulfillment
of national aspirations for four basic reasons. Firstly, it was
constantly under the shadow of the British army of occupation with its

superior technology and organization. Secondly, fraternization
between officers and enlisted men was discouraged by the British
staff. Describing the situation in 1888, William Willcocks wrote that
there were "no bonds between officers and men."[26] Thirdly, most
positions of importance within the upper ranks of officers were filled
by Britons, and fourthly, Egyptian officers were constantly spied
upon. They were not allowed to hold command unless they joined the
British masonic lodge supervised by the British Director of
Intelligence.[27] Thus the Turko-Circassians who monopolized the upper
ranks within the army before 1881 were supplanted by Britons after the
brief nationalist interlude of the 'Urabi revolution. Even before all
the 'Urabi rebels had been sentenced, the British moved to assert
control over the civil administration through control of finances .

The fiscal key to British domination of the Egyptian government
was the appointment of a powerful Financial Adviser. Lord Dufferin's
reorganization of the Egyptian state centered on an indirect system of
British control of finances via a Financial Adviser rather than a dual
control or a European minister of Finance. The Egyptian Minister of
Finance and his colleagues provided the "native screen" behind which
the Financial Adviser could control affairs. Dufferin's
reorganization proposal of January 10, 1883 was rapidly accepted on
January 22 by the Egyptian ministry of Sharif Pasha. [28]

Lord Milner summarized the importance of this official, stating
that

        The Financial Adviser is the corner-stone of English

233

influence inside the Egyptian Administration.... The English
Government laid it down that "no financial decision should be
taken without his consent," and this interpretation was never
called into question by the Egyptian government. [29]

In this way the level of expenditures and therefore the size and
impact of every branch of the Egyptian government could be manipulated
through fiscal control. This control was tightened by the creation of
a Finance Committee on March 6, 1884. Edgar Vincent, the Financial
Adviser at that time, explained how this committee aided him in
monitoring expenditures.

> It is now known that all grants of money have to be approved
> by the Committee of Finance, and that no sum will be given away
> except in accordance with the Regulations in force. The
> consequence has been that a great dimunition has taken place in
> the number of irregular demands for money presented to the
> Government. [30]

British control of Egyptian government finances was improved by a
steady influx of European and espeically British appointees into the
upper ranks of the Ministry of Finance. [31]

The Ministry of Public Works was another early target for British
takeover because national prosperity and governmental solvency so
obviously depended on the irrigation system maintained by this
ministry. Again, following Lord Dufferin's scheme of reorganization,
an English Adviser was appointed to the ministry in 1883, who then
brought in Anglo-Indian experts and irrigation inspectors who
supervised the agricultural life of the country in minute detail by
1890. [32]

British irrigation inspectors were to become the arbitrators
of Egypt's agricultural life. Their responsibilities brought
them in contact with local Egyptian officials - the <u>mudir</u>, the
<u>ma'mur</u>, and the village shaykh.... Scott-Moncrieff (the
British Adviser) insisted that his engineers live among the
people, and encouraged them to learn the language of the
country. [33]

The Ministry of Public Works was given extremely high priority in

budget allocations at the start of the occupation. This ministry grew

in size and expenditures almost constantly throughout the first

twenty-six years of the occupation. Available evidence argues for an

influx of Europeans into this minstry from 1882 to 1907. [34]

The Ministry of Justice was the next target for British control.

All judicial affairs concerning Europeans had long been out of

Egyptian hands. In 1875 authority over most of these matters was

transferred from consular courts to the Mixed Courts. New Egyptian

"Native Tribunals" were set up in November of 1883. [35]

Two early British Advisers proved unsuccessful in controlling the

ministry and were removed. In 1887 a Belgian Procurer-General was put

at the top of the ministry. In 1889 the Native Court of Appeals was

stacked in favor of Britian by the addition of two Englishmen,

bringing its membership to three English and three Belgian judges.

The following year a British judge from the Indian service was put at

the head of the ministry as Advisor. [36] Though these appointments

gave the British control over judicial affairs outside Muslim and

Coptic courts of personal status, they did not improve the quality of

justice for Egyptians in the first decade of the occupation. A

British observer wrote that

> The new Native Courts do not seem to have inspired any
> confidence whatever, while the cumbrous and intricate procedures
> are ill adapted to their views, and are, in fact, quite
> incomprehensible....[37]

The British Inspector-General wrote three years later

> Every judge is considered bribable. No one dreams of
> justice. Chance, expediency, and a large purse are considered as
> the best weapons to win a case.[38]

By the turn of the century, even judges before the Mixed Courts
could find their employment terminated if Lord Cromer learned of their
"expressed Anglophobia."[39]

Thus by 1890 the Ministries of War, Justice, Public Works and
Finance were firmly under British control. In 1893 Cromer showed how
this control was formalized on the highest level.

> The Ministers of Justice, War and Public Works are under an
> obligation to show respectively to each of the English
> functionnaries concerned any proposal which they may send up for
> discussion in Council (i.e., the Council of Ministers.) The
> latter may then, should they think fit, express a wish to be
> present at the discussion. The President of the Council will
> then be under an obligation to invite ("invitera") to the Council
> the officials concerned.[40]

The Ministry of the Interior came under direct British control
only after a long and bitter struggle. This ministry had crucial
importance because it extended state police powers down to the village
and neighborhood levels. The first attempt at direct British control
was made in 1884 and failed when Nubar, the Prime Minister, threatened
to resign and remove the native screen covering British rule.[41]

As the occupation took on a more permanent character and after
'Abbas Hilmi's ineffectual resistance to Cromer had been broken in
1892, Englishmen moved into the intermediate and lower levels of the
Ministry of the Interior. This takeover has been admirably detailed
by El-Messady.[42] It should suffice to say that the

> turning point came in 1894 when the post of
> Inspector-General of Police was abolished and local police
> officials were made responsible to English inspectors under a
> British Adviser to the ministry rather than to the _mudir-s_ or
> Egyptian provincial governors. Permanent European employees in
> this ministry rose from 91 in 1896 to 150 in 1906.[43]

British officials in the Interior then brought village headmen
(_'umda-s_) under their control by regulating selection and defining
their duties in decrees of March 16, 1895 and April 25, 1898.[44]

Toward the end of Cromer's rule, British control was extended
into traditional Islamic institutions such as the Islamic _Shari'a_
courts and the Department of Awqaf. The Ministry of Finance began to
audit and control _Waqf_ accounts after the turn of the century. When
the chief Islamic legal scholar, Muhammad 'Abduh, the Grand Mufti,
died in July, 1905, Cromer forced the Egyptian government to wait
until he could return from vacation to name a replacement.[45]

Thus by 1905 Britain controlled all departments of the Egyptian
government. Mixed administrations were run harmoniously in
conjunction with other European powers after the Entente with France

in 1904. Ministries such as War or the Interior were directly staffed
with British officers and inspectors after 1895 and traditional
Islamic institutions were ruled with a combination of fiscal control
and the appointment of cooperative Muslims.[46]

Composition of the Egyptian Bureaucracy, 1882-1907

It has been shown how the British changed the structure of the
Egyptian government and how they assumed control over each of the
ministries and departments. This section will analyze changes in the
social composition of the cadres within the upper ranks of government.

This analysis is based upon two complementary sources. The first
is Al-Waqa'ia al-Misriyya, in which all appointments to posts with a
salary of sixty pounds or more were to be made public as of
February,1887.[47] This official journal yielded a list of 1,593
individuals who worked in positions of authority in government from
1880 to 1907 with at least the rank of Bey, Second Class. The second
source is the pension files of the Ministry of Finance located in Dar
al-Mahfuzat in which the pensions of all employees were recorded upon
retirement. Detailed information for two hundred public servants was
taken from these files, 116 of which offered complete career histories
including every government post held by the employee.

The composition of government elites is a vital topic for the
student of social history because the state forms the location where
the most decisive power in society is exercised. Even though the
state is not necessarily the source of this power, it is necessary to
analyze the social composition of those groups exercising power in
order to understand the relationship between the state, those factions
with state power, and the groups competing for power and wealth in
society as a whole.

As the British seized control of each of the departments of the
Egyptian government, they restructured the process of recruitment into
each area as well as the process of retirement. Control of hiring was
crucial to British domination of the state apparatus and it had the
important side effect of slowly changing the social composition of
government cadres. When the dust cleared after the battle of Tall
al-Kabir, the British discovered that recruitment into the Egyptian
government was not a rationalized process under firm central control,
but an informal one fraught with nepotism and patronage. In March of
1883 Lord Dufferin forwarded a very critical report by a European
observer.

> In regard to the supply of subordinate officials for the
> Government Offices, experience has thus far shown that the
> Government schools are incapable of furnishing competent public
> emplyoyees. The reason is obvious. Almost all the Public
> Offices are encumbered with a number of boys whom their
> relations, themselves employees, bring with them to sit beside
> them during office hours. These youths have seldom attended any
> school, and as they grow up they gradually learn the pure routine
> work of the offices in which they have been sitting for years,
> and being in due course inscribed as "supernuméraires" they then
> take a permanent foothold in the public administrations. The
> result is that there is no inducement for a young Egyptian to
> seek a public career by means of the government schools.[44]

In the following month the British began a total restructuring of
government hiring. Each department was re-ordered into a strict
hierarchy with upper and lower cadres, presided over by a Council for
Administration and Discipline and a Central Personnel Office. All
appointments or promotions had to be approved by these two bodies.
Important posts could be filled only by competitive examination and

nominations could be confirmed only after a probationary period.[49]

By 1888 control over state superior schools was sufficient to permit preferrence in government hiring for graduates. During the following years this restructuring of hiring and promotion was rationalized further, with important turing points in 1892 when a higher cadre for provincial administrators was organized and in 1901, when the entire process was brought under tighter control under redrawn administrative orders.[50]

This rationalization of hiring gave preference to those with access to modern education, a knowledge of European languages and acquaintance with the new cadres of cooperative Egyptian or foreign bureaucrats. However, the transformations in the social composition of the state were not as radical as one might have expected, perhaps because of the size of the bureaucracy and the time it took for the British to bring all segments under full control.

Systematic analysis of the Egyptian governmental elite reveals a broad shift of power in the ranks of government parallel to the accelerating changes in property distribution in Egyptian society. There were distinct gains for foreigners, non-Muslim Egyptians and urban residents. Those displaced were Turko-Circassians within the middle ranks and Muslims in all but the lowest ranks. On the other hand, there were important limits to these shifts. There may have been a slowdown in the entry of non-Muslims into the upper middle ranks of government from 1900 to 1907. Secondly, government rank was

by no means a guarantee to a rapid rise into the heights of the rural
and urban property holding elite for those below the ministerial
level. It is curious to note that even the highest ranking foreign
employees of the government owned very little real estate in Cairo in
1894. Instead, they invested heavily and some amassed personal
fortunes in commerce and financial services.

Foreigners were numerous and extremely powerful within the
Egyptian bureaucracy, despite their limited representation within the
country. Foreigners constituted 6.18% of the Egyptian political elite
although they numbered only 1.23% of the population in 1897.[51]

Non-Egyptians were particularly numerous in the Mixed
Administrations (20.26%), Finance (12.50) and Public Works (9.52%).
Omitting the Ministry of the Interior with its numerous and
predominantly Muslim employees (90.34%), almost ten percent (9.66%) of
all elite functionaries from 1882 to 1907 were foreign.[52] Hence this
analysis corroborates the observation above that after 1882, Egyptians
were increasingly ruled by foreigners.

When government positions are classified from one to eight by
rank, it becomes apparent that foreigners were particularly numerous
on levels two, Wakil Minister or Advisor (19.08%), three , Nazir
Idara (Head of Administration, 6.90%) and five Mufattish
(Inspector, 10.95%),as can be seen in Appendix 41. On the three
lowest levels, foreigners were almost absent, constituting only 1.64%.
Levels two and three contained the foreigners who made basic policy

decisions for the Egyptian government under Lord Cromer's overbearing
tutelage. Other Europeans on level five extended foreign power down
to neighborhoods, <u>markaz-s</u> and irrigation districts.

Religion as well as nationality was highly correlated with power
rank and power within the state apparatus. Non-Muslims were extremely
numberous among the government elite, constituting 18.84% of the total
though they accounted for only 7.77% of the national population in
1897.[53] Most of these minority group employees were Christian,
numbering 253 out of the 1503 whose religion could be determined, or
16.83%. Non-Muslims were especially numerous in the ministries of
Finance (56.52%), the Mixed Administrations (44.76%), Health (43.75%)
and Justice (23.59%). Some low level posts such as <u>sarraf</u> may have
become more accessible for Muslims after the turn of the century.[54]

Non-Muslims were disproportionately represented on all levels of
the government bureaucracy except that of <u>'umda</u>, level seven, where
they constituted 7.92% of the total. Christians were particularly
numerous on approximately the same levels as were non-Egyptians.
Non-Muslims accounted for a suprising 36.84% of all employees at the
level of <u>Wakil</u> Minister , 27.85% at the level of Mufattish I, 18.72%
at the level of Mufattish II and 33.96% at the level of simple
employee or clerk.

Government Employment by Level by Religion,1882-1907

Level	Muslim		Non-Muslim		Total
	N	%	N	%	N
1 Minister	58	85.29	10	14.71	68
2 Wakil Minister	48	63.16	28	36.84	76
3 Nazir Idara	117	83.57	23	16.43	140
4 Wakil Idara	156	83.87	30	16.13	186
5 Mufattish I	158	72.15	61	27.85	219
6 Mufattish II	165	81.28	38	18.72	203
7 'Umda	337	92.08	29	7.92	366
8 Employee	35	66.04	18	33.96	53
Total	1074	81.92	237	18.08	1311

We can conclude that Copts began to replace Turko-Circassian
ministers and wakil ministers after the occupation while entry into
the position of clerk became easier for Muslims. Important positions
such as inspector, judge and wakil idara were opened up to Copts on
the intermediate levels where they could act to extend the power of
their British co-religionists. There may have been a dimunition in
this process after 1900, although my information is not complete
enough to make a firm assertion here. When goverenment employment is
broken down by period and religion, it appears that the percentage of
non-Muslims was relatively stable at 23.81% from 1882 to 1890 and
25.77% from 1891 to 1899 but then decreased to perhaps seventeen

percent through 1907. Unfortunately full data is not available for
the last ten years of Cromer's rule, so no firm conclusion can be
drawn. See Appendix 42.

Career Patterns of High Level Officials

Mobility is the most striking characteristic of the career
patterns of successful bureaucrats in the Egyptian government in the
latter half of the nineteenth century. Officials who reached the rank
of <u>Nazir</u> <u>Idara</u> or above were very mobile geographically and moved
considerably between different departments of government. Of the 116
high level bureaucrats for whom complete employment records were
consulted in the pension files, fifty-nine or 50.86% were employed by
several administrations during their careers.

Isma'il Safwat's career offers a good example of the great career
mobility possible for Egyptian government officials. A freed slave of
Muhammad 'Ali Pasha, he began government service as a Sergeant in the
Mafruza military academy in 1849, reaching the rank of Major in 1859.
After leave of absence he re-entered government service as a <u>Mu'awin</u>
of the Muhafaza of Cairo later that year. After leaving the
government for part of 1861 and 1862, he was appointed <u>Ma'mur</u> of the
provincial police garrison of Gharbiyya province. Next he became
<u>Nazir</u> of coal stores for the Railway Administration, then he was
appointed Director of Customs at Alexandria. After a brief stay in
the Daira Saniyya Administration he was appointed Governor of Isna
province in 1875, then of Qalyubiyya in 1876. Leaving this post in
1880, he became Judge of the Tanta Native Court for six years and in
1886 a member of the Maglis al-Ahkam. After three months' service as
<u>Wakil</u> of the Estate of Tusun Pasha, he returned to the Maglis
al-Ahkam for two years until he was appointed Governor of Minya in

1889. He retired from government service February 5,1890 and lived in al-Darb al-Gadid in the Sayyida Zaynab quarter of Cairo where he collected a pension of 53 L.E. per month until his death there on April 16, 1902. His widow, Aisha Hanem, then collected a pension of 6.66 L.E. per month until 1909. His two daughters were married at the time of his death and so were not entitled to pensions. Although Isma'il Pasha Safwat followed the predominant mixed career pattern of employment with several administrations, there were also a number of other distinctive patterns of advancement for high officials.

The Ministry of the Interior seems to have offered its employees great career stability and for some, a chance of steady advancement. Excluding the fifty-nine mixed career patterns exemplified by Isma'il Safwat above, twenty-four out of the remaining fifty-nine officials worked predominantly in the Ministry of the Interior where two paths of advancement dominated. Eighteen officials moved from the Egyptian army into the Interior in their late twenties or early thirties and of these, most went on to rise to the level of provincial governor. Of the eighteen, at least five and perhaps several more were Turko-Circassian in origin. Most of the Turks graduated from the al-Mafruza military school. The other six officials in the Interior spent their entire careers in that ministry or moved from the muhafaza-s of Cairo or Alexandria into the ministry.

Following the Interior, the Ministry of Justice offered the second largest block of career paths for high officials. Two paths of advancement stand out in this ministry. Nine officials received law

degrees in France and on returning to Egypt, moved up rapidly within
the judicial apparatus. Of these, three were Turko-Circassians, two
Egyptian Muslims, two Europeans, one a Copt and one a Muslim whose
origins could not be determined. It is clear that the advantages
enjoyed by Europeans and Turko-Circassians before 1882 made law
studies in France more readily available and hence offered them great
prospects of success in the Ministry of Justice. The second path of
steady advancement began with law studies in Egypt for seven
officials, none of whom was identified a Turk in the pension files.
Four were Egyptian Muslims, one a Copt, one an Armenian and one a
Muslim of unknown origins. Of the Egyptian Muslims, Ahmad Fathi
Zaghlul mauy have partially owed his advancement to <u>Wakil</u> Minister
of Justice on February 28, 1907, to the influence of this brother Sa'd
Zaghlul with Lord Cromer.

Four other distinct career paths stand out in our sample. Three
men returned with medical degrees from Europe and rose steadily in the
Department of Public Health or were attached to the royal family. Two
Muslim Egyptians had long careers of steady advancement serving
members of the royal family. Four men, of which one Copt, one Turk
and two Egyptian Muslims, had long careers in the Mixed
Administrations. Five men with diplomas from al-Azhar rose steadily
through that hierarchy or within the Ministry of Justice. A schematic
diagram of career paths is presented in Appendix 43.

Two careers fit no recognizable pattern, and can only be labeled
as miscellaneous. It is significant that the only govenment official

who also had several important positions in Egyptian private companies
was a Copt, Barsum Bey Hanain, who graduated from a Coptic school in
Cairo, and then worked in the Suez Canal Company, the Ministry of
Public Works, the Railway Administration, a foreign company in
Alexandria, a private match company in the same city, the Khassa of
the Khedive, the Muhafaza of Cairo, and the Cairo Police Service
before being appointed Judge of First Instance in the Cairo Native
Courts in 1884. He died in 1889 after a total of twenty years of
government service.

From this analysis of the career patterns of 116 high government
officials we can draw several conclusions. Though most Ministers
under Cromer were Turko-Circassians, this group effectively lost its
monopoly of high positions and real power in government after the
'Urabi revolution. Egyptian Muslims, Copts and Armenians moved into
important positions in the early decades of the British occupation.
Officials with European diplomas advanced more steadily than their
colleagues except in the Interior, where Turks were favored until the
1890's. By 1907, a secular education had become the _sine qua non_
for steady advancement, replacing schooling in the military academies
such as al-Mafruza which had been crucial at mid-century.

In a memo on foreigners in the Egyptian service, Cromer noted the
changes in the composition of the bureaucracy and stressed the
importance of European education on recruitment during the first
eleven years of the occupation.[55] He observed the increased hiring
of Europeans, European educated Copts and especially Syrians after the

establishment of the Mixed Courts in 1876, where a working knowledge of French was essential. Cromer correctly observed that native Egyptians and especially Muslim Egyptians were jealous of the few Armenians in high positions and remarked on the Coptic bureaucrats' fear of displacement by Syrians. He concluded that the only cure for such imbalance in government hiring would be increased stress by Muslim Egyptians on the education of their sons. As we have seen above, the Egyptian government under Cromer devoted only minimal funds to public education until 1904.

There was also a broad pattern of career mobility for Egyptian officials in the latter half of the nineteenth century, but this probably decreased after the turn of the century as more jobs came to require specialized secular training. The possibilities of mobility that are always available for the highest level of administrators were reserved for Egyptian puppets and foreigners after 1900, as we have seen earlier. Finally, the ministries of Interior and Justice appear to have offered the most secure paths of steady advancement for those who retired before World War I. See Appendix 43.

It appears that more members of the political elite lived in villages after 1900, 19.42%, than those before this date, 7.47%, although these percentages are suspect for several reasons. Firstly, residence could not be established for 299 out of the 1,593 government employees. Secondly, Europeans, who usually lived in towns, were systematically undercounted after 1894. Thirdly, nominations to certain ministries such as War appear consistently under-recorded in

our sources. Desipte these caveats, we can infer that rural notables
were more frequently coopted into the government after 1900, were
given titles and were often connected with the Ministry of the
Interior where most appointments were made after 1899.[56]

Analysis of urban property holding in 1894 by government
employees suggests that the bureaucracy can be seen as a microcosm of
Cairene society, but one where shifts in property distribution
occurred more slowly. Those losing rank were the older elite, often
Turko-Circassian, who had risen to wealth in a previous period because
of connections to the royal family or to traditional Muslim
institutions. There was some gain for non-Muslim Egyptians and for
the holders of newly created offices such as Native Court Judge or
Appeals Court Judge. These shifts were not as striking or as
statistically significant as in Cairene society as a whole.

Several holders of older posts, such as the Bash Agha of the
Khedival Palace, wakil-s of royal domains or al-Khazandar, held vast
waqf property or had bequeathed large urban properties to their heirs
in 1894. However, newer appointees to these posts do not appear among
the urban elite and in some cases the posts were eliminated under
Cromer. Holders of traditional posts continued to appear among the
urban elite in cases where the appointment was made automatically
because of a man's position in Cairene society. Two typical cases are
the head of a Sufi order and shaykh of a guild, but newer appointees
owned considerably less property than their predecessors who had died
or commuted their holdings to waqf by 1894.[57]

Thus the holders of traditional posts connected with the royal family or traditional Muslim institutions were still wealthy property holders in Cairo in 1894, but were not renewing their economic status.[58]

The ten top categories were:

Post	Average Urban Property Tax (L.E.)	N
Bash Agha Khedival Palace	371	1
Sirr Tagir Cairo	364	1
Wakil Daira Khedive's Mother	120	1
Minister	50	12
Khuga	49	2
Director Bulaq Press	45	1
Ma'mur Baladiyat Cairo	45	1
Director Medical School	33	1
Head Physician Royal Family	33	1
Prime Minister	32	2

Some low status government posts were filled by wealthy Cairene property holders. A simple scribe in the Shari'a courts ranked twelfth, paying 26 L.E. and a department head (rais qalam) ranked twentieth, paying 18 L.E. These anomalies suggest that government employment may have been a hobby for wealthy Cairenes or agricultural property holders who chose the diversions of city life over close supervision of their estates.[59]

Copts in government appear to have improved their position in the
urban elite somewhat between 1882 and 1894. Holders of jobs
traditioally going to Copts ranked in the second level of the urban
elite, from rank 20 for department head to rank 32 for scribes
(<u>Katib</u>.) Christians in government held about the same average urban
property as Muslims.[60] However, posts often filled by Christians
were secured by wealthier men as the date of appointment approached
1894. For example, an early President of the Appeals Court paid only
5.2 L.E. while a later appointee paid 18 L.E. annual urban property
taxes.

Rural Landholding of Government Employees, 1882-1907

Shifts in rural landholding by state officials parallelled those
for the sale of royal lands under Cromer, but with foreigners and
non-Muslims making less decisive gains. Both proteges and foreigners
had greater average holdings according to our records than Egyptians
outside the royal family, as can be seen in the following table.

Nationality	N	Average Holdings (feddans)
Royal Family	7	6,602
Proteges	3	2,996
Foreigners	3	861
Egyptians (excluding Royal Fam.)	378	592

Because few foreigners in the Egyptian government purchased land
in our records, the great majority of land held by public servants
remained in Egyptian hands (95.89%). Aggregate figures for
landholding as a whole indicate, in contrast, that foreigners held
more than ten percent of the country's arable land during this period.

Muslim officials were more likely to purchase land than their
Christian colleagues, but when they bought land, Christians purchased
more as can be seen in the following table.

Total Feddans of Government Employees by Religion

Religion	N	Total	Mean Feddans
Muslim	323	213,250	660
Christian	44	45,651	1037
Jewish	1	538	538 [61]

Officials with higher positions usually but not always purchased more land. Ministers took great advantage of their ability to acquire land as did 'umda-s, while wakil idara-s purchased less land than others with lower rank. See Appendix 44.

Residence could be established for few officials who held land in our sources, but the data available indicate that town dwellers held more land on the average than those who lived in villages.[62] In this government employees follow very closely the pattern in Egyptian society as a whole.

When the different administrations are ranked by average holdings, it is clear that those with the highest percentage of non-Muslims were often ranked highest, e.g. Foreign Affairs, Interior and Finance. See Appendix 45.

If landholding by officials is broken down by period and by administration, it is again clear that Muslims had an overwhelming comparative advantage in most administrations. Christians achieved relative superiority in a few after 1890, for example Foreign Affairs, Interior, and Justice, only to lose it there and gain it in others like Towns and Miscellaneous Administrations. See Appendix 46.

why did so many non-Muslims end up with title to the former royal lands by 1907? There are three obvious hypotheses: (1) The Egyptian state under British control handed out most of the former royal lands to collaborating Christian and Jewish government officials. (2) The state favored non-Muslim purchasers in the private sector who sought to buy the land in competition with the Muslim the majority. (3) Non-Muslims were not favored by the state in the land sales but merely emerged as holders of a large share of the royal lands after 1882 by virtue of their superior access to capital and entrepreneurial sophistication. Hypotheses one and two point to the primacy of politics in this crucial process of land transfers. The third hypothesis argues for the primacy of purely economic factors. Our data support the accuracy of the second hypothesis and point to the primacy of politics.

The state did not hand the land to minority sect government officials. There was not a great flood of non-Muslims into the government bureaucracy after 1882. There may even have been a slowdown in entry of non-Muslims after 1900. Though almost half of the Domains and Daira Saniyya lands that make up the bulk of our category "total feddans" went to non-Muslim purchasers, Muslims held a comparative advantage in landholdings in most administrative departments.[63] Thus the first hypothesis cannot be substantiated.

The third hypothesis is likewise invalid. The Muslim landholding elite benefitted from the cotton boom and the rise in land values under Cromer. Muslims were sophisticated enough to mortgage their land, switch to the biennial crop rotation system and invest in expanded acreage. Had they been given a chance, they would have purchased all of the former royal lands on the attractive terms offered. Non- Muslims were the great benefactors of these land sales because the mixed Domains and Daira Saniyya administrations were controlled by non-Muslims, foreigners and Copts, who discriminated against Muslim purchasers. A close study of the records of the Daira Saniyya Company for the period of sales from 1898 to 1907 makes this abundantly clear. Each sale had to be approved by the London office. In going through the records I noticed that almost all sales proposed by the regional offices to Christians were routinely approved. Those to Muslims were sometimes cancelled by the head office in London.

The Egyptian government lost its independence of action after 1882, becoming a formidable instrument for the extension of British power down to successively lower levels of provincial and local administration. Control began at the top, when the weakened Khedive Tawfiq was restored to the throne by British arms. He had little choice but to appoint ministers who would provide a native screen for British rule. Caught between a weak Khedive and British advisers, these ministers and their subordinates progressively lost their ability to obstruct British directives. The most crucial ministries such as War and Public Works were the first to be fully dominated and in the following decades the other departments were increasingly controlled and often staffed by non-Egyptians and European educated minority sect Egyptians at the middle levels. Turko-Circassians lost their near monopoly of the post of minister and the Muslim Egyptians who predominated in the middle ranks of the Interior and Muhafaza administrations were slowly displaced because of the time lag in the effect of new recruitment procedures. Though young Copts and Syrians with European training were hired preferentially in the 1880's, they rose to the level of wakil governor only toward the end of the century. After 1904 even the traditional Muslim institutions such as the Department of Waqf-s and the Azhar university became somewhat compliant. The entire judicial apparatus of Egypt was transformed, with power flowing away from the Muslim Shari'a courts to the new Native Courts and especially to the European staffed Mixed Courts created six years before the occupation where those with foreign status received preferential treatment. A broad pattern of growing British control and Egyptian compliance is clear inside the government.

Egypt's representative institutions show an almost opposite pattern. In the early years of the occupation Lord Dufferin's plan to use the Legislative Council and General Assembly as a forum for collaboration by large landowners worked admirably. However, after 1892 and especially in 1906 and 1907, the national representative institutions provided a focal point for nationalist criticism of the occupation. This growing agitation at the end of Cromer's period of rule coincided with the re-emergence of indigenous political parties whose goals were greater power for local elites.

Footnotes: Chapter Seven

1. Baring to Salisbury , PRO,FO, 407/106, No.80, Cairo, May 15, 1891.

2. Granville to Baring, PRO,FO, 407/60, No.6, Secret, January 4, 1884.

3. This analysis omits the cabinet proposed by Abbas Hilmi on May 15, 1893, which he was forced to withdraw two days later.

4. Jacques Berque, Egypt, Imperialism and Revolution, 1972, p.177.

5. Cromer to Grey, PRO,FO, 407/168, No.22, Cairo, October 27, 1906.

6. Lloyd to Chamberlain, PRO,FO, 371/12388, May 23, 1927, forwarding a description of 1920.

7. Baring to Salisbury, PRO,FO, 407/106, No.80, Cairo, May 15, 1891.

8. Cromer, Abbas II, p.xxiii.

9. Louis Brehier, L'Egypte de 1798 à 1900, Paris, n.d., p.261

10. Baring to Salisbury, PRO,FO, 407/106, No.80, , May 15, 1891.

11. Dufferin to Granville, PRO,FO, 407/627/31, No.118, Cairo, 6 February, 1883, "Europeans in Egyptian Civil Service," p.112.

12. Morroe Berger, <u>Bureaucracy and Society in Modern Egypt.</u>
<u>A Study of the Higher Civil Service</u>, (Princeton, N.J.: Princeton
University Press, 1957), pp.30-32; Tignor, <u>Modernization</u>,
pp.180-182. The <u>Census of 1897</u> listed 12,085 civil servants of
all sorts. (v.1, pp.lxi-lxiii.)

13. <u>Berger</u>,p.30, citing Great Britian, Egypt No.11, (1887),
<u>Further Correspondence Respecting the Finances of Egypt</u>,
(Cd.4942), pp.6-7.

14. Dufferin to Granville, PRO,FO, 407/627/31, No.118, 6
February, 1883, p.112.

15. Europeans in the Egyptian service increased from 1,263 in
1882 to 1,662 in 1886, excluding proteges. Sir E. Baring to the Earl
of Iddesleigh, November 4, 1886, <u>House of Commons Sessional</u>
<u>Papers</u>,(Hereafter abbredviated as <u>HCSP</u>) in Egypt No.1, (1887),
vol.XCII, C.4997 ,pp.587-588. Even after proteges were excluded, the
European contingent had swollen to 1,157 in 1893. Lord Cromer to the
Earl of Rosebery, No.163, PRO,FO, 407/119, Inclosure in No. 163,
p.143. By 1896, European permanent government employees (excluding
the Mixed Courts and non-commissioned officers and men of the police)
numbered 690 and increased to 1,252 by 1906. Cromer, Annual Report
for 1906, No.31, <u>HCSP</u> (1907), C, 617, p.36. Although these figures
are not directly comparable because of the exclusions, one gets the
impression that the absolute number of Eurpoeans increased constantly.
In any case, British officials increasingly monopolized the upper

ranks of the bureaucracy, at the expense of both other Europeans and Egyptians, so that by 1905 the number of Egyptians in the highest posts was reduced to 27.7 percent. Egypt No.1, 1921, Report on the Special Mission to Egypt, <u>HCSP</u>, vol.xlii, Cmd. 1131, p.629-631, cited by Tignor, <u>Modernization</u>, p.181.

16.   Dufferin to Granville, No.173, April 3,1883, p.178.

17.   <u>Census of 1897</u>, v.1, p.lxiii. Male "functionnaires et employes civils et administratifs de toutes categories" numbered 12,085. <u>Loc.Cit</u>. It is not clear to what extent these figures for 1882 and 1897 are compatible.

18.   <u>Census of 1907</u>, p.282.

19.   A memo of the Ministry of War set the effective strength at this figure in June, 1881, and nominal forces at 11.000. Alexander Schölch, <u>Ä gypten den Ä gyptern</u>! ,p.137.

20.   Muhammad Mahmud al-Saruji, <u>Al-Gaysh al-Misri fi al-Qarn al-Tasi 'Ashar</u> (The Egyptian Army in the Nineteenth Century), (Dar al-Ma'arif: Cairo, 1967), pp.385-386.

21.   Baring to Granville, PRO,FO, 407/61, 9 April, 1884.

22.   Baring to Salisbury, PRO,FO, 407/107, No.285, Cairo, 12 December, 1891.

23.   Cromer to Salisbury, PRO,FO, 407/144, No.80, 12 October,1897.

24. <u>Census</u> <u>of</u> <u>1907</u>, p.282.

25. I have not been able to obtain reliable statistics about
this category of government employment. Dufferin's plan to reorganize
the Egyptian state spoke of 3,402 urban police in 1883 whose numbers
were to be reduced to 2,536 and of 4,400 gendarmes. Special Mission
from Lord Dufferin, PRO,FO, 78/3565, Cairo, January 1, 1883. The
<u>Census</u> <u>of</u> <u>1907</u> listed 29,201 members of the army, coastguard and
police forces. The army stood at 23,000 men at this time, so we may
estimate police forces at about six thousand. <u>Census</u> <u>of</u> <u>1897</u>, vol.
1, p.xxiii. The <u>Census</u> <u>of</u> <u>1907</u> lists 49,888 male members of the
"police" forces. These probably included at least 35,000 <u>ghaffir-s</u>
and guardians, who numbered 33,931 a decade before. <u>Census</u> <u>of</u> <u>1897</u>,
v.1, pp.lxi-lxiii. Thus the police and gendarmerie may have increased
to as much as 14,000 by 1907. See <u>Statistical</u> <u>Yearbook</u> <u>for</u> <u>1909</u>,
p.50. Here it is inferred that 80,000 L.E. of police expenses were
transferred to the Central Administration of the Ministry of the
Interior after 1895. This increase in expenditures would support the
assumption that police and gendarmerie forces increased considerably
from 1897 to 1907.

26. Willcocks to Baring, Inclosure 1 in No.44, PRO,FO, Tanta, 25
April, 1888.

27. <u>El-Messady</u>, p.72.

28. Dufferin to Cherif Pasha, PRO,FO, 78/3565, 10 January, 1883

and Cherif Pasha to Sir A. Colvin, <u>Loc</u>.<u>Cit</u>., 22 January, 1883.

29. Milner, <u>England</u> <u>in</u> <u>Egypt</u>, pp.105-106.

30. Sir Edgar Vincent, Appendix No.6 to "Report on the Financial Administration of Egypt", in No. 183, The Earl of Northbrook to Earl Granville, No.15, PRO,FO, October 5, 1884.

31. In September of 1882, there were 213 European employees in the ministry, or 3.71% of the total 5,743. By 1896 there were 281 Europeans, and by 1906 the European contingent had grown to 356. The source of the 1882 figures is a "Report by Mr. Fitzgerald on the Administrations in Egypt," Inclosure 3 in No.230, PRO,FO, 407/23/2879, Alexandria, 10 September, 1882, p.114. The 1896 and 1906 figures are not directly comparable with those òf 1882 because they include only permanent employees and thus understate the number of Europeans, but possibly understate their percentage of the total: 18.13% in 1896 and 15.49% in 1906.

32. Walid Kazziha, "The Evolution of the Egyptian Political Elite, 1907,1921", Thesis submitted to the University of London, September, 1970, pp.21-24.

33. Tignor, <u>Modernization</u>, p.115.

34. European employment exceeded 100 in 1882 when there were only five Englismen of the staff. "Report by Fitzgerald," PRO,FO, 407/23/2879, Alexandria, 10 September, 1882, p.114. All sources agree that there was a great influx of Europeans, especially Britons, into

this ministry after 1882 but the only available statistics give no
clear picture:

Europeans in the Ministry of Public Works

	1882	1896	1906
Europeans	101	52	99
% Europeans	3.21%	9.19%	15.49%
Total Employees	3127	566	639

The 1882 figures are drawn from Fitzgerald's report cited above.
The figures for 1896 and 1906 are from Cromer's _Annual_ _Report_ _for_
_1906_, cited above ,but these include only permanent employees unlike
the earlier data. The percentage figures, the evidence of ministry
expenditures and all contemporary accounts lead us to believe that
there was a sizable influx of British employees into the ministry.

35. _Moniteur_ _Egyptien_, December 10, 1883.

36. Kazziha, _Political_ _Elite_, pp.22,23.

37. Mr. Kent to Consul Burg, Inclosure 3 in No.20, Baring to
Granville, PRO,FO, 407/65, Mehella Kibir, 18 March 1885.

38. Willcocks to Baring, Inclosure 1 in No.44, PRO,FO, Tanta, 25
April, 1888.

39. _El-Messady_, p.106.

40. Cromer to Rosebery, No.150, PRO,FO, 407/119/3459, Cairo,

March 2, 1893, p.89.

41. Tignor, Modernization, p.72.

42. El-Messady, pp.178-185.

43. Cromer, "Report for 1906," Egypt No.1, HCSP, vol.C,
Cd.3394, 617, p.36.

44. Kazziha, Political Elite, pp.143,144.

45. Op.Cit., pp.153,306.

46. European Christians were appointed to technical positions in
the Department of Awqaf as early as 1885, when a France Bey was named
Bash Muhandis, or Chief Engineer. Al-Waqa'ia al-Misriyya,
February 25, 1885, p.1.

47. Gelat, Législation, vol.2, p.538.

48. Dufferin to Granville, PRO, FO, 78/3567, Cairo, 7, March,
1883.

49. Decree Regulating State Employees, April 10, 1883, quoted in
Gelat, vol.2, pp.532-533.

50. Decree of October 23, 1888, quoted in Gelat, vol.2,
pp.547-548; Baring to Salisbury, PRO,FO, 407/113, No.232, Cairo, April
12, 1892 and Decree of June 24, 1901, quoted in Gelat, vol.2

51. Census of 1897, v.1, p.xiii.

52. These figures represent an incomplete sample of the foreigners nominated to government posts from 1894 to 1907. All other categories of information about government employment are complete as stated in Al-Waqa'ia al-Misriyya. Thus the percentage of foreigners indicated above should probably be somewhat increased.

53. Census of 1897, vol.1, p.xiv.

54. There is no reason to believe Jacques Tagher's statement that most civil servants in the lower ranks were Copts before 1882. He is probably more accurate in asserting that more sarraf-s were Muslim after 1900. Jacques Tagher, Coptes et musulmans, Cairo, 1952, p.248.

55. See Cromer to Rosebery, No.163, PRO,FO, 407/119, Cairo, April 2,1893, pp.133-140.

56. Titles proliferated after 1890. Government employees without the title of Bey or above shrank from 24.93% (1882-1890), to 19.42% (1891-1899) and to 13.95% (1900-1907.) Of the 271 elite appointments to the Ministry of the Interior recorded between 1882 and 1907, 137 came after 1899.

57. Four older heads of Sufi orders paid an annual average tax of 24.6 L.E., while the two newer office holders paid a smaller average of 9.6 L.E.

58. An exception to this observation was the Sirr Tagir or Head

Merchant of Cairo in 1894 who paid an annual urban property tax of 364
L.E.

59. The latter phenomenon was observed by A. Behmer in 1868 in
his Observations sur l'état actuel de l'agriculture en Egypte,
pp.7-8, quoted in Owen, Cotton, p.151.

60. A chi square test of religion as an indicator of above or
below average urban property taxes in 1894 yielded a significance of
.2789; i.e., the correlation was low and not statistically
significant.

61. Of the 227 Chrisitan high officials, 19.38% purchased land
while 30.07% of the Muslims made purchases.

62. Employees living in towns numbered 198 with an average
holding of 950 feddans; the 103 in villages held an average of 440
feddans.

63. Of the total 281,873 feddans held by government employees
that can be broken down by level and religion, 75.65% or 213,250
feddans belonged to Muslims. Although non-Muslims purchased 228,113
of the coded Domains and Daira Saniyya lands transferred or 43.38%,
government employees bought only 120,677 (Daira Saniyya) and 68,997
(Domains) feddans, for a total of 189,674 feddans, or only 34.01% of
the total royal lands transferred. Of the 300 government buyers of
Domains land, only 24 were Christian and none Jewish. Of the 585
non-government buyers of Domains land, 117 were Christian and eleven

Jewish. For details of the religious breakdown of Domains buyers by
occupational sector, see Appendix 47.

Chapter Eight

Conclusions

This final chapter will repeat the conclusions of each of the
seven preceding chapters which outlined transformations in demography,
foreign trade, commerce, manufacturing, urban and rural society, the
Khedivate, representative institutions and the bureaucracy in Egypt
from 1882 to 1907. The discussion then will focus on connections
between these different levels of change and take up the problem of
whether political or economic relationships were dominant in Egypt
from 1882 to 1907.·

Chapter one showed that the population of Egypt grew considerably
during the first twenty-five years of the British occupation though
not all sectors grew at the same rate. Differences in the growth rate
point to several significant changes in the composition and balance of
power within Egyptian society.

The rural population grew more rapidly than that of urban areas
and Lower Egypt grew faster than Upper Egypt. Up to 1897 the foreign
community grew somewhat faster than the total population and then
increased at twice the national rate up to 1907. Egyptians were
forced out of some desirable urban neighborhoods such as al-Muski in
Cairo. The Muslim majority declined somewhat relative to other groups
while the Christian population increased significantly. The
Protestant Coptic and Catholic Coptic sects grew at the expense of the

orthodox Coptic community from 1897 to 1907. The non-Coptic orthodox population almost doubled during this period because of the influx of Greeks. Among the non-Coptic Christian communities of Egypt, Protestant and Catholic sects grew little from 1897 to 1907. The Jewish community grew, probably due to immigration from Europe. The rural Coptic community was squeezed into a narrower band of sub-provinces during this period. Finally, some provinces grew much more rapidly than others.

Where there was demographic growth, especially relative to other groups within Egyptian society, we might be tempted to read in shifts in wealth or power. As we have seen this was true in some cases. The decline in the Muslim majority population relative to Christians reflected a major structural transformation as did the shift away from orthodox Coptic communities to non-orthodox Coptic sects. The rapid influx of foreigners after 1897 again mirrored real shifts in national wealth and power. On the other hand, though the rural sector grew in population it suffered a real decline in economic power and political influence relative to the urban sector. Thus demographic data enable us to focus our attention on three axes of structural shifts in Egypt under Cromer but cannot explain them: urban versus rural, foreign versus Egyptian and Muslim versus non-Muslim.

Chapter two showed that both foreign trade and internal commerce were increasingly dominated by cotton during the first twenty-five years of the British occupation. The trend toward a dual economy accelerated during this period. Large scale commerce and the

lucrative export sector were dominated by foreigners, proteges,
minority sect Egyptians and clients of the royal family. Small scale
commerce remained in the hands of Muslim Egyptians. Egypt exported
cotton, imported manufactured goods from Europe and exported a few
locally manufactured goods abroad such as cigarettes. By 1900 the
country became a net importer of foods. Though Great Britain remained
Egypt's major trading partner, its overall share of imports and
exports declined. Government institutions made some progress
supplying credit to middle level agricultural producers after 1898
although small farmers remained at the mercy of local money lenders
who charged usurious rates.

Chapter three showed that Egyptian industry in the first decades
of the British occupation was marked by many of the traits of a
colonial or dual economy. Most modern production was oriented toward
the agricultural export sector, construction and luxury goods for the
urban rich. Elsewhere the level of technology was archaic, depending
largely on human or animal energy sources. The evolution of a fully
modernized manufacturing sector was blocked during the first decades
of the occupation. The impediments of the guild system were replaced
by fluid wage labor in the towns, but though traditional manufacturing
declined the emergence of fully developed modern industry was blocked
by Britain.

Large blocks of capital in industry were almost completely owned
and manged by foreigners, proteges, a few high government officials
and members of the royal family. In relation to the entire work

force, employment in manufacturing grew little from 1882 to 1907. It appears that the last vestiges of the guild system of artisanal production disappeared by 1907 and were replaced by modern wage labor, at least in the larger towns where information is available.

Chapter four demonstrated that non-Muslims and foreigners were penetrating all levels of the urban elite in Cairo at the start of the British occupation and that they were increasing their share of property at each of the three upper levels of society: (1) small scale merchants and lower level civil servants, (2) middle ranking functionaries, professionals and employees, and (3) high government officials, merchants, industrialists, financiers and successful professionals in the liberal arts. Most inhabitants of Cairo, on the other hand owned no urban property or so little that they were not listed as tax payers. Urban property holding was extremely concentrated.

There appear to have been major obstacles limiting social mobility out of the bottom level of the elite where urban property taxes reached a maximum of 3.5 L.E. per year. Movement into the two upper sectors where 1,997 owners held 55.43% of Cairo's taxable property in 1894 was becoming more and more difficult for Muslim Egyptians, though government employment opened doors for a few. Most were elbowed aside by proteges and non-Muslims who became increasingly over represented in those occupations that were to prove the greatest sources of wealth and power in modern Egyptian society: government, manufacturing and finance. At the apex of the elite, foreign status

under the Capitulations, membership in the royal family and access to
foreign capital helped families to acquire far greater wealth than
mere government employment. Muslim Egyptians were being forced out of
neighborhoods like al-Muski and Cairo was becoming a city where
residence followed patterns of social stratification. Women improved
their relative position at some levels, but only marginally. Cairo
remained a city where men dominated property holding.

Chapter five showed that a massive shift took place in the
distribution of agricultural land and the balance of power among
social groups in the Egyptian countryside. The predominance
established by non-Muslims in large scale commerce was transferred
into the rural sector during the first twenty-five years of the
British occupation. In general, rural society became less homogeneous
and more stratified by religion while the opportunities for upward
social mobility decreased sharply.

During the first twenty-five years of the British occupation
massive investment in irrigation and in the national transport
infrastructure increased agricultural output, which became more and
more dominated by cotton. These shifts increased the total wealth in
the agricultural sector, but mismanagement by Anglo-Indian irrigation
advisors led to a sharp decline in yield per feddan at the same time
as Egypt became more dangerously dependent on fluctuating world market
prices for its dominant cash crop.

On the eve of the occupation, elite landholders, i.e., those with

over five feddans, were divided into two groups, those holding more
and those holding less than about thirty-two feddans. The lower
group, middle landholders, was relatively homogeneous and
representative of the national population. The wealthier group of
large landholders was stratified by occupation and residence. By 1885
non-Egyptians and non-Muslims had established a large presence among
middle elite groups in the commericalized areas of the delta and were
beginning to gain a disproportionate share of large agricultural
estates. The apex of the rural elite was beginning to lose its
homogeneity by 1885.

Aggregate statistics on land distribution from 1896 to 1907 show
that the overall spread of holdings by size of plot changed little.
However, the social consequences of this seeming stability were great.
The increase in the cultivated area lagged behind the growth in rural
population so that the ranks of landless peasants greatly increased.
Placed against the background of growing absentee ownership,
competition for land increased considerably during the first quarter
century of the British occupation. This competition was exacerbated
by the sharp inflation in land prices and rent after 1900.

Sales records of the Domains and Daira Saniyya estates indicate
that the processes of social differentiation within the elite,
competition for land, and the shift away from continued dominance by
the Turko-Circassian and Muslim rural elite families all accelerated
through 1907. These sales show wealth and power flowing out of the
hands of the royal family and the old rural elite families and into

the hands of a new spectrum of elite groups dominated by urban
dwellers, Muslim government employees, non-Muslims and non-Egyptians.

Agricultural relations of production shifted simultaneously in
the following ways from 1882 to 1907: (1) forced labor without
compensation was almost completely eliminated by 1889, (2) the
'ezbah system remained dominant and the pattern spread to many
estates between thirty and fifty feddans, (3) cash rental, by itself
or within the 'ezbah system, bacame more common, (4) sharecropping
remained important but may have decreased slightly in order to permit
the rise of cash rental and (5) small plots under five feddans
continued to be cultivated by their owners though there were cases of
rental here as well.

These simultaneous shifts in output, land distribution and the
organization of agricultural production had tremendous social
consequences. The swelling population of landless peasants was
absorbed partly by the prosperous 'ezbah plantations while other
segments of this displaced group became wage laborers for middle
estate owners. Demographic statistics cited in chapter one show that
Egypt's urban areas absorbed few peasants up to 1907 though they
opened their doors to a great flood of foreigners. Because all land
became alienable by 1896 and forced labor almost completely
disappeared, farm laborers became increasingly mobile. Here the trend
was for excess labor in Upper Egypt to migrate to the delta during the
cotton season. In general rural society became much more stratified
and opportunities for upward mobility diminished. The elite group of

large landowners which developed under Cromer was able to maintain its
dominant position in rural society down to the revolution of 1952.

Chapter six demonstrated that the royal family was the great
loser in the 'Urabi revolution and the British occupation, both
economically and politically. The occupation reaffirmed the Law of
Liquidation of 1880, by which the family of Khedive Isma'il lost title
to 934,637 feddans, retaining approximately 150,000 feddans of
'ushuriyya land. The Khedive also lost effective control over the
Egyptian government. When Abbas Hilmi tried to reassert Khedival
power on accession in 1892, he was outmaneuvered by Cromer and
abandoned by his own ministers.

Egypt's pseudo-parliamentary institutions under the occupation
were designed by the British to have a powerless advisory role.
Parliamentary government in general offers a vehicle for stable rule
of the middle class. In a semi-colonial context such as that of Egypt
at the end of the nineteenth century, the indigenous middle class was
too weak to provide stable government and prevent foreign invasion.
In an unstable political environment, many elements of the Egyptian
political and economic elites welcomed the foreign invasion. Once
British troops had defeated organized resistance, the occupying power
naturally emasculated local parliamentary institutions and made them
into a legitimizing screen for foreign rule.

There were several reasons why members of Egypt's national
representative istitutions were likely to collaborate with their

British rulers in the first years of the occupation: (1) they were large landowners; (2) they were also often government employees whose rank increased after 1882; (3) those who sat in more than one assembly were wealthier and held higher offices ; (4) they were increasingly Christian and Christians were happy to cooperate with their foreign co-religionists and (5) they were increasingly residents in the large urban centers whose elite members flourished under the occupation. In other words, they were well rewarded for their collaboration.

After 1892 however, and especially in 1906 and 1907, the national representative institutions provided a focal point for moderate nationalist criticism of the occupation. This growing agitation at the end of Cromer's period of rule coincided with the re-emergence of indigenous political parties whose major goal was greater power for local elites.

Chapter seven showed that Egyptian government lost its independence of action after 1882, becoming a formidable instrument for the extension of British power down to successively lower levels of provincial and local administration. Control began at the top, when the weakened Khedive Tawfiq was restored to the throne by British arms. He had little choice but to appoint ministers who would provide a native screen for British rule. Caught between a weak Khedive and British advisers, these ministers and their subordinates progressively lost their ability to obstruct British directives. The most crucial ministries such as War and Public Works were the first to be fully dominated and in the following decades the other departments were

increasingly controlled and often staffed by non-Egyptians and
European educated minority sect Egyptians at the middle levels.
Turko-Circassians lost their near monopoly of the post of minister and
the Muslim Egyptians who predominated in the middle ranks of the
Interior and Muhafaza administrations were displaced slowly because of
the time lag in the effect of new recruitment procedures. Though
young Copts and Syrians with European training were hired
preferentially in the 1880's, they rose to the level of wakil
governor only toward the end of the century. After 1904 even the
traditional Muslim institutions such as the Department of Awqaf and
the Azhar university became somewhat compliant. The entire judicial
apparatus of Egypt was transformed, with power flowing away from the
Muslim Shari'a courts to the new Native Courts and especially to the
European staffed Mixed Courts created six years before the occupation
where those with foreign status received preferential treatment. A
broad pattern of growing British control and Egyptian compliance is
clear inside the government.

The basic organizational scheme of this thesis should now be
explicitly stated again. Chapter one outlined the demographic
background to our study of Egypt under Cromer, stressing quantitative
evidence. Chapters two through five concentrated upon economic
structures and transformations in the distribution of wealth and the
orgainization of production. Chapters six and seven summarized the
changes in political structures and access to state power from 1882 to
1907. Given the fact that this study excludes the field of

intellectual history, the essential remaining question is that of
basic predominance or causation. In other words, were changing
economic relationships essentially motivated by transformations on the
political level, or were economic changes behind the shifts in
political institutions?

The answer is that of temporary predominance by the level of
politics. This basic question must now be put into the perspective of
shifts during the entirity of the nineteenth century. During the
period from 1813 to 1840, a period where political relationships
dominated and reshaped economic structures, power rested in the hands
of Muhammad 'Ali and the Turko-Circassian elite which he placed at the
apex of the state apparatus. During periods of political level
dominance, economic institutions are often rapidly transformed.
During the ensuing period of economic supremacy from 1840 to 1881,
political institutions were relatively stable and passively reacted to
the maturation of the economic structures in place at the onset of the
period. By the end of this forty year period of economic maturation
and dominance, the social and political consequences of the maturing
economic institutions - cash crop agriculture for export to the
European dominated world market, the formation of large agricultural
estates, growth of a landless rural labor force, private property in
land, a modernized export sector and an urban commercial elite with
ties to European cotton purchasers - had become intolerable to many
cadres near the apex of the indigenous political institutions.

The 'Urabi revolution was an attempt to realign political and

economic structures and to restore Egyptian supremacy in the face of
foreign economic influence. The Egyptian army officers realized that
their Turko-Circassian superiors no longer held the key to power in
Egyptian society and therefore there was hope of toppling the
autocratic Turkish general staff. Some Egyptian politicians had
adopted European ideas of democratic government and used the Egyptian
representative assembly as a forum to promote ideas of parliamentary
government. Had they succeeded, what emerged would have been
indigenous representative government in the hands of the landowning
elite in perfect congruence with the local distribution of economic
power. The great mass of Egyptians resented the growing influence of
Europeans over all aspects of life in Egypt. Many landless and
smallholding peasants disliked the growing affluence of the great
estate holders and supported those elements around 'Urabi who argued
that the land belonged to those who tilled it. When the danger of
land seizure by <u>fallahin</u> became obvious to the Muslim estate holders
who joined 'Urabi out of xenophobia , dislike of the Turks or desire
to restore Egyptian power over local economic structures, they
abandoned 'Urabi and went over to Tawfiq and the British army.

Thus the suppression of the 'Urabi rebellion began another period
of political supremacy in which British control of the government of
Egypt protected those economic processes detailed directly above that
benefitted foreigners, proteges, some members of the royal family,
minority sect Egyptians and cooperating Muslim estate holders. The
period of rule by Cromer was characterized by the energetic

intervention of government into economic developments.

The British worked rapidly to eliminate any centers of resistance within the Egyptian government. Beginning with the army and moving finally into the Department of Awqaf, all those who refused to collaborate were swept aside. The entire judicial apparatus was tranformed with power flowing from the Shari'a courts to the new Native Courts and the Mixed Courts. Powerless representative institutions were erected to provide a forum where the country's large estate holders could lend legitimacy to the native screen behind which the British governed. The structure and cadres of the government were slowly transformed under Cromer.

The rhythm of government expenditures under Cromer reflected the semi-colonial environment of foreign domination. Firstly, debt service dominated all government expenditures. It was extremely high until 1890, then began a phase of slow decline until 1904, when the decline became more rapid. Taking into account heavy irrigation expenses in the 1880's and increased revenues after the turn of the century, there was a constant commitment to heavy debt service without much interest in retiring the debt. It should be recalled that the creditors of the Egyptian government were all Europeans. These European investors benefitted by the continued high indebtness of Egypt. Secondly, defense expenditures were extremely low after the defeat of 'Urabi , except during the reconquest of the Sudan. Thirdly, the British rulers of Egypt spent very little on public education during a period when private schooling increased rapidly.

Public health was also neglected for most of the period, though there was some increase in spending for both health and education after 1896. Fourthly, public works received extremely high priority, with expenditures rising from eight to ten percent per year during the decade that began in 1886. Expenditures for public works constituted the second largest block of expenses until 1899, when railways moved up to second place. However, the railways brought in a net profit for the government of Egypt as it was a "revenue earning administration." Again, it was European industrialists who benefitted from the high quality, steady supply of long staple cotton from Egypt during a period when Cromer impeded the creation of a modern textile industry in Egypt. See Appendix 40.

The reorganized political structures dominated and transformed economic structures from 1882 to 1907. The government supervised massive investment in irrigation to promote the export of cotton. Under British administration, Egypt was increasingly turned into a large cotton farm and became a net importer of food products about 1900. This transformation made life more precarious for all Egyptian groups below the rural and urban elites, made Egypt's export earnings dependent on the world market for cotton over which it had little control and benefitted most those groups in control of the export sector, namely foreigners, proteges and minority sect Egyptians.

Under political pressure, the continued development of Egypt's dual economy proceeded rapidly. Only middle and small scale commerce remained in the hands of Muslim Egyptians. Large scale commerce and the lucrative export sector were dominated by the new multi-national

elite. The British allowed cheap European imported goods to displace

traditional local manufactures but manipulated tariff policy to

prevent the emergence of a modern local textile industry, even in the

hands of foreigners. Cromer remained true to the principles of free

trade, however, in one significant way. He did not and perhaps could

not have intervened to stop the slow decline of Britain's share of

Egyptian imports and exports which shifted to the benefit of Germany.

Those provinces that increased in populaion more rapidly than

others benefitted from the expansion of the irrigation system carried

out to increase the cultivation of cotton for export. Again, this

served the purposes of European industrialists and the mediating

Egyptian landed elite that used _fallah_ labor to produce the cotton.

There was a strong relationship between population growth and the area

of land under cultivation. The correlation between the population

growth rate from 1897 to 1907 and the growth rate in the total

cultivated area by province was very high, .6904688. Taking only the

six delta provinces, the correlation was even higher, .7678159. These

correlations were computed from data in the _Annuaire_ _Statistique_ of

1909.

The broad movement of crucial changes in the Egyptian social

formation proceeded from the levels of politics to economics to

intellectual and social concerns. It has been shown how the British

influenced the direction of economic development. The ramifications

for social and intellectual life in Egypt were massive. Elite

Egytians came to identify with their conquerors. They imitated them in language ,in dress, in the style of their clothes and in the style of their houses. Villas built during this period by Muslim politicians in Garden City, an elite district of Cairo, are indistinguishable from those commissioned by British, Belgian and French residents.

The increasing wealth and power of foreign Christians in Egyptian society, Christians who were either Catholics, Greek orthodox or Protestants, led orthodox Copts to emulate the powerful by converting to the Catholic and Protestant Coptic rites. Hence the shifts within the Coptic community can be explained by a desire to emulate the new dominant groups within Egypt. This was merely one of many levels on which the powerful foreigners were aped. Egyptians had imitated their dress, learned their languages and constructed houses in the European fashion since the time of the Khedive Isma'il. However, these mass conversions within the Coptic community offer striking evidence of the desire of indigenous minority groups to emulate their powerful European co-religionists.

Starting in approximately 1890 there were, nonetheless, several signs of resistance to the new status quo. Firstly, peasant and lower class urban discontent manifested itself in a rising crime rate. Misdemeanors classified as "indignities and violence offered to public authority" rose from 580 in 1897 to 3,814 in 1907, as reported in the Annuaire Statistique of 1909. Secondly, toward the end of Cromer's rule the urban Muslim elite began to form political parties to press

for greater indigenous access to political power. It was this elite
demand for greater local power that made Cromer's position so
difficult that he returned to England in 1907, thus ending a momentous
period in Egyptian history.

Appendix 1

The Foreign Population in Egypt, 1882-1907

(1882)

	Foreign Pop.	Total Pop.	% Foreign
Cairo	21,650	463,414	4.67
Alexandria	49,693	256,921	19.34
Lower Egypt	9,202	3,797,165	.24
Upper Egypt	1,895	3,227,501	.06
All Egypt	90,868	7,840,271	1.16

(1897)

	Foreign Pop.	Total Pop.	% Foreign
Cairo	35,385	570,062	6.21
Alexandria	46,118	300,172	15.36
Lower Egypt	11,212	4,719,335	.24
Upper Egypt	3,395	4,026,218	.08
All Egypt	112,574	9,717,228	1.34

(1907)

	Foreign Pop.	Total Pop.	% Foreign
Cairo	55,987	654,476	8.55
Alexandria	59,368	332,246	17.87
Lower Egypt	16.082	5,519,194	.29
Upper Egypt	4,460	4,658,045	.10
All Egypt	151,414	11,287,359	1.34

Annual Rate of Increase

	(1892-1897)	(1897-1907)
Cairo	.0332944	.0469521
Alexandria	-.004965	.0255768
Lower Egypt	.013258	.0276601
Upper Egypt	.039677	.0367301
All Egypt	.0143826	.0300844

The figures were taken from the respective censuses. Aswan is excluded from Lower Egypt in 1882.

Appendix 2

Religion in Egypt, 1897-1907

Sect	N--1897	% 1897	N--1907	% 1907
Muslim	8,977,702	92.23	10,269,445	91.77
Copts (total)	609,511	6.26	706,322	6.31
Orthodox	592,374	6.09	667,036	5.96
Protestant	12,507	.13	24,701	.22
Catholic	4,630	.05	14,576	.13
All Christians	731,235	7.51	881,692	7.88
Orthodox	645,775	6.63	771,926	6.90
Catholic	61,051	.63	72,320	.65
Jews	24,409	.25	37,446	.33
Others	268	.01	206	.01
Total	9,734,405	100.00	11,189,978	100.00
Non-Coptic Christian				
Orthodox	53,381	.55	104,890	.94
Protestant	11,902	.12	12,736	.11
Catholic	56,421	.58	57,744	.52

	%	AGR	AGR- Nat. AGR
Muslim	-.46	.0135337	-.0004991
Copts (total)	+.05	.0148506	+.0008178
Orthodox	-.13	.0119413	-.0020915
Protestant	+.09	.0704637	+.0564309
Catholic	+.08	.1215167	+.1074839
All Christians	+.37	.0188869	+.0048541
Orthodox	+.27	.0180039	+.0039711
Catholic	_.02	.0170834	+.0030506
Jews	_.08	.0437237	+.0296248
Others	___	-.025968	-.0400008
Total	___	.0140328	----
Non-Coptic Christian			
Orthodox	+.39	.0698792	+.0558464
Protestant	-.01	.0067956	-.0072372
Catholic	-.06	.0023205	-.0117123

In 1907 'Orthodox' indicates Greek Orthodox plus Eastern
Christians. <u>1907 Census</u>, p.117. AGR means annual growth rate;
AGR - Nat. means annual growth rate minus national annual growth.
All growth rates were calculated by the author. Other data come from
the the respective censuses.

Appendix 3   Provincial Growth Rates, 1882-1897

<u>Province</u>	<u>Rate of Annual Increase</u>	<u>Rank</u>
Buhaira	.028920	5
Daqahliya	.019285	12
Gharbiya	.021998	9
Minufiya	.019588	11
Qalyubiya	.021171	10
Sharqiya	.032338	4
Beni-Suef	.023722	6
Fayyum	.032776	3
Giza	.023526	7
Minya	.038017	1
Assyut	.022313	8
Girga	.018656	13
Qena	.032810	2
Aswan Mark.	.0110703	14

McCarthy, "Nineteenth Century Egyptian Population", p.27. The rankings have been indicated by the author.

Appendix 4   Provincial Growth Rates, 1897-1907

Province	Pop.in 1897	Pop.in 1907	Rate of Increase	Rank
Buhaira	656,419	830,015	.0237419	1
Daqahliya	780,480	912,428	.0157426	7
Gharbiya	1,297,656	1,484,814	.0135642	11
Minufiya	864,206	971,016	.0117213	13
Qalyubiya	371,602	434,575	.0157777	6
Sharqiya	748,972	886,346	.0169832	5
Beni-Suef	312,115	372,412	.0178198	3
Fayyum	371,006	441,583	.0175673	4
Giza	401,234	460,080	.0137796	10
Minya	550,971	663,144	.0187038	2
Assyut	782,720	907,435	.0148945	9
Girga	688,011	797,940	.0149333	8
Qena	711,457	780,849	.0093501	14
Aswan	208,704	234,604	.011766	12

The figures were taken from the respective censuses. The rates
and rankings were caluclated by the author.

Appendix 5

Egyptian Exports, 1885-1907 (L.E.)

	1885-89	%	1890-94	%
Cotton Exports	7.518.161	57.10	8,561,245	56.66
Other Goods	3,494.637	26.54	4,351,185	28.80
Specie Exports	2,154,168	16.36	2,198,257	14.55
Total Exports	13,166,966		15,110,687	

	1895-99	%	1900-1904	%
Cotton Exports	9,682,571	63.32	14,227,651	69.13
Other Goods	3,625,526	23.71	4,107,465	19.96
Specie Exports	1,982,366	12.96	2,277,248	10.92
Total Exports	15,290,463		20,582,364	

	1905-07	%
Cotton Exports	19,977,429	71.41
Other Goods	4,439,488	15.87
Specie Exports	3,557,944	12.72
Total Export	27,974,861	

Statistical Yearbook of 1909, p.85.

Appendix 6

Large Scale Public and Private Debt in Egypt,
1884-1907   (L.E. 1000's)

Years	1884-92	1893-97	1898-902	1903-07
Payments abroad on public debt	4,564	5,043	4,379	5,453
Payment abroad of debt of joint stock companies	277	387	994	3,465
Payment abroad public & private debt (C)	4,841	5,430	5,373	8,918
Exports excluding specie	11,921	12,768	15,810	22,728
Above increased by 1/9 (E)	13,246	14,187	17,567	25,244
C/E	36.55	38.27	30.59	35.33
Public Debt	103,078	104,633	103,201	98,392
Capital Held Abroad	6,030	8,747	16,770	26,198

Public & Private

Debt Abroad   109,108   113,380   119,971 124,590

Exports/Total

Debt Abroad   10.93   11.26   13.18   18.24

Inflow of Private

Capital   12   1,065   2,144   8,616

     The figures in the above table are drawn from Crouchley,

Investment, pp.148,21. All ratios were calculated by the author.

Appendix 7

Cotton Prices, 1880-1908

Season	Cotton Price/Cantar	Season	Cotton Price/Cantar
1880-1	3.076	1895	2.229
1881-2	3.139	1896	2.124
1882	3.271	1897	1.597
1883	3.007	1898	1.757
1884	2.792	1899	2.410
1885	2.602	1900	2.417
1886	2.785	1901	2.181
1887	2.736	1902	3.035
1888	2.951	1903	3.520
1889	2.979	1904	2.708
1890	2.563	1905	3.361
1891	2.014	1906	3.750
1892	2.069	1907-8	3.201
1893	1.889		
1894	1.882		

Owen, _Cotton_, p.197.

Appendix 8

Loans Made by the Credit Foncier Egyptien 1880-1907

Amount of Loan	Number of Loans	Total Loaned
Under 100	158	20,375
100-200	1,678	263,495
200-300	1,134	307,996
300-400	932	347,213
400-500	770	385,029
500-1000	2,359	1,835,139
1000-2000	1,785	2,958,403
2000-3000	1,002	2,511,002
3000-5000	987	3,967,729
5000-10000	878	6,360,433
10,000-40,000	731	13,757,294
40,000-60,000	58	2,922,832
60,000-70,000	13	768,098
70,000-90,000	11	899,342
Over 90,000	25	3,740,398
Total	12,521	41,044,780

Credit Foncier Egyptien, Rapports..., 1901-7. The average loan
in the category "less than 100 L.E." actually exceeds that amount
because of the entry for 1906, where the average loan under 100 L.E.
equals 430.07 L.E.

Appendix 9

Paid-Up Capital and Debts

of Agricultural and Urban Companies

(L.E. 1000)

Year	1883	1892	1897	1902	1907
Capital & Debts Held Abroad	0	221	360	2,096	7,135
%	0	37.52%	26.83%	70.48%	36.86%
Capital & Debts Held in Egypt	180	368	982	878	12,221
%	100%	62.48%	73.17%	29.52%	63.14%

Crouchley, <u>Investment</u>, pp.147,154. The total paid up capital
of these companies amounted to 1,719,438 L.E. <u>Ibid</u>., pp.9-20.

Appendix 10

A Discussion of Mortgages on Real Estate

Assuming that the value of private property was six percent of
the rental value, the total would come to 16,627,400 L.E. in Cairo
and about eleven million pounds in Alexandria in 1902. Roger Owen has
estimated the value of private property in Alexandria loca tax. Owen,
"The Cairo Building Industry and the Building Boom of 1897 to1907, "in
Colloque International sur l'Histoire du Caire, German Democratic
Republic, 1972, pp.339,345. Alfred Eid calculated that the value of
all buildings in Cairo and Alexandria in 1907 was 56,700,000 L.E. and
the value of the land was 122,000,000 L.E.

Alfred Eid, La fortune immobilière de l'Egypte et sa dette
hypothécaire, Paris, Felis Alcan, 1907, p.46.

Eid's estimate seems more accurate than that of Owen because he
undertook a detailed study of rents and land values in each
neighborhood of both cities. Eid found that to reduce the house tax.
Multiplying the area of each quarter by the market price for land
there, and adding the corrected value of the buildings, he arrived at
estimates which should be more accurate than those of Owen.

In 1902 the tax on urban property in Cairo and Alexandria was
83,137 + 53,263 = 136,400 and in 1907 it had increased to 119,614 +

80,124 = 199,738 L.E.

Owen, "The Cairo Building Industry...", pp.339,345.

Multiplying Eid's 1907 estimate for the total value of real
property in Cairo and Alexandria for 1907, 178,700,000 L.E. by the
ratio of property tax levied in 1907, the result is a reasonable
estimate of the value of Cairo and Alexandria real property in 1902 =
122,033,260 L.E.   (178,700,000 times (136,400/199,738) = 122,033,260.)
Thus the total paid-up capital of the seventeen joint stock companies
investing in urban property stood at only 1.41% of the total estimated
value of real property in the two major cities of Egypt.
(1,7179,438/122,033,260 = 1.41%).   If we consider both the paid up
capital and debentures of these seventeen companies, totalling
2,494,938, this represents still only 2.04% of Cairo and Alexandria's
estimated real property.

Appendix 11

Employment in Transportation, 1897-1907

Profession	Egyptian('97)	Foreign('07)	1907
Railroads			10,662
Post and Telegraphs			2,475
Mechanic	4,644	1,068	1,286
Mule Driver	10,801	-	
Camel Driver	8,281	-	
Coachman or Carter	15,959	140	23,688
Harbor Agent, etc.			2,527
Shipowner, Broker			324
Sailor (Excluding Navy)	41,582	2,940	39,352
Roadcrew			2,781
Street Porter			17,762
Carriage Maker	288	37	48
Boat Maker			1,399
Other Transport Construction			33
Saddler	1,721	50	2,386

Data in the above table are drawn from the censuses of 1897 and
1907.

Appendix 12

Manufacturing Companies in Egypt, 1901 and 1908

Company	Established	Type
Kafr-el-Zayat Cotton Company,Ltd.	1894	A
Société d'Engrenage de Mehalla-el-Kibira	1897	A
Société d'Engrenage de Coton à Zagazig	1893	A
Société Anonyme de Presses Libres Egyptiennes	1892	A
Société Générale de Pressage et de Dépôts	1889	A
Anglo-Egyptian Spinning and Weaving Co.,Ltd.	1899	A
Egyptian Cotton Mills, Ltd.	1899	A
Egyptian Sugar and Land Co.,Ltd.	1896	A
Société Générale des Sucreries et de la Raffinerie d'Egypte	1892	A
Société des Huileries et Savonneries d'Egypte	1889	A
Daira Sanieh Sugar Corporation	1898	A
Egyptian Salt and Soda Company,Ltd.	1899	A
Savonnerie du Gabbari	1898	A
Société Industrielle de Karmous, Selim Saraya and Company (soap and cotton oil production)	1899	A
Cairo Sewage Transport Company	1897	A
Société Anonyme des Moulins d'Egypte	1857	A
Associated Cotton Ginners of Egypt, Ltd.	After '01	A
Port Said Salt Association, Ltd.	" "	A

Rosetta and Alexandria Rice Mills Co.	" "	A
Société Anonyme des Presses Allemandes	1906	A
Société Anonyme des Ciments d'Egypte	1900	B
Egyptian Hydraulic Stone Co., Ltd.	After 01	B
Egyptian Brick and Lignolite Co.,Ltd.	" "	B
Platreries du Ballah	" "	B
Boulangerie Mechanique d'Egypte	1899-04	C
British Beer Breweries (Egypt) Ltd.	After 01	C
Crown Brewery of Alexandria	1897	C
Crown Brewery of Cairo	1897	C
The Egyptian Aerated Water Co.Ltd.	1899	C
Fabrique Egyptienne de Papier	1897-01	C
Cleopatra Cigarette Co.	After 01	D
Société Anonyme Le Khedive	1896	D
Société Egyptienne des Tabacs	1899	D
Tabacs et Cigarettes Matossian	1899	D
Société Anonyme pour la Fabrication des Cigarettes Egyptiennes (Hadges Nessim)	After 01	D
Egyptian Swiss Iron Works	" "	

All thirty-six companies listed above fall into three general
categories with one exception. These are the processing of
agricultural products, chiefly cotton, sugar (A) and tobacco (D), the
construction of building materials (B), and the production of luxury
goods for the urban rich (C). The exception is the Egyptian Swiss
Iron Works which was not an important industrial enterprise. For

companies in existence in 1901, <u>List of Financial</u>..., pp.
18-21,26-36; for those from 1901 to 1909. Egypt, Ministry of Finance,
<u>Alphabetical Index of Joint Stock Companies</u>, Cairo, 1908, 24 pps.,
also in <u>Statistical Yearbook for Egypt for 1909</u>, pp.292-299; for
Societe Anonyme des Presses Allemandes, Owen, <u>Cotton</u>, p.221.

Appendix 13

Net Fixed Capital Formation in Egypt, 1899-1908

Year	Net Fixed Capital Formation (1,000)	Net Fixed Cap. Stock (1960 L.E.)	Price Deflator	Annual Growth Rate%	NFCS Contemp. Prices
1899		89,000	15	-	13,350
1900	5,100	94,100	17	5.7	15,997
1901	6,100	100,200	16	6.5	16,032
1902	4,200	104,400	15	4.2	15,660
1903	5,200	109,600	16	5.0	17,536
1904	11,900	121,500	16	10.9	19,440
1905	6,900	128,400	17	5.7	21,828
1906	9,200	137,600	18	7.2	24,768
1907	6,300	143,900	19	4.6	27,341
1908	1,300	145,200	19	0.9	27,588

Samir Radwan, _Capital Formation_, pp.98,162,251.

Appendix 14

Male Occupations in Manufacturing for 1897 and 1907

Occuption	Egyptians	Foreigners	Total'97	1907
Wood & Construction	79,191	2,976	82,167	111,331
Textile	71,660	1,137	72,797	94,677
Iron & Metals	34,497	2,720	37,217	30,047
Leather & Shoes	15,530	1,021	16,551	18,836
Terra Cotta (Pottery)	5,018	5	5,023	9,377
Jewelry	4,666	339	5,005	5,849
Printing & Bookbinding	1,344(1)	331	1,675	2,519
Candle & Soapmaking	240	7	247	84
Glassmaking	86	0	86	26
Tobacco	7,947(2)	1,679	9,626	3,147
Others	1,337(3)	1	1,338	449
Total	221,516	10,216	231,732	276,342

(1)This category includes booksellers in 1897 and journalists in 1907. (2) This includes workers and merchants in 1897, but only workers in 1907. (3) This category treats items not duplicated in the two censuses: for 1897, sleeve makers (1338) and for 1907, sugar refiners (130), brewers (243) and distillers (76). Census of 1897, v.1, pp.lxi-lxii; Census of 1907, pp.279-283. The occupational categories differed slightly in the two censuses, so there is some difficulty in comparing activity. For example, candle makers were listed alone in 1897 but were with soap makers in 1907.

Appendix 15

Weaving Centers in Egypt

Location	Rank	Male Weavers in 1907
Mahalla al-Kubra	1	3,183
Cairo	2	2,869
Qaliub	3	2,405
Menouf	4	2,394
Chebin al-Kom	5	1,628
Sennoures	6	1,530
Damietta	7	1,431
Akhnim	8	1,226
Belbis	9	1,230
Abou Tig	10	1,157
Kous	11	1,108
Mit Ghamr	12	1,084
Embaba	13	1,057
Tahta	14	1,035
Total		23,377

The provinces employing the largest number of weavers were
Menufiya (4,891), Gharbiya (4,829), Girga (4,070), Assyut(4,022),
Daqahliya(3,839) and Qalyubiya (3,030).

Sidney H. Wells, "Note préliminaire sur l'industrie du tissage
en Egypte",Egypte Contemporaine, November, 1910, No.4, p.580.

Appendix 16

Residence of Guild Heads vs. All Elite Property Holders
in Cairo, 1894

Quarter	Guild Heads	%	All Owners	%	Male Pop.'97(1)	%
'Abdin	1	10	417	17.27	26,304	8.69
Bulaq	1	10	93	3.85	40,049	13.22
Darb al-Ahmar	2	20	300	12.43	39,049	12.89
Misr al-Qadima	1	10	23	.95	17,215	5.68
Sayeda Zaynab	4	40	271	11.23	26,823	8.86
Others	1	10	1310	54.27	153,417	50.66
Total	10	100	2414	100.00	302,857	100.00

1. Census of 1897, v.1, pp.44-45.

Appendix 17

The Cairo Urban Property Tax Records of 1894

The major new source utilized in this study for analysis of ubran

property holding and the changing social structure of Cairo in the

late nineteenth century is the Cairo Urban Property Tax Records stored

in the Archives of the Ministry of Finances, the Dar al-Mahfuzat.

These records were compiled to allocate the city's property taxes

following the decree of January 1, 1884, as follows:

> A partir du ler janvier 1884, l'impôt du douzième sur la
> valeur locative sera perçu dans les conlditions specifiées
> ci-après, sur les maisons d'habitation, hôtels, entrepôts ou
> magasins, usines ou fabriques, batîments d'exploitation, et
> généralement sur toutes les propriétés baties de l'Egypte et
> jardins y attenant, qu'elles soient occupées par le propriétarie,
> l'usufrutier ou par d'autres, à titre gratuit ou onéreux. Sont
> exempts de l'impôt: 1. Les cabanes non productives de revenus;
> 2. Les maisons dont la valeur locative annuelle n'excède pas 500
> p.t. et qui sont habitées par les propriétaires ou usufruitiers;
> 3. Les edifices affectés au service des cultes, tels que
> mosquées, églises, temples, couvents et les immeubles consacres à
> des oeuvres de bienfaisance ou de charité; L'Etat, toutefois,
> désignera les immeubles qui doivent bénéficier de cette
> exemption, laquelle ne s'etend pas aux biens immeubles productifs
> de revenus appartenant aux wakfs, aux communautés religieuses ou
> aux établissements de charité; 4. Les immeubles appartlenant à
> l'Etat et destinés à un service publique; 5. Les hôtels
> consulaires appartenant à des Puissances étrangères.

Moniteur Egyptien, 17 March 1884.

Starting in 1887, the tax was also applied to the property of

foreign nationals and proteges.

Statistical Yearbook for 1909, p.40.

So theoretically, urban property tax records should provide an

excellent source to describe the distribution of all urban property in
Egypt after 1886. In reality, these records proved to be easily
available only for Cairo. Also, though the Dar al-Mahfuzat presumably
had all the dossiers recording urban property taxes in Cairo from
their inception, it proved impossible to locate any preceding 1894.
Luckily the 1894 records were intact.

All taxes assessed on property in Cairo for 1894 are recorded in
120 notebooks stored in the Dar al-Mahfuzat. The city at that time
was divided into twelve districts. Tax records for each district were
kept separately in a series of notebooks, numbering from five (for
Misr al-Qadima and al-Waili) to sixteen (for 'Abdin). The unit of
taxation was defined as each property that was (1) inhabited by the
taxpayer and his relatives or (2) rented to one 'person' by the
taxpayer. The taxable unit guild therefore have been a shop, a
warehouse, a house, an apartment merely a room, or any other structure
lived in or rented as a unit. The taxable units in each series of
notebooks for each distrinct were organized in loose alphabetical
order by the given name of the taxpayer. Within each group of
repeated names, Muhammad for example, the tas units were again
organized by street, thus enabling bureaucrats to find an individual's
taxable property in each location within a reasonable amount of time.
One page was devoted to each tax unit and each notebook contains 400
pages. It should be noted that not all notebooks were filled and that
there were blank pages between some letters of the alphabet.

Because the notebooks together contained space for 48,000 tax

units, a way had to be found to limit the amount of transcription.
Since this study is focussed on the Egyptian elite. I arbitrarily
chose to copy full records for only the top 5% of property holders.
The task was then to find the cut off point for the tax properties
which would separate the bottom 95% of owners from the elite 5%.
Random sampling combined with some elementary statistics enables one
to calculate such a point, which turned out to be approximately four
Egyptian pounds.

A sample was taken for four districts: al-Gamliyya, al-Khalifa,
al-Waili and 'Abdin. I first listed the tax on each 50th unit, then
realized that sometimes one owner had 50 to 100 units in a row. Since
each property is described, it became clear that large numbers of
adjacent units constituted one recognizable property, such as an
apartment house or <u>wikala</u>, a large rectangular building with open
interior court divided into numerous small shops rented to craftlsmen
or retailers. I then revised the sampling technique to include the
tax on each 50th unit plus the tax on all directly adjacent units held
by the same taxpayer. This modified technique gives a more accurate
picture of the distribution of urban property because it reflects the
fact that most taxpayers held only one small property in one district,
but that a few wealthy individuals owned large rental properties
sometimes comprising entire blocks.

To compute the cut-off point precisely, it is necessary that the
data be distinguished normally. Normality in statistics is defined
quite carefully. A histogram can give good intuitive idea of a normal

311

curve. A histogram graphs the number of data points versus the size
of each data point, and if normal looks like a bell-shaped curve. In
such a normal curve, the mean or arithmetic average falls exactly in
the middle of the curve and 68% of the area under the curve falls
within one standard deviation of the mean. To calculate the cut off
point with any exactitude, it is also necessary to calculate the mean
and standard deviation.

Although the mean and standard deviation can be easily calculated
from any set of data points with a small hand held calculator, it is
helpful to graph the data points in a histogram beforehand to see if
the curve is normal.

A sample of every fiftieth adjacent property unit in al-Gamaliyya
yielded 66 data points that varied from .36 L.E. to 35.1 L.E. The
histogram below plots the number of data points on the vertical axis
and the size of data point by one pound increments on the horizontal
axis. Here the data points are, of course, adjacent property unit
taxes. It is obvious from the shape of the histogram that the curve
is not normal.

TAX UNITS
40
30
20
10
0 2 4 6 8 10 15 20 25 30 35
URBAN PROPERTY TAXES L.E.

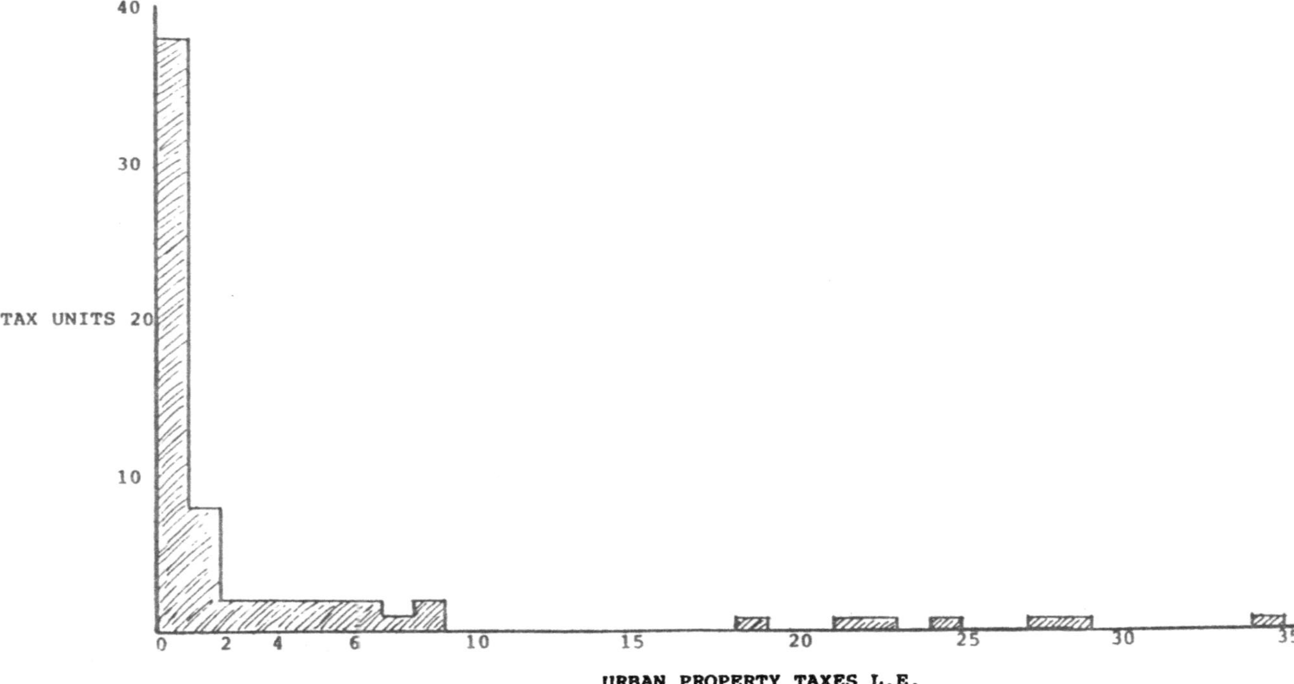

313

The curve comes considerably closer to normality if we simply
eliminate the "deviant" data points over ten pounds. Without the
seven high data points, the mean tax is 1.7117119 L.E. and the
standard deviation 2.1554935 L.E. Nonetheless, it is best to bear in
mind that both the mean and standard deviation are non-resistant
statistics; that is, a few extremely high or low points will throw off
these statistics a great deal. Therefore in a curve like that for
al-Gamaliyya, both the mean and standard deviation are likely to be
exaggerated because many of the points "skew" the curve to the left.

For a discussion of non-resistant statistics, see Frederick
Hartwig and Brian E. Dearing, <u>Exploratory</u> <u>Data</u> <u>Analysis</u>, in the
series, Quantitative Applications in the Social Sciences of Sage
University Publications, Beverly Hills, 1979, pp.9-31.

Looking at a table of the areas of a standard normal
distribution, to select a cut-off point to exclude all but the top 5%,
the point must be equal to the mean plus 1.645 times the standard
deviation. For al-Gamaliyya this equals 5.257. The same procedure
was followed for al-Khalifa, which yielded 57 data points from .136 to
31.8 With two extreme points eliminated, the mean was 1.3522182 and
the standard deviation 1.4949814. Using the same formula, the cut off
point equals 3.8114625. Al-Waili yielded 22 data points that varied
from .18 to 4.8 The mean was 1.9322727 and the standard deviation
2.0618793. The cut off point thus equal 5.3240642. 'Abdin yielded 49
data points ranging from .18 to over fifty. With three extreme data
points excluded, the mean was 1.0779565 and the standard deviation

1.5663115. The average of these four cut off points is 4.512.
Because the curves are all skewed a bit to the left, the cut off point
should be nearer to four. Therefore I recorded all cases of urban
property owners whose adjacent property tax exceeded four pounds. In
practice, all units that exceded three pounds were recorded as well as
all taxes for members of the political elite.

When the sample data from the four districts are taken together,
the result is a skewed histogram that plots 176 data points that vary
from .136 to 7.0. Eighteen extreme data points above seven have been
eliminated. The data is clustered around one pound, though there are
numerous points above two pounds as can be seen in the histogram
below. The mean is 1.2755682 and the standard deviation is 1.5234077,
so the five percent cut off point should theoretically be 3.75 L.E.
and 40.9% above. On the other hand, 17 owners paid more than 3.75
L.E. while 159 paid less. Thus, in view of owners, a cut off point
of 3.75 gives the top 9.7% of all property owners, a cut off point of
3.75 gives the top 9.7% of all property owners. By inspection, we can
see that the cut off point to separate out the top 5%, or 9/176,
should be 5.5 L.E. Supposing that this sample is representative of
the distribution of urban property tax in Cairo in 1894, the cut off
point of four pounds should theoretically yield the top 16/176 or 9.1%
of all property owners, who should own 39.20% of Cairo's taxable
property, counting the area under the line to the right of four
pounds. Because 18 extreme data points were eliminated from the
histogram above, a cut off point of four pounds will probably yield

315

somewhat more than the top ten percent of all owners and as will be
shown, they owned in fact over half of all the city's taxable property
in 1894.

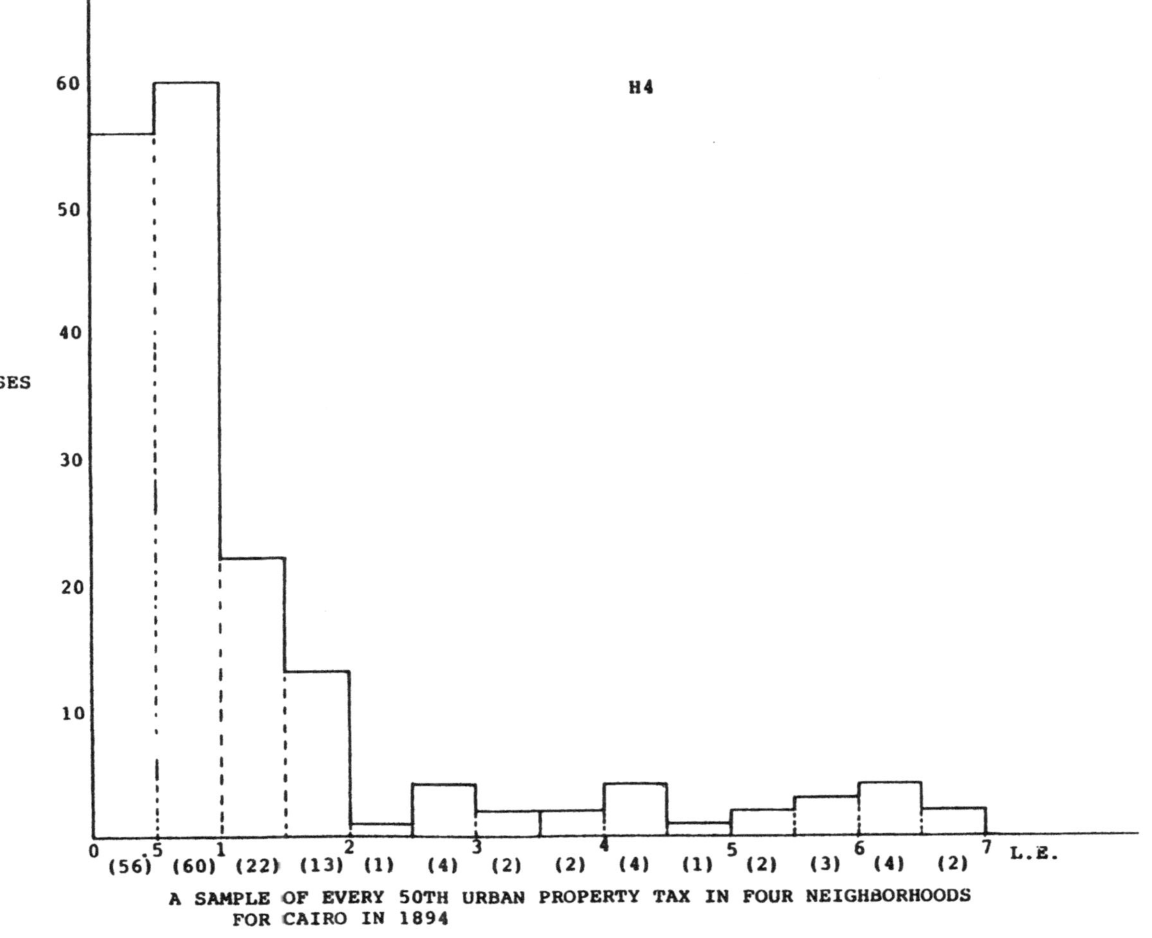

H4
CASES
60
50
40
30
20
10
0   5   1   2   3   4   5   6   7   L.E.
(56) (60) (22) (13) (1) (4) (2) (2) (4) (1) (2) (3) (4) (2)
A SAMPLE OF EVERY 50TH URBAN PROPERTY TAX IN FOUR NEIGHBORHOODS
FOR CAIRO IN 1894

The following information was recorded for all such property owners: annual tax, name, title(s), nationality, occupation when listed, quarter, dossier number and page number(s) within each dossier. From the name and title(s), both sex and religion were almost always obtainable. Ownership type was also recorded: (1) heirs of deceased, (2) waqf, (3) business,(4), owner and co-proprietors (5) co-proprietors and heirs, (6) heirs and waqf (7) personal property and waqf or (8) personal property. When the owner's place of residence was not the unit being taxed, residence was sometimes stated and this was recorded as well.

Appendix 18

Primary and secondary sources reveal serious discrepancies about
the total tax levied on Cairo property in 1894.

The statistical yearbook for 1909 shows that the total tax on
urban property in Egypt remained relatively constant from the time of
its application to foreigners' property in 1887 through 1895.

Year	House Tax for Egypt (L.E.)
1887	110,281
1888	132,930
1889	167,926
1890	137,243
1891	126,556
1892	133,728
1893	131,242
1894	120,618
1895	130,783

<u>Statistical Yearbook for 1909</u>, p.40.

The average house tax during this period was 132,367 L.E. and
the standard deviation, a measure of variation around this average,
was 15,627 L.E. This large deviation, both upward and downwards, is
important to note because it points out the fact that these figures
indicate the taxes collected rather than the taxes levied on urban
property. The tax was supposedly re-valued every two years. See

Gelat Bey, Répertoire, v.3, p.80, which provides the full text of

the 1884 decree. The taxes, as is common, were slowly raised but the

amount varied widely. It is also important to note that the urban

property tax collected in Cairo in 1895, 56,000 L.E. according to

Clerget, Le Caire, v.1, p.258; cited by Roger Owen, "The Cairo

Building Industry ...", p.339, would theoretically amount to 42.82% of

the taxes collected in the country that year. A close examination of

the tax dossiers for 1894 shows that both the taxes levied and those

collected in Cairo were considerably greater. The urban property tax

registers for Cairo stored in the Dar al-Mahfuzat break down the taxes

due and those actually paid.

Cairo Property Taxes 1893-1894

Quarter	Back Tax '93	Tax '94	Back Tax'94	Dossiers
	(Paid '94)			
'Abdin	2894.853	12952.563	?	16
B.al-Shariya	525.925	3396.224	793.071	9
Bulaq	583.403	2861.116	1348.220	11
D.al-Ahmar	?	?	?	14
Azbakiyya	3318.601	12015.209	2515.547	12
Gamaliyya	?	?	?	10
Khalifa	732.120	2267.420	430.163	9
Muski	1637.462	6485.892	1354.274	8
M.al-Qadima	136.033	779.044	215.808	5
Sayeda	1347.992	10478.303	839.839	15
Shubra	635.629	2281.571	402.197	6
Waili	145.430	641.144	200.245	5
Total		54158.486	10994.217	120

In estimating the total back taxes for 1894, the back taxes for
1893 have been used for 'Abdin.

The total tax levied in 1894 was 65,152.703 L.E., excluding
al-Gamaliyya and al-Dard al-Ahmar. Since these two districts
accounted for 20% of the dossiers, it would seem logical to estimate
the taxes levied there at an equal percentage of the total. Thus the
total urban property tax levied in Cairo in 1894 was probably close to
81,440.879 L.E. This would seem to be a much more accurate estimate

than Clerget's figure because it takes into account the difference between taxes levied and taxes actually collected. If we assume that the back taxes for 1893 collected in 1894 were not included in the category "House Tax," for 1894 from the Statistical Yearbook, Cairo would account for 56.13% of all urban property taxes collected that year. 54,158.486 + 1/4 = 67,698.108 divided by 120,618 = 56.13%. In 1897 the major urban areas of Egypt, the governorates and provincial capitals, had a population of 1,409,732.

The populus of Cairo, 570,062, constituted 40.44% of the total urban population. The difference in the percentages for taxes and population is probably due to the fact that Cairo was much more built up than the provincial capitals and Alexandria. Although the population of Alexandria began to increase rapidly in the 1860's, the real building boom began only near the end of the century. Cairo had been a fully developed urban center centuries before Alexandria began to expand in the nineteenth century.

The last dossiers for three of the twelve districts contain the number of property owners in the entire district. 5893 owners held taxable property in Sayeda Zaynab, 786 in Misr al-Qadima and 4195 in 'Abdin. On the average, each dossier contained the taxable property units of 149.44 owners. Therefore taxable property was probably held by 17,933 owners in Cairo. (One hundred and twenty times 149.44 = 17,933.)

Our sample of the elite property owners of Cairo yielded a total

of 66 individuals who held property in more than one district. We can
conclude that taxes were probably levied on about 17,867 owners of
property in Cairo in 1894.

Appendix 19

Residence Patterns of Small Property Holders
in 1882

| | SPH | | Total Pop. (1882) |
	N	%	%
'Abdin	11	10.68	9.56
Bab al-Sha'riyya	3	2.91	13.65
Bulaq	5	4.85	13.97
Al-Darb al-Ahmar	20	19.42	7.73
Azbakiyya	10	9.71	12.94
Gamaliyya	26	25.24	8.03
Khalifa	5	4.85	9.80
Muski	0	0	3.26
Old Cairo	2	1.94	5.37
Sayeda	14	13.59	9.10
Shubra	3	2.91	2.96
Waili	4	3.88	3.65

Appendix 20

Residence Patterns of Small Property Holders

Compared with the Total Male Population

in 1897

Quarter	New SPH N	New SPH %	Old SPH %	Tot.Pop.'97 %
'Abdin	46	14.74	10.68	8.69
Bab al-Sha'riyya	25	8.01	2.91	8.79
Bulaq	24	7.69	4.85	4.50(1)
Al-Darb al-Ahmar	43	13.78	19.42	12.89(1)
Azbakiyya	27	8.65	9.71	6.35
Gamaliyya	35	11.22	25.24	10.24
Khalifa	25	8.01	4.85	7.94
Muski	13	4.17	0	4.31
Old Cairo	1	.32	1.94	5.68
Sayeda	37	11.86	13.59	8.86
Shubra	20	6.41	2.91	5.45
Waili	16	5.13	3.88	6.77
Total	312	100.00	100.00	100.00

There are large discrepancies for the percentages of 1882 and
1897 that are probably due to errors in the census or in publication
of the figures.

Appendix 21

Residence Patterns of Middle Property Holders

MPH

	1882		1894		%1882 Pop.
	N	%	N	%	
'Abdin	33	12.99	101	15.26	9.56
Bab al-Sha'riyya	22	8.66	64	9.67	13.65
Bulaq	8	3.15	26	3.93	13.97
Al-Darb al-Ahmar	47	18.50	84	12.69	7.73
Azbakiyya	32	12.60	117	17.67	12.94
Gamaliyya	32	12.60	50	7.75	8.03
Khalifa	10	3.94	21	3.17	9.80
Muski	15	5.91	57	8.61	3.26
Old Cairo	1	.39	8	1.21	5.37
Sayeda	40	15.75	70	10.57	9.10
Shubra	13	5.12	45	6.80	2.96
Waili	1	.39	19	2.87	3.65

Appendix 22

Occupation of Middle Property Holders in 1894

MPH 1894

Occupation	N	%	% Men Working in Cairo (1897)
(1) Finance	12	4.63	3.87
(2) Architecture, Engineering	6	2.32	.88
(3) Manufacturing	23	8.88	20.26
(4) Transport	3	1.16	8.99
(5) Trade	33	12.74	15.23
(6) Building	10	3.86	6.62
(7) Hotels, etc.	1	.39	5.00
(8) Fuel	1	.39	.18
(9) Government	104	40.15	11.78
(10) Religion	5	1.93	3.15
(11) Liberal Arts	29	11.20	.75
(12) Domestics	3	1.16	10.64
(13) Other	29	11.20	4.66
(14) Students	0	0	7.99
Total	259	100.01	100.00

Appendix 23

Reigion and Occupation of Middle Property Holders

in 1894

	Muslims		Christians		Jews	
	N	%	N	%	N	%
Finance	7	3.55	2	4.76	2	28.57
Architecture	6	3.05	0	-	0	-
Manufacturing	14	7.11	4	9.52	4	57.14
Transport	3	1.52	0	-	0	-
Trade	28	14.21	2	4.76	1	14.29
Building	7	3.55	2	4.76	0	-
Hotels	1	.51	0	-	0	-
Fuel	0	-	1	2.38	0	-
Government	80	40.61	19	45.24	0	-
Religion	4	2.03	1	2.38	0	-
Liberal Arts	24	12.18	5	11.90	0	-
Domestics	3	1.52	0	-	0	-
Other	20	10.15	6	14.29	0	-
Total	197	100.00	42	100.00	7	100.00

Appendix 24

Average Property Taxes in 1882 by Group

Large Property Holders (1882)

Group	Total Tax (L.E.)	N	Average Tax (L.E.)
Jewish Proteges	1516.1	2	758.05
Royal Family	986.2	8	123.18
Muslim Public Institutions	174.0	2	58.00
Christian Proteges	251.2	6	41.87
Muslim Proteges	250.8	6	41.80
Foreign Christians	228.0	11	38.91
Christian Private Institutions	116.7	3	38.90
Egyptian Christians	976.6	28	34.89
Muslim private Institutions	147.1	5	29.42
Egyptian Muslims	8268.1	290	28.51
Foreign Muslims	22.8	1	22.80

Within each religious community, proteges held more urban property than Egyptian subjects. Muslims owned less than Christians, who in turn owned less, on the average, than Jews. Unlike those for small and middle property holders, the curve of urban property taxes for those at the top of the old elite is not normal, but is skewed far

to the right by a few extreme values. If members of the royal family
are excluded, the distribution of taxes by religion is as follows.

	Tax: Low (8.3-37.7)	High (37.8-Top)
Muslim	246	59
Christian	39	11

Though the group average for Christians is higher, 36.93 L.E.,
than that for Muslims, 31.47 L.E., much of the discrepancy might be
caused by a few extreme values. Although we have the entire group in
question here and not just a sample, it is best to use the Chi square
test to see if the group means are a relatively valid indication of
differences between the two religious communities considered as a
whole. The Chi square test indicates that the difference is not
statistically significant. Chi square equals .1913928.

Appendix 25

Residence Patterns of Old Large and Middle
Property Holders

	Old LPH		Old MPH
Quarter	N	%	%
'Abdin	79	21.18	12.99
Bab al-Sha'riyya	31	8.31	8.66
Bulaq	8	2.14	3.15
al-Darb al-Ahmar	59	15.82	18.50
Azbakiyya	46	12.33	12.60
Gamaliyya	41	10.99	12.60
Khalifa	12	3.22	3.94
Muski	27	7.24	5.91
Old Cairo	5	1.34	.39
Sayeda	51	13.67	15.75
Shubra	10	2.68	5.12
Waili	4	1.04	.39

Appendix 26

Average Property Taxes for Large Property Holders

by Group in 1894

Large Property Holders

Group	Average Taxes (L.E.)	N	Rank
Christian Private Institutions	242.80	5	1
Egyptian Jews	102.54	5	2
Jewish Proteges	59.08	10	3
Royal Family	47.48	16	4
Muslim Proteges	47.25	14	5
Christian Proteges	37.39	34	6
Foreign Christians	32.28	85	7
Egyptian Muslims	27.80	365	8
Egyptian Christians	24.13	110	9
Muslim Private Institutions	17.60	1	10
Foreign Muslims	15.90	3	11
Foreign Jews	15.86	5	12

Appendix 27

Residence Patterns of Large Property Holders

Quarter	Old LPH %	New LPH %	N	Change
'Abdin	21.18	21.15	147	Little
Bab al-Sha'riyya	8.31	7.05	49	Little
Bulaq	2.14	3.17	22	Little
al-Darb al-Ahmar	15.82	6.33	44	Down
Azbakiyya	12.33	25.32	176	Up
Gamaliyya	10.99	3.88	27	Down
Khalifa	3.22	2.88	20	Little
Muski	7.24	13.24	92	Up
Old Cairo	1.34	.86	6	Little
Sayeda	13.67	8.49	59	Down
Shubra	2.68	6.47	45	Up
Waili	1.07	1.15	8	Little

Azbakiyya made the largest gains in percentage of elite residence
(12.99%), followed by Muski (6.00%) and Shubra (3.79%). During this
period Cairo was becoming less homogeneous by social class. The
shifts in elite residence did not follow the pattern of population
growth by neighborhood. The districts that increased their overall
share of Cairo's population most were al-Darb al-Ahmar (5.15%), Waili
(3.12%) and Shubra (2.49%). Though Azbakiyya made the greatest gains

in the percentage of large property owners by 1894, it was next to
last in percentage change for the general population, as can be seen
in the following table. Shubra was the only district that made
substantial gains in its share of both the general population and of
large property holders.

Appendix 28

Residence Patterns Ranked by Neighborhood

	1897 % Pop.	1882 % Male Pop.	Change %	Rank
'Abdin	8.69	9.65	-.87	8
Bab al-Sha'riyya	8.79	13.65	-4.86	10
Bulaq	4.50	13.97	-9.47	12
al-Darb al-Ahmar	12.89	7.73	5.16	1
Azbakiyya	6.35	12.94	-6.59	11
Gamaliyya	10.24	8.03	2.21	4
Khalifa	7.94	9.80	-1.86	9
Muski	4.31	3.26	1.05	5
Old Cairo	5.68	5.37	.31	6
Sayeda	8.86	9.10	-.24	7
Shubra	5.45	2.96	2.49	3
Waili	6.77	3.65	3.12	2

Raw figures for population were taken from the 1882 and 1897 censuses. All percentages and rankings were calculated by the author.

Appendix 29

Occupations of Elite Groups in Cairo

	LPH (1894)		% Men Working	MPH (1894)
	<u>N</u>	<u>%</u>	<u>in</u> <u>Cairo</u>	<u>%</u>
Finance	13	4.63	3.87	4.63
Architecture	13	4.63	.88	2.32
Manufacturing	32	11.39	20.26	8.88
Transport	3	1.07	8.99	1.16
Trade	22	7.83	15.23	12.74
Building	9	3.20	6.62	3.86
Hotels,Etc.	1	.36	5.00	.39
Fuel	1	.36	.18	.39
Government	118	41.99	11.78	40.15
Religion	2	.71	3.15	1.93
Liberal Arts	28	9.96	.75	11.20
Domestics	2	.71	10.64	1.16
Students	0	0	7.99	0
Other	307	13.17	4.66	11.20

Appendix 30

Remarks on the Validity of Data on Land Distribution in The
Statistical Yearbook for 1909

Firstly, this table provides the distribution of property by plot
rather than by owner. Only late in 1907 was the cadaster completed
and it was found necessary to redo the property registers because many
small plots recorded under one owner's name actually belonged to
several landholders. This problem was noticed by J.I. Craig who
commented in 1914 that

> the Cadastral Survey ... had the result of splitting up
> single holdings recorded under one man's name onto two or more
> under the names of his successors, where all or part had been
> sold, and more rarely under the names of his heirs....(The
> observed increase from 1896 to 1910 of owners of small plots) is
> also to some extent due to the operations of the Agricultural
> Bank. Small joint proprietors, the writer has been told, found
> it easier to obtain loans when this land was split into shares
> each recorded under an individual's name.

J. I. Craig, "The Distribution of Landed Property in Egypt,"
Egypte Contemporaine, v.4, January, 1913, pp.35-36.

During the resurvey of Sharquiyya province, it was found that an
average of 25% of all plots registered to one owner were actually held
by an average of three owners, varying from 2.8 average owners in
Faqus to 6.3 in Hehya. In other provinces the percentage of shared
plots formerly registered in the name of one owner was even higher.
The number of small plots with multiple owners was probably
underestimated by 38.75%.

Lyons, <u>Cadastral</u> <u>Survey</u> <u>of</u> <u>Egypt</u>, pp.319-320. The math of the above argument is the following: $y = x + (2x (.3875))$; $y = 1.775 x$; $x + 77.5\% x = y$.

Thus the number of owners should be increased by at least 77.5%, of we follow the proportion observed in Sharqiyya where the ratio of recorded owners to actual owners was one to three.

Secondly, much of the apparent increase in the area that was held in plots of under five feddans from 1896 to 1907 was due to the reduced costs of registering small land holdings. Thus the table of land distribution underestimates both the number of owners holding less than five feddans and the area they held, because some plots in the five to ten feddan range undoubtedly belonged in the smallest category.

Thirdly, the table records the numbers of plots held by separate owners in each village and a man owning land in several villages would be counted several times. Because middle and large landowners were those most likely to own land in more than one village, the table underestimates the concentration of land in the top categories. Fourthly, the table includes waqf lands but excludes State Domain and untaxed lands.

Baer, <u>Landownership</u>, pp.71,73.

Fifthly and finally, these statistics do not include the lands of the Domains Administration and Daira Saniyya Administration that were sold to private buyers from 1896 to 1907. This is evident from a comparison of the sales records with the figures for private land and the cultivated area from the Statistical Yearbook.

The Domains sales during this period transferred 94,242 feddans and the Daira Saniyya sales 162,263 feddans, for a total of 256,505 feddans. The number of privately held feddans according to the data in the Statistical Yearbook rose from 5,001,001 in 1896 to 5,435,789 in 1907, up 434,788 feddans. However, according to the same source, the number of cultivated feddans increased from 6,004,803 to 6,426,056 in the same period, up 421,253 feddans. Yet we know that the number of privately held feddans should have increased by an equal to the sum of the sales plus the new acreage brought into cultivation. That this did not occur indicates that the Statistical Yearbook data on private landholdings exclude the land sold by the Domains and Daira Saniyya Administrations.

Statistical Yearbook for 1909, pp.266-268.

Calculation of Gini indexes for land distribution for the years from 1896 to 1907 from the raw data in the table seems to indicate that no change took place in the in the concentration of landholding. The indexes calculated as described above are as follows.

Year	Gini Index	Year	Gini Index
1896	.6959	1902	.6955
1897	.6969	1903	.6961
1898	.6923	1904	.6959
1899	.6935	1905	.6935
1900	.6946	1906	.6997
1901	.6925	1907	.6958

The raw data were taken from the above table from the
Statistical Yearbook for Egypt for 1909, p.244-245.

This approach produces a false impression of stability in land
distribution because the raw data are based on partial registration of
real ownership. Evaluating the published statistics on land
distribution from 1896 to 1902, Lord Cromer concluded that

> They confirm the conclusion which I had arrived at as to the
> unreliability of the statistics .... The true facts will,
> however, never be obtained until the dues on the sale and
> mortgage of property are reduced so low as to render registration
> almost universal.

Cromer, *Report of His Majesty's Agent...* for *1906*, Cd.3994,
v.100, p.15.

Appendix 31

Sales of the Royal Domains, 1878-1907

On October 26,1878, the royal family abandoned title to 425,729 feddans of the best agricultural land in Egypt, which had previously been mortgaged to European banking establishments. In return the government of Egypt was granted a loan of 8,500,000 pounds sterling by the firm of Rothschild and Sons of London.

Gelat Bey, _Répertoire_, v.2, pp.100-101.

The lands were distributed as follows:

Province	Feddans
Behera	35,088
Daqahliyya	18,167
Gharbiyya	223,170
Minufiyya	3,015
Qalyubiyya	5,582
Sharqiyya	42,768
Assyut	15,048
Beni-Suif	23,418
Fayyum	46,131
Girga	647
Giza	12,694
Minya	0
Qina	0
Total	425,728

The discrepancy of one feddan is due to rounding off the figures to the nearest feddan. _Ibid._, p.108.

A convention between the Egyptian government and Rothschild and Sons set up the Domains Commission to administer the mortgaged properties and guarantee the debt. The convention was signed on October 31, 1878. The Domains Commission was headed by a committee of three directors, one English, one French and one Egyptian. The Egyptian was nominated by the Egyptian Council of Ministers and the two foreigners named by their respective governments. The commissioners were granted authority to (a) administer the property,

(b) collect renenues and (c) turn the net revenues over to the firm of
Rothschild and Sons.

 Ibid., p.101.

On January 30, 1879, the Egyptian government authorized the
commissioners to sell the Domains lands to pay off the debt. Sales
were neglibible until 1883 when Lord Dufferin accepted the suggestion
that the Domains land be divided into large lots to ensure their rapid
sale. Dufferin, as the highest British official in Egypt at this
time, had near absolute power over Egyptian affairs, backed as he was
by the army of occupation that had defeated the 'Urabi rebels and set
Tawfiq back on the throne as puppet Khedive.

The Domains Commission divided the 420,000 feddans remaining to
be sold into 393 lots and a company was formed to expedite their sale.
The company was kindly permitted to receive a 20% commission on all
sales. This scheme was approved by the Egyptian government and
Rothschild and Sons on April 29,1883, but by the end of 1884, only
42,600 feddans had been sold. The Commission then realized its error,
took back control of the lands and paid the company a large penalty,
which it described as "une perte sensible." Next the Commission
subdivided the lots into much smaller parcels and after 1884 began
demanding only fifty percent downpayment and offered mortgages for the
rest at the low rate of five percent per annum. The interest was
reduced to 4.5% in 1890. Starting in 1887, the Egyptian government
began to offer Domains lands to government pensioners in exchange for

their fixed pensions.

Commission des Domaines de l'Etat, <u>Compte Générale des</u>
<u>Operations Effectuées du 26 Octobre 1878 au 31 Mars 1898</u>, E.
Bouteron, J.Gibson and S.E. Muhammad Chekib Pacha, Paris, 1898,
pp.20-21.

By December 31, 1897, all Domains lands had been carefully
surveyed and the actual land held by the Commission turned out to be
429,539 feddans. A total of 210,913 feddans was sold between 1878 and
1898, and so on January 1, 1898, the Commission possessed 218,626
feddans. By December 31, 1906, a total of 283,195 feddans had been
sold or conceded to various departments of the Egyptian government,
for a total of 6,492,469 L.E. The transfers of land involved 2,212
contracts, the first of which was dated January 30,1879 and the last
December 31, 1906. Each numbered sale is described in table H of the
annual reports of the Domains Commission and furnishes (1) the date,
(2) the <u>taftish</u> or administrative unit of the Commission, (3) the
"Culture" or sub-division, (4) the name of each village where the land
was located, (5) the total land per village in feddans, (6) the
name(s) of the principal purchaser(s) and (7) the price. The series
of annual reports from 1881 to 1906 was nearly complete in the Dar
al-Mahfuzat library and a few missing volumes were located in the
Egyptian National Library.

Administration des Domaines de l'Etat Egyptien Affectues en
Garantie de l'Emprunt de 8.500.000 Liv.st. contracte le 31 octobre

1878, <u>Cahier</u> <u>des</u> <u>Charges</u>, <u>Clauses</u> <u>et</u> <u>Conditions</u> <u>Générales</u>
<u>Applicables</u> <u>à</u> <u>la</u> <u>Vente</u> <u>Des</u> <u>Biens</u> <u>Dominaux</u> ..., Cairo, Imprimerie du
Journal Les Pyramides, 1900, Dar al-Mahfuzat Library, 55/3/2/683,594,
pp.57-58, Dar al-Kutub, No. H15470.

A total of 1,195 Domains sales were coded. All sales were
included of over forty feddans, those involving over 500 L.E. up to
March, 1904, or over 1000 L.E. thereafter, and those to any member of
the political elite. Free grants of land to the Egyptian government
and land exchanges were not coded. The 1,195 purchases were made by
885 parties, who signed from one to twenty-three deeds, as shown in
the following table.

<u>Number</u> <u>of</u> <u>Sales</u>	<u>Frequency</u>
1	716
2	112
3	33
4	10
5	7
6	1
9	2
10	1
11	1
13	1
23	1

For each buyer, the total price varied from 23 L.E. to 201,978
L.E. and the total land purchased from 2 to 9,040 feddans. The mean
cost of land purchased per buyer was 5,605 L.E. and the mean land
261.6 feddans. The price per feddan varied widely, depending not only
on the quality of the land but on the general level of land values,
which increased greatly after 1900 until the speculative bubble burst
in 1907.

Appendix 32

The Daira Saniyya Estate Sales, 1882-1906

The Daira Saniyya estate sales made during this twenty-four year
period added five percent to the total of Egypt's private landed
property. This enormous transfer of productive land at once brought
about and reflected major changes on all levels of relationships in
the rural sector. Most of the land was purchased in large tracts,
increasing the concentration of privately controlled productive forces
in the countryside. These estates belonged to the Khedive until 1877.
They were then in custody of an international administration which
sold about forty percent to private buyers and then handed over the
remainder to a joint stock company in 1898. This company sold the
rest of the land by 1906. This section will briefly trace the history
of the estates down to the sales of 1898-1906, discuss the
characteristics of the land transferred and describe the sale of the
land from 1898 to 1906.

The Daira Saniyya, or Estate of the Khedive, existed before
Isma'il became Khedive of Egypt in 1863. The term Daira Saniyya stood
for all properties and obligations of the Khedive. Later Isma'il
detached certain properties from these, establishing the Daira of the
Queen Mother, the Daira Khassa or Civil List and the Daira Seraiat or
land allocated for the maintenance of the Khedive's palaces. Thus
Daira Saniyya came to signify the lands which the Khedive retained for
himself, the debts and the obligations contracted for the upkeep of

his properties.

"Note Presentee a la Commission de Liquidation sur la Daira
Saniyya," in _Rapport Presentée à S.A. le Khedive sur la Situation
de la Daira Saniyya en 1897_, Cairo, 1880, stored in Dar al-Mahfuzat,
278/13/42.

On March 26, 1870, the Khedive took out a loan for 125 million
French francs, giving a mortgage on 157,000 feddans of the Daira
Saniyya estates. On February 11, 1871, Isma'il borrowed another large
sum, giving as mortgage a further 364,930 feddans of Daira land. On
July 12, 1877, these and other Daira Saniyya debts were converted to a
new loan of 8,815,430 pounds sterling with a mortgage of 434,975
feddans of Daira land as well as 50,156 feddans of the Daira Khassa,
which became an integral part of the Daira Saniyya.

Gelat Bey, _Répertoire_, v.2, pp,44,47 and 93.

The Law of Liquidation of 1800 made several important changes in
the status of the Daira Saniyya. The Daira Saniyya and Daira Khassa
were joined together and made property of the Egyptian state. These
properties were to be used exclusively to pay the General Debt of the
Daira Saniyya. The product of any alienation of Daira land would go
to pay off the General Debt, and not into the coffers of the Egyptian
government. The Daira would be administered by a Director General and
a High Council, named by the Khedive "on the designation of the
English and French governments."

Op. Cit., pp.123-124.

Thus the Khedive lost control of his Daira Saniyya estates to an international administration that ran them for the exclusive purpose of paying off the usurious loans contracted by the unlucky Khedive. For example, the loan of March 26, 1870 was for 125 million francs, of which only seventy percent was paid to the Daira, whereas the Daira contracted to pay back one hundred percent of the capital plus seven percent interest per annum. One only needs mention that Isma'il was deposed by British pressure in part because he balked at paying back his loans in full. The new Khedive, Tawfiq, suited the plans of the bondholders much better. Any doubt that Europeans fully controlled Daira finances was terminated with the British occupation in 1882.

Op. Cit., p.44.

The half million feddans of the Daira Saniyya, comprising ten percent of the conutry's cultivated land, was quietly administered by the European controllers from 1882 to 1897. The report of the Daira for that year ended with a cheerful reminder of its prosperity:

> Nous terminerons cet exposé en faisant remarquer que malgré la baisse constante du prix des sucres, nous parvenons à maintenir la situation satisfaisante à laquelle la Daira est arrivée depuis quelques années, çela grace à l'équlibre qui s'établit fort heureusement entre nos deux grands sources de revenus: le sucre et les fermages.

Daira Sanieh Report for 1897, located in Dar al-Mahfuzat, 288/13/42, p.21.

There has been some confusion about the amount of land belonging
to the Daira Saniyya from 1880 until 1897 and the amount sold from
1898 to 1906. Gabriel Baer has stated that

> It seems clear that only about 66,000 feddans were disposed
> of by the end of 1900, and 224,000 between the beginning of 1901
> and the end of 1905; and that the operation was completed by the
> sale of some 160,000 feddans between October 1905 and March 1906.

Gabriel Baer, A History of Landownership in Modern Egypt
1880-1950, London, 1962, p.95.

It is clear nonetheless from the detailed records of the Daira
Saniyya Administration conserved in Dar al-Mahfuzat that the
Administration sold almost forty percent of its land before 1898. Let
us recall that the total lands of the Daira in 1877 amounted to
434,975 plus 50,156 feddans, or a total of 485,031 mortgaged feddans.
According to the Daira Report of 1879, the land of the Daira was
505,098 feddans. I would explain this difference by citing
differences in bookkeeping, constant buying and selling of land by the
Administration and constant changes in the area caused by the desert
and the Nile. In 1882 the total was 490,671 feddans, the difference
here caused land sales. Large scale sales had begun as early as 1882,
inasmuch as 5,602 feddans were sold between June 1, 1882 and June 30,
1883. So by the end of 1897, just before the period of publicized
sales, the Daira Saniyya had only 308,122 feddans.

Daira Saniyya Report of 1879, pp.56-57; Daira Saniyya Report
of 1897, p.9.

Despite the fact that the international Daira Saniyya
Administration was able to pay all interest on the Daira debt, reduce
the outstanding capital from 8,815,430 pounds sterling in 1877 to
6,431,500 in 1898, a decision was made to sell the rest of the lands
held on June 21, 1898, including

> Factories, agricultural railroads, supplies, storehouses,
> workshops, houses, buildings of all kinds, fixed and moveable
> engines, crops in the field, cattle, receipts, credits to be
> called in, everything hereafter indicated as the properties of
> the Daira Sanieh.

Gelat Bey, _Repertoire_, v.2, pp. 165-168.

The false claim was made that the Daira Saniyya was losing money
and should therefore be sold off as the best means of stemming a
fiscal hemmorage that might eventually drain the Egyptian government
treasury. For the incredibly low price of the remaining debts,
6,431,500 pounds sterling, four parties were allowed to buy the entire
Daira Saniyya in the following proportions.

Name	Percentage	Residence
E. Cassel	50	London
E. Cattaui	12 1/2	Paris
E. Cronier	12 1/2	Paris
R. Suares	25	Cairo

These men formed the Daira Sanieh Company, Limited, in 1898, with
its head office in London. The object of the company was "the sale to
third parties of the lands of the Daira Sanieh mortgaged in guarantee

of the public loan amounting on the 1st January 1898 to L. 6,431,500." The London Board consisted of Sir V. Caillard, Chairman; Sir W. Ward; Sir E. Sasson; Earl Cairns; C. Meyer and R. Miller. The local board was composed of Sir E. Palmer, Chairman; R. Suares; S. Rolo; Aly Bey Charawi; Borelli Bey; F. Dusseigneur and W. Willcocks. Note that several of the board members and one of the principals were high officials of the Egyptian government and thus open to a charge of conflict of interest in which they used their position as government employees for private gain at the expense of the country they were supposed to serve. These investors made a considerable side profit by selling public shares in the company. The 118,000 ordinary shares issued at five pounds reached a high of eight pounds for the year of 1900, and the 10,000 deferred shares issued at one pound each reached a high of twenty-eight pounds in 1900. Deferred shares participated for 40% of the company's profits.

The British Chamber of Commerce of Egypt, Alexandria, <u>List of Financial</u>, <u>Manufacturing</u>,<u>Transport</u> <u>and</u> <u>Other</u> <u>Companies</u> <u>Established in Egypt</u>, Alexandria, June, 1901, p.22.

At the end of November, 1899, William Willcocks, Esq.C.M.G, Managing Director of the company, wrote in a report for the directors that the Daira Saniyya estates totalled 293,000 feddans, as follows.

<u>Location</u>	<u>Feddans</u>
Upper Egypt	48,000
Ibrahimiyya Tract	162,000

Fayyum	70,000
Lower Egypt	13,000
Total	293,000

William Willcocks, <u>Reports upon the Lands of the Daira Sanieh</u>, (<u>Confidential-For Directors Only</u>), London, no date, Dar al-Mahfuzat, 289/13/42, pp.78-79.

In the conclusion to his report, Willcocks proposed to gradually sell

> between 1900 and 1905 to the fellaheen and
> neighboring landed proprietors certain lands of the
> Daira, on the condition one-tenth of the purchase
> money were paid in installments before October, 1905,
> with power to the purchasers to enter into possession
> of the lands on October, 1905, when the remaining
> annuities would begin to be paid.

<u>Op.Cit.</u>, p.85.

Appendix 33

Analysis of Representative Institutions in Egypt

<u>Institution</u>: Electoral Lists

<u>Mode of Election</u>: 1. In the eight towns, drawn up under
Mamours and the Sheikhs. 2. In the other towns and
villages, under a nominee of the Governor, and four
proprietors also named by him.

<u>Composition</u>: Manhood suffrage, over 20 years of
age, excepting soldiers with the colours, officials
dismissed for serious offences, bankrupts, outaws, and
criminals.

<u>Regulations</u>: No elector shall vote twice. Electoral
lists to be published every January. Appeals to be made
February 1-15, and decided before March 15.

<u>Functions</u>: Election of "Electeurs délégues."

<u>Institution</u>: "Electeurs Délégues"

<u>Mode of Election</u>: 1. One from each section of Cairo
and Alexandria and from the six other towns. 2. One from
every other town and village.

<u>Composition</u>: 1. Twelve from Cairo, four from Alex.
2. One from every town and village.

<u>Regulations</u>: 1. To meet at the Prefecture of Police or
the Governor's residence. 2. To meet at the Governor's
Residence.

354

<u>Functions</u>: 1. To elect members for Legislative
Council and General Assembly. 2. To elect members for
Provincial Councils and General Assembly.

<u>Institution</u>: Provincial Councils
<u>Mode</u> <u>of</u> <u>Election</u>: Elected by "Electeurs délégues" by
ballot, under superintendence of a Committee, each
elector having as many votes as there are Councillors.
Members must be 30 years old, pay a certain amount of
taxes, and have been electors for five years.
<u>Composition</u>: Selected from "Electeurs délégues."
The size of the Councils varies from three to eight
members.
<u>Regulations</u>: Convoked by Mudir (Governor) in virtue
if a Decree fixing limits of session, at least once a
year. Mudir presides. Chief engineer is a member.
Members are elected for six years, and are unpaid.
Sittings are held in private.
<u>Functions</u>: To vote extraordinary taxes for the
province, subject to Government sanction. To be
consulted on changes of boundary, roads, canals,
irrigation, fairs, etc. May advise on other subjects.

<u>Institution</u>: Legislative Council
<u>Mode</u> <u>of</u> <u>Election</u>: Cairo sends one member, chosen
by "Electeurs délégues." Alexandria and the six other
towns send another. Each Provincial Council sends one

of its own members, elected by ballot.

<u>Composition</u>: President, Vice-President, twelve
members - nominated. (14) One member from Cairo, one
from Alexandria, etc., fourteen from provinces -
elected by ballot. (16)Ministers may take part.

<u>Regulations</u>: Convoked first by Decree; then to meet
on first of every second month. Elected members choose
a second Vice-President. They sit for six years, and
get expenses paid. Permanent members get an allowance.
Sittings are held in private.

<u>Functions</u>: Must be consulted on general Laws and
Decrees. May suggest such Laws. To examine Petitions.
Budget to be laid before them Dec.1. They cannot
interfere with Public Debt. Yearly accounts to be
presented to them.

<u>Institution</u>: General Assembly

<u>Mode</u> <u>of</u> <u>Election</u>: Elected by "Electeurs délégues."
The members must be over 30 years old, pay a certain
amount of taxes, and have been electeurs for five years.

<u>Composition</u>: Ministers (8), Legislative Council (30),
eleven members from eight towns, thirty-five from
fourteen provinces (46).

<u>Regulations</u>: Convoked at least once in two years.
Members elected for six years. President of Legislative
Council presides. Sittings are held in private. Elected

members get an allowance for expenses.

<u>Functions</u>: No new tax can be levied without being
discussed and voted by them. To be consulted on
public loans, ralilways, and canals, classification
of land for land tax. Government shall state reasons
for not following their advice.

Note: The eight towns which are independent of the Provincial
Governors and Councils are Cairo, Alexandria, Damietta, Rosetta, Port
Said, Suez, Ismailia, and El Arish.

W. Chauncy Cartwright, Inclosure in No 132, PRO,FO 407/28/2921,
Cairo, September 7, 1883, p.120.

Appendix 34

The Social Composition of Egypt's Representative Institutions,
1866- 1912

ASBY	N	%UMD	DS,M	%MUSLIM	%GOVT	%TOWNS	MEAN-FDNS
MSN1	74	71.62	2	95.83	86.49	17.57	333
MSN2	93	65.22	2	96.74	81.72	17.20	74
MSN3	91	64.84	6	94.32	78.02	15.38	41
MN	73	43.84	8	95.83	61.64	24.66	253
MSQ1	35	14.29	9	97.06	60.00	45.71	898
GA1	51	25.49	6	93.75	41.18	45.10	161
MSQ2	32	6.25	6	96.77	53.13	56.25	658
GA2	48	16.67	4	91.49	25.00	37.50	52
MSQ3	33	9.09	11	90.63	54.55	54.55	309
GA3	53	16.98	5	96.08	20.75	35.85	60
MSQ4	39	10.26	13	86.84	41.03	35.90	381
GA4	51	19.61	7	90.20	19.61	39.22	119
MSQ5 (Data not available)							
GA5	47	12.77	5	97.73	14.89	48.94	65
AVG.	55	28.99	6	94.10	49.08	36.45	262

The abbreviations used in this table are to be interpreted as
follows:

ASBY   The name of the representative institution.

N   The number of members in the body.

358

%UMD   The percentage of 'umda-s in the body.

DS,M   Percent purchased Domains or D.Saniyya land.

%MUSLIM   Percentage of Muslims of all those whose
            religion could be determined.

%GOVT   Percentage Govt. Employees in the body.

%TOWNS   The percentage of large town resdients.

MEAN-FDNS   The mean feddans owned by all members
            of the body, based on records of property
            holding used in this study.

AVG.   The average for the thirteen representative
            institutions for which information was
            available.

Appendix 35

Government Employment of Members of National

   Representative institutions

Level of post	1866-1882		1883-1913		Total	
	N	**%**	**N**	**%**	**N**	**%**
Minister	4	1.75%	11	3.58%	14	4.91%
Wakil Minister	4	1.75%	3	3.70%	6	2.11%
Mudir	6	2.63%	7	8.64%	13	4.56%
Nazir Qism	9	3.95%	12	14.81%	17	5.96%
Ma'mur	11	4.82%	12	14.81	21	7.37%
Mufattish	10	4.39%	4	4.94%	14	4.91%
Umda,Skilled Employee	184	80.70%	32	39.51%	200	70.18%

Appendix 36

Government Administration Employment of Members of Egypt's

National Representative Institutions, 1866-1913

	1866-1882		1883-1913		Total
Govt. Admin.	N	%	N	%	N
Khedivate	1	.44%	2	2.53%	3
Council of Ministers	2	.88%	1	1.27%	3
Finance	1	.44%	4	5.06%	5
Interior	212	93.81%	48	60.76%	238
(Umda-s)	(184)		(32)		(200)
Public Works	1	.44%	1	1.27%	2
Justice	2	.88%	5	6.33%	5
War	1	.44%	1	1.27%	3
Public Instruction	1	.44%	3	3.80%	3
Miscellaneous	2	.88%	10	12.66%	11
Mixed Administration	2	.88%	1	1.27%	3
Awqaf	0	0	1	1.27%	1
Town Administrations	1	.44%	1	1.27%	3
Churches	0	0	1	1.27%	1
Total	266	100.00%	79	100.00%	280

Appendix 37

Egyptian Cabinets, 1882-1908

P.M.	N	%Mus	%T-C	%Egy	Feds	DS+DM	URT
Sharif	9	9/9	8/9	1/9	4704	2387	26.8
1882-84		100	88.89	11.11			
Nubar	7	6/7	5/7	1/7	942	827	32.5
1884-88		85.7	71.43	14.29			
Riyaz	6	6/6	5/6	1/6	3826	3594	33.6
1888-91		100	83.33	16.67			
M.Fahmi	6	5/6	5/6	0	513	483	24.7
1891-93		83.33	83.33				
Riyaz	6	4/6	4/6	1/6	1185	1149	28.8
1893-94		66.67	66.67	16.67			
Nubar	6	4/6	3/6	2/6	1555	1416	16.3
1894-95		66.67	50.00	33.33			
M.Fahmi	6	5/6	4/6	2/6	605	600	11.1
1895-06		83.33	66.67	33.33			
M.Fahmi	7	6/7	4/7	3/7	576	514	10.7
1906-08		85.71	57.14	42.9			

The abbreviations above are to be interpreted as follows:

P.M.   Prime Minister and dates of his ministry

N   The number of members of the ministryat time

%Mus   The percentage of Muslims in the ministry

%T-C   The percentage of Turko-Circassians in the
          ministry. This assumes that Ibrahim Fu'ad
          was not a Turko-Circassian.

%Egy   The percentage of Egyptian nationals in the
          ministry

Feds   The mean feddans of ministers in our records

DS+DM   The mean Daira Saniyya and Domains feddans
          purchased from 1882 to 1907 by ministers

URT   The mean urban property tax paid in Cairo in 1894
          by ministers

Appendix 38

The Organization of the Egyptian Government

1.Khedivate

2.Cabinet of Khedivate

3.Family of Khedivate

4.Council of Ministers

5.Ministry of Foreign Affairs

6.Ministry of Finance

7.----- Under Secretary of State

8.----- Director General of Accounts

9.----- Legal Affarirs

10.----- Director of Revenue

11.----- Archives

12.----- Pensions

13.----- Land Survey

14.----- Mint

15.----- Octroi

16.----- Salt Department

17.----- Financial Services of the Provinces

18.Ministry of Public Instruction

19.Ministry of the Interior

20.----- Central Administration

21.----- Office of the Advisor

22.----- Legal Affairs

23.----- Police and Gendarmerie

24.----- Sanitation

25.----- Prisons

26.----- Office of the Suppression of Slavery

27.----- Civil Administration of the Provinces

28.Ministry of Public Works

29.----- Central Administration

30.----- Administrative Services

31.----- Director General of Tanzim

32.----- Techincal Services

33.----- Dredging

34.----- Legal Affairs

35.----- Irrigation

36.----- Under Secretary of State

37.Ministry of Justice

38.----- Central Administration

39.----- Mixed Courts

40.----- Native Courts

41.----- Mehkemehs Chariehs

42.----- Personnel

43.Ministry of War

44.Miscellaneous Services of the Provinces

45.Department of Health

46.Customs

47.Coastguard

48.Ports

49.Railways

50.Telegraphs

51.Post Office

52.Government Stores

53.Department of Awqaf

54.Caisse de la Dette

55.Domains Administration

56.Daira Saniyya Administration

57.State Lands

58.Bait al-Mal

59.Sudan Administration

60.Town Muhafaza

61.Other Town Administrations

62.Maglis al-Ahkam

63.Churches

Appendix 39

Egyptian Government Expenditures

	(Thousands of L.E.)			Index
Year	Ordinary	Extraordinary	Total	(1882 = 100)
1882	8,977	0	8,977	100
1883	9,793	341	10,134	113
1884	9,796	205	10,001	111
1885	10,335	3,594	13,929	155
1886	10,066	275	10,341	115
1887	9,609	926	10,535	117
1888	9,374	2,000	11,374	127
1889	9,500	369	9,869	110
1890	9,590	1,512	11,102	124
1891	9,607	413	10,020	112
1892	9,552	114	9,666	108
1893	9,555	118	9,673	108
1894	9,470	15	9,485	106
1895	9,429	0	9,429	105
1896	9,605	0	9,605	107
1897	9,709	0	9,709	108
1898	9,800	0	9,800	109
1899	9,929	0	9,929	111
1900	9,895	10	9,905	110
1901	9,924	713	10,637	118
1902	10,040	353	10,393	116

1903	10,262	264	10,526	117
1904	10,588	242	10,830	121
1905	11,668	106	11,774	131
1906	12,393	6	12,399	138
1907	13,231	0	13,231	147

Source: <u>Statistical Yearbook for 1909</u>, pp.49,55. All figures were rounded to the nearest 1,000 L.E. The Extraordinary Expenses included (1) heavy indemnities for the fire in Alexandria paid in 1885, (2) commutation of pensions paid in 1888, most of which went to the royal family, and (3) expenses for the railway system made from 1901 to 1905. The Ordinary Expenses for 1887 include salaries of 340,000 not actually paid until the following year. The Ordinary Expenses for 1888 have been adjusted accordingly. The index was calculated by the author.

Appendix 40

Areas of Egyptian Government Expenditures(%)

Year	Fin.	Ed.	P.Wks.	Army	Health	Debt	RR
1880	1.25	.70	5.87	5.76	.79	45.88	5.91
1882	1.19	.84	6.25	9.62	.98	41.78	4.49
1886	1.25	.67	8.96	3.25	.92	42.59	5.55
1887	1.07	.60	10.20	3.81	.88	40.04	5.59
1892	.82	.92	10.36	5.77	.77	41.37	8.30
1896	.90	1.03	9.81	6.14	1.23	39.38	8.20
1899	.87	1.07	9.43	8.32	.97	37.27	9.57
1900	.88	1.08	9.75	8.15	1.05	37.10	10.78
1904	.85	1.11	8.94	6.55	1.42	34.18	15.57
1907	1.70	2.66	9.54	6.58	1.98	28.50	14.85

This table was calculated on the basis of the figures from the
Statistical Yearbook for 1909 cited above. This source offers a
reliable comparision figures for percentages used in comparisions,
although reports by British officials indicate that not all data were
exact. For example, see Baring to Granville, Inclosure 2 in No.8,
PRO,FO, 407/45, Cairo, 29 December, 1883, and compare the above
figures.

Appendix 41

Government Posts by Level by Nationality, 1882-1907

	Egyptians		Foreigners		Total
Level	N	%	N	%	N
1 Minister	65	100.00	0	0	65
2 Wakil Minister	123	80.92	29	19.08	152
3 Nazir Idara	135	93.10	10	6.90	145
4 Wakil Idara	183	95.31	9	4.69	192
5 Mufattish I	187	89.05	23	10.95	210
6 Mufattish II	161	99.40	7	.60	168
7 'Umda	389	99.74	1	.26	390
8 Employee	51	96.23	3	3.77	53
Total	1294	94.11	81	5.89	1381

Note: This listing includes six ministers who served before
1882. Small discrepancies between this table and previous data are
due to the fact that some jobs were not classified by level and were
excluded here.

Appendix 42

Government Employment by Level by Period

Level	1882-1890		1890-1899		1900-1907	
	N	%	N	%	N	%
1 Minister	22	45.83	18	37.50	8	16.67
2 Wakil Minister	19	27.14	25	35.71	26	37.14
3 Nazir Idara	33	26.40	39	31.20	53	42.40
4 Wakil Idara	45	24.73	49	26.92	88	48.35
5 Mufattish I	61	30.05	64	31.53	78	38.42
6 Mufattish II	54	27.41	78	39.59	65	32.99
7 'Umda	56	29.17	41	21.35	95	49.48
8 Employee	6	11.76	42	82.35	3	5.88
Total	296	27.72	356	33.33	416	38.95

Remembering that Non-Muslims were traditionally numberous on levels one, two, five and eight, five comments are in order. With very few appointments on level eight during the period from 1900 to 1907, we can account for some of the overall decrease after 1900 of non-Muslims. On the other hand, after 1900 there were increases on level four, where Muslims tended to predominate. Had there been more appointments on level one where Muslims held a monoploy, the overall percentage of Muslims would have been somewhat higher. There were no appointments of foreigners to the very numerous departments of Justice and Interior for the final period of 1900 to 1907, which again lowered the percentage of foreigners. Finally, the recording of nominations

of foreigners was not complete after 1900. We can only conclude there
may have been a decrease in the percentage of Non-Muslim appointments
after the turn of the century.

Appendix 43

Career Paths of High Government Officials

	Total	Muslims			Non-Muslims		
		Turks	Egys.	Unk.	Copt	Arm.	For.
Mixed Careers	59	16	7	28	5	2	1
Army to Interior	18	5	1	12	0	0	0
Justice (Egy.Deg.)	7	0	4	1	1	1	0
Justice (For.Deg.)	9	3	2	1	1	0	2
Mixed Admin.	4	1	0	2	1	0	0
Muhafaza to Int.) Interior)	6	2	1	3	0	0	0
Azhar to Justice	4	0	1	3	0	0	0
Azhar	1	0	1	0	0	0	0
For. to Govt. Dr.	3	1	1	1	0	0	0
Service Royal Fam.	0	2	0	0	0	0	0
Govt.and Pri.Sect.	0	0	0	0	1	0	0
Misc.	2	0	2	0	0	0	0
Total	116	28	20	53	9	3	3

Arm. indicates Armenians. For.Ed. to Govt. indicates men
who received medical degrees in Europe and then worked as government
physicians. One man, a Copt, worked both in the private sector and
for the government. Unk. denotes Muslims who origins,
Turko-Circassian or Egyptian, could not be determined. Egy.Deg.
designates a man who received a university or law school diploma in
Egypt, and For.Deg. one whose degree was granted in Euproe.

Appendix 44

Feddans Held by Officials by Rank

Level	Total High Officials	Average Holdings
1 Minister	71	1404
2 Wakil Minister	79	187
3 Nazir Idara	148	134
4 Wakil Idara	197	98
5 Mufattish I	229	127
6 Mufattish II	216	103
7 'Umda	389	142
8 Employee	53	14

Appendix 45

Ranking of Administrations by Average Feddans of Officials

Rank	1882-1890	1891-1899	1900-1907
1	Council of Min.	Unknown	Unknown
2	Pub. Inst.	For.Affairs	Misc.
3	Finance	Interior	For. Affairs
4	Justice	Misc.	Interior
5	Interior	War	Finance
6	Awqaf	Finance	Maglis Markaz
7	Khedivate	Council of Mn.	Awqaf
8	Mixed Admin.	Awqaf	War
9	War	Pub. Inst.	Council of Min.
10	Pub. Works	Khedivate	Mixed Admin.
11	Maglis Markaz	Mixed Admi.	Pub. Inst.
12	Misc.	Health	Khedivate
13	Unknown	Towns	Pub. Works
14	--	Justice	Towns
15	--	--	Justice
16	--	--	Health

Appendix 46

Feddans by Administration by Period

	1882-1890			1891-1899			1900-1907		
	M	MM	CM	M	MM	CM	M	MM	CM
Khed.	76	27	0	36	30	0	73	83	46
Cou.Min.	3761	3452	0	100	133	0	0	0	0
For.Afr.	-	-	-	1024	600	1448	69	92	0
Fin.	70	120	0	53	82	34	180	421	18
Int.	168	177	141	271	178	633	177	183	163
Pub.Wks.	87	104	0	0	0	0	47	55	0
Just.	113	32	5	4	3	5	33	33	32
War	101	108	0	71	79	0	117	130	0
Health	0	0	0	17	21	0	29	36	0
Pub.Ins.	305	305	0	58	24	0	110	110	0
Misc.	36	39	0	157	183	0	840	755	1345
Mixed	43	79	6	14	28	0	181	213	149
Awqaf	146	146	0	89	89	0	197	236	0
Towns	0	0	0	8	8	0	64	32	128

M designates the mean, MM the mean for Muslims alone and CM the mean for Christians alone.

Appendix 47

Employment and Religion of Domains Buyers

<u>Religion</u>	<u>Govt.</u>	<u>Non-Govt.</u>
Muslim	252	389
Christian	24	117
Jewish	0	11
Not Muslim	2	3
Not Jewish	5	10
No Info.	17	55
Total	300	585

Bibliography

<u>Archives</u>

Egypt. Ministry of Finances. Tribunal Mixte du Caire.
Etat des inscriptions hypothecaires a partir de
l'annee 1786 jusqu'au 14 novembre 1883.

------. -----. Pension File.

------. Secrétariat, Echanges des Pensions. Affaires
terminées, 14/7/1887 jusqu'au 3/4/1889. des
Pensions. Dar al-Mahfuzat, 664/27/42.

------. Sagal al-Awa'id 'ala al-Mabani fi Madinat Misr,
1894-1901 (Schedule of Taxes on Property in Cairo).
Dar al-Mahfuzat.

------. Idara al-Amwal al-Muqarrara (Administration of
Direct Taxes). Kashf 'an al-matlub min al-mumawwilin
al-ladhina 'atyanuhum tablaghu mi'tani faddan fa'fuqu
wa muta'akhar 'alihim min al-amwal li-ghayat shahr
fibrayar sanat 1885 min mablagh mi'tani gineh fa ma
fawqa ma'ada al-ladhina muta'khar 'alihim aqall min
hadha al-mablagh (Schedule of taxes solicited from
owners of over two hundred feddans who have back
taxes of over two hundred pounds due up to February,
1885). Dar al-Mahfuzat, 33/3149/326.

------. Liste des Contribuables qui possèdent deux cent
feddans et au-dessus et qui sont en retard pour le
paiement de l'impôt foncier à fin novembre, 1884, non
compris ceux dont la dette n'excèdent pas Lst. 200.
Dar al-Mahfuzat, 54/12/1 646.

Great Britain. Public Records Office, Foreign Office,
Series 78, 371 and 407.

------. House of Commons Sessional Papers.

Publications

Adam, Juliette. Angleterre en Egypte. Paris, 1922.

Amir, Ibrahim. Al-ard wal-fallah al-mas'ala al-zira'iyya fi misr
(The Land and the Fallah, the Agricultural Question in Egypt).
Cairo, 1958.

Amin, Ahmad. Zu'ama' al-islah fi al-'asr al-hadith (Leaders of
Reform in the Modern Age). Cairo, 1949.

Artin, Yacoub Bey. La Propriété foncière en Egypte. Cairo, 1883.

Asaf, Yusuf. Dalil misr li-'amay 1889-1890. Cairo, 1889.

Baer, Gabriel. Egyptian Guilds in Modern Times. Jerusalem, 1964.

------. A History of Landownershop in Modern Egypt, 1880-1950.
London, 1962.

Barakat, 'Ali. Tatawwur al-milkiyya al-zira'iyya fi misr 1813-1914
    (The Development of Agricultural Property Holding in Egypt,
    1813-1914). Cairo, 1977.

Berques, Jacques. Egypt: Imperialism and Revolution. London,
    1972.

Brehier, Louis. L'Egypte de 1798 à 1900. Paris, 1901.

Brinton, Jaspar Yeates. The Mixed Courts of Egypt. New Haven,
    1930.

British Chamber of Commerce of Egypt. List of Financial,
    Manufacturing, Transport and Other Companies Established in
    Egypt, Prepared by the British Chamber of Commerce.
    Alexandria, 1901.

Cantori, L. J. "The Organizational Basis of an Elite Party: The
    Egyptian Wafd". Ph.D. Diss., University of Chicago, 1966.

Chafik, Ahmad Pasha. L'Egypte moderne et les influences
    étrangères. Cairo, 1931.

Chelu, A. Le Nil, le Soudan, l'Egypte. Paris, 1891.

Chenouda, Atyya. "Notes sur l'industrie du tissage," Egypte
    Contemporaine. 1 (January, 1910), 187-191.

Cleland, W. "A Population Plan for Egypt," Egypte Contemporaine.

185 (May, 1939), 461-484.

Craig, J.I. "The Distribution of Landed Property in Egypt," Egypte
Contemporaine. 13 (January, 1913), 33-39.

Credit Foncier Egyptien. Rapports de Conseil d'Administration et
des Censeurs : Résolutions de l'Assemblée, Exercise 1883-1907.
Cairo, 1884-1908.

Cromer, Earl of. Abbas II. London, 1915.

-------. Modern Egypt. London, 1908.

Crouchley, A. E. "The Development of Commerce in the Reign of
Muhammad 'Ali," Egypte Contemporaine. 28 (February, 1937),
305-318.

-------. The Economic Development of Modern Egypt. London, 1938.

-------. Investment of Foreign Capital in Egyptian Companies and
the Public Debt. Cairo, 1936.

-------. The Visible Balance of Trade since 1884," Egypte
Contemporaine. 156 (April, 1935), 491-512.

Dearing, Brian E., and Hartwig, Frederick. Exploratory Data
Analysis. Beverly Hills, California, 1979.

De Chamberet, Raoul. Enquête sur la condition du Fellah Egyptien
au triple point de vue de la vie agricole, de l'éducation, de
l'hygiène et de l'assistance publique. Dijon, 1909.

Dassuqi, 'Asim. Kubar mullak ul-iradi al-zira'iyya wa duruhum fi
al-mujtam' al-misri min 1914 - 1952 (Large Agricultural
Landowners and their Role in Egyptian Society, 1914 - 1952).
Cairo, n.d.

Dollar, Charles, and Jensen, Richard. Historian's Guide to
Statistics: Quantitative Analysis and Historical Research.
New York, 1971.

Egypt. Journal Officiel. Cairo.

------. Al-waqa'i al-misriyya (Official Journal in Arabic).
Cairo.

------. Customs Administration. Le Commerce Extérieur de l'Egypte
pendant l'année 1909. Alexandria, 1910.

------. Daira Saniyya Commission. Rapport Presenté à S.A. le
Khedive sur la Situation de la Daira Saniyya en 1880-1907.
Cairo, 1881-1908, stored in Dar al-Mahfuzat, 278/13/42.

------. Domains Administration. Rapport présenté pour les
commissaires des domaines à S.A. le Khedive à l'appui du compte
général des recettes et des dépenses de l'exercise 1880-1907.
Alexandria and Cairo, 1881-1908.

------. ------. Cahier des Charges, Clauses et Conditions
Générales Applicables à la Vente des Biens Dominaux. Cairo,

1900.

------. Domains Commission. <u>Compte Générale des Opérations</u>
<u>Effectuées</u> <u>du</u> <u>26</u> Octobre <u>1878</u> <u>au</u> <u>31</u> <u>Mars</u> <u>1898</u>. Paris, 1898.

------. Ministry of Culture. Center of Documentation and History of
Modern Egypt. <u>Al-nizarat</u> <u>wal'wizarat</u> <u>al'misriyya, al-juz'</u>
<u>al-awwal</u> <u>mundhu</u> <u>insha'</u> <u>hiyyat</u> <u>nizara</u> <u>fi</u> <u>28</u> <u>Augustus</u> <u>1878</u> <u>hatta</u>
<u>qiyam</u> <u>al-gumhuriyya</u> <u>fi</u> <u>18</u> <u>juniu</u> <u>1953</u> (Egyptian Ministries and
Ministers, Part One, from the Foundation of the Ministry on
August 28, 1878 to the Establishment of the Republic on June 18,
1953). Fu'ad Karam ed., Cairo, 1969.

------. Ministry of Finance. <u>Alphabetical</u> <u>Index</u> <u>of</u> <u>Joint</u> <u>Stock</u>
<u>Companies</u>. Cairo, 1904.

------. ------. Census Department. <u>TheCensus</u> <u>of</u> <u>Egypt</u> <u>Taken</u> <u>in</u>
<u>1907</u>. Cairo, 1909.

------. ------. ------. <u>Recensement</u> <u>générale</u> <u>de</u> <u>l'Egypte</u>, <u>15</u>
<u>Gamad</u> <u>Akher</u> <u>1299</u> - <u>3</u> <u>Mai</u> <u>1882</u>. Cairo, 1884.

------. ------. ------. <u>Recensement</u> <u>générale</u> <u>de</u> <u>l'Egypte</u> <u>ler</u>
<u>juin</u> <u>1897</u> , <u>ler</u> <u>moharrem</u> <u>1315</u>. Vol. 1. Cairo, 1884.

------. ------. Survey Department. <u>Collection</u> <u>of</u> <u>Statistics</u> <u>of</u>
<u>the</u> <u>Areas</u> <u>Planted</u> <u>in</u> <u>Cotton</u> <u>in</u> <u>1909</u>, <u>by</u> <u>E</u>. <u>M</u>. <u>Dawsun</u> <u>and</u> <u>J</u>.
<u>I.Craig</u>. Cairo, 1910.

------. Statistical Department. <u>Annuaire</u> <u>Statistique</u> <u>de</u>

l'Egypte, 1909. Cairo, 1910.

------. ------. Joint Stock Companies Operating Chiefly in Egypt,
December 31, 1907.Cairo, 1909.

------. ------. Statistique des sociétés anonymes par actions
travaillant principalement en Egypt. Cairo, 1911.

------. Survey Department. The cadastral survey of Egypt,
1892-1907. By Captain H. G. Lyons. Cairo, 1908.

Eid, Alfred. La Fortune immobilière de l'Egypte et sa dette
hypothécaire. Paris, 1907.

Fahmi, Qalini. Mudhakirrat Qalini Fahmi Pasha. (Memoirs of Qalini
Fahmi Pasha). Two vols. Cairo, 1934 and 1943.

Gelat, Philippe. Répertoire général annote de la législation et de
l'administration égyptiennes 1840-1908. Alexandria, 1909.

Ghali, Ibrahim. L'Egypte nationaliste et liberale de Moustapha
Kamel à Saad Zagloul, 1892-1927. The Hague, 1969.

Gran, Peter. Islamic Roots of Capitalism in Egypt, 1760-1840.
Austin, Texas, and London, 1979.

Guemard, Gabriel. Le Regime hypothécaire égyptien. Aix, 1914.

Haikal, Muhammad Husain. Mudhakirat fi al-siyasa al-misriyya
al-juz' al-awwalu min 1912 ila 1927 (Memoirs of Egyptian
Politics, Part One, from 1912 to 1927). Cairo, 1951.

------. _Tarajim misriyya wa gharbiyya_ (Egyptian and Western Biographies). Cairo, n.d.

Hamid, Ra'uf 'Abbas. _Al-nizam al-ijtima'i fi misr fi dhul al-milkiyya al-zira'iyya al-kabira 1837-1914_ (The Social Structure in Egypt in Light of Large Agricultural Property Holding). Cairo, 1973.

Hamza, 'Abd al-Maksud. _The Public Debt of Egypt 1854-1876_. Cairo, 1944.

Hanin, Girgis. _Al-Atyan wal-Dara'ib_ (Land and Taxes). Cairo, 1904.

Heyworth-Dunne, John. _An Introduction to the History of Education in Modern Egypt_. London, 1938.

Holt, P. M., ed. _Political and Social Change in Modern Egypt_. London, 1968.

Holynski, Alexandre. _Nubar Pasha devant l'histoire_. Paris, 1885.

Issa, Hossam M. _Capitalisme et sociétés anonymes en Egypte_. Paris, 1970.

Issawi, Charles. "Egypt since 1800: A Study in Lop-sided Development", _Journal of Economic History_. 21 (March, 1961) 1-26.

------. _The Economic History of the Middle East_. Chicago, 1966.

Kazziha, Walid. "The Evolution of the Egyptian Political Elite, 1907
    - 1921". Thesis submitted to the University of London, London,
    1970.

Kyriakos, Mikhail. Copts and Moslems under British Control in
    Egypt. London, 1911.

Lahita, Ahmad Ahmad. Tarikh misr al-iqtisadi fi al-qarn al-tasi
    'ashar (Economic History of Egypt in the Nineteenth Century).
    Cairo, 1958.

Landau, Jacob. "The Jews in Nineteenth Century Egypt: Some
    Socio-Economic Aspects." in P. M. Holt, ed. Political and
    Social Change in Modern Egypt. London, 1968.

Landes, David. Bankers and Pashas in International Finance and
    Economic Imperialism in Egypt. Cambridge, Mass., 1958.

Lashin, 'Abd al-Khaliq Muhammad. Sa'd zaghlul duru fi al-siyasa
    al-misriyya hitta sana 1914 (Sa'd Zaghlul's role in Egyptian
    Politics up to 1914). Cairo, 1971.

Lutfi al-Sayyid, Afaf. Egypt and Cromer, A Study in Anglo-Egyptian
    Relations. New York, 1969.

Maunier, Rene. "L'Apprentissage dans la petite industrie en Egypte"
    Egypte Contemporaine. 11 (May, 1912), 341-369.

McCarthy, Justin. "Nineteenth Century Egyptian Population,"

Middle Eastern Studies. 12 (October, 1976), 1-39.

El-Messady, Mohammad Gamal El-Din. "The Relations between 'Abbas Hilmi and Lord Cromer," Ph. D. Thesis, University of London, 1966.

Milner, Alfred. England in Egypt. London, 1893.

Mitchell, B. R. European Historical Statistics, 1750-1970. New York, 1975.

Le Moniteur Egyptien. (Cairo).

Al-Muayyad. (Cairo).

Mubarak, 'Ali. Al-Khitat al-tawfiqiyya. Bulaq, 1889.

Mustafa, Ahmad 'Abd al-Rahim. Misr wal-masala al-misriyya min 1876 ila 1882 (Egypt and the Egyptian Question from 1876 to 1882). Cairo, 1965.

O'Brien, P. K. D. "The Long-term Growth of Agricultural Production in Egypt, 1821-1962, " in P. M. Holt, ed. Political and Social Change in Modern Egypt, London, 1968.

Owen, E. R. J. "Cairo Building Industry" in Colloque International sur l'Histoire du Caire. German Democratic Republic, n.d., Pp.337-351.

------. Cotton and the Egyptian Economy 1820-1914: A Study in Trade and Development. Oxford, 1969.

Radwan, Samir. Capital Formation in Egyptian Industry and
     Agriculture 1882-1967. Oxford, 1974.

Al-Rafi', 'Abd al-Rahman. 'Asr Isma'il (The Age of Isma'il). Cairo,
     1948.

------. 'Asr Muhammad 'Ali (The Age of Muhammad 'Ali). Cairo, 1930.

------.Mustafa Kamil ba'ith al-haraka al-wataniyya (Mustafa Kamil
     Leader of the Nationalist Movement). Cairo, 1962.

Raymond, André. Artisans et commercants au Caire au xviiiè
     siècle. Damascus, 1973.

Richards, Alan. "Primitive Accumulation in Egypt, 1798-1882,"
     Review. 1 (Fall, 1977), 3-49.

------. "The Political Economy of Gutwirtschaft: A Comparative
     Analysis of East Elbian Germany, Egypt, and Chile," Comparative
     Studies in Society and History. 21 (October, 1979) 483-518.

Rivlin, H. A. B. The Agricultural Policy of Muhammad 'Ali in
     Egypt. Cambridge, Mass., 1961.

Al-Saruji, Muhammad Mahmud. Al-gaysh al-misri fi al-qarn al-tasiᶜ
     'ashar (The Egyptian Army in the Nineteenth Century). Cairo,
     1967.

Schölch, Alexander. Ägypten den Ägyptern.Die politische und

gesellschaftliche <u>Krise</u> <u>der</u> <u>Jahre</u> <u>1878-1882</u> <u>in</u> <u>Ägypten</u>.
Freiburg, *1972.*

Shearer, W. V. "Report on the Weaving Industry in Assiout, <u>Egypte</u>
<u>Contemporaine</u>. 1 (January, 1910), 184-186.

Subhi, Muhammad Khalil. <u>Tarikh</u> <u>al-haya</u> <u>al-niyabiyya</u> <u>fi</u> <u>misr</u> <u>min</u>
<u>'ahd</u> <u>sakin</u> <u>al-jinan</u> <u>Muhammad</u> <u>'Ali</u> <u>Basha</u> (The History of
Representative Institutions in Egypt from the Time of His Majesty
Muhammad 'Ali Pasha). Cairo, 1947.

Tagher, Jacques. <u>Coptes</u> <u>et</u> <u>musulmans</u>. Cairo, 1952.

Tignor, Robert. <u>Modernization</u> <u>and</u> <u>British</u> <u>Colonial</u> <u>Rule</u> <u>in</u> <u>Egypt</u>,
<u>1882-1914</u>. Princeton, 1966.

Wells, Sidney H. "Note préliminaire sur l'industrie du tissage en
Egypte," <u>Egypte</u> <u>Contemporaine</u>. 4 (November, 1910), 578-581.

Willcocks, William. <u>Reports</u> <u>upon</u> <u>the</u> <u>Lands</u> <u>of</u> <u>the</u> <u>Daira</u> <u>Saniyya</u>
(<u>Confidential-</u> <u>for</u> <u>Directors</u> <u>Only</u>). London, n.d., stored in
Dar al-Mahfuzat, 289/13/42.

Zakhura, Ilyas. <u>Kitab</u> <u>mirat</u> <u>al-'asr</u> <u>fi</u> <u>tarikh</u> <u>wa</u> <u>rusum</u> <u>kabir</u>
<u>al-rijal</u> <u>li-misr</u> (Mirror of the Age for the History and
Sketches of the Greatest Men of Egypt). Cairo, 1897.

Zaydan, Jurgi. <u>Tarajim</u> <u>mashahir</u> <u>al-sharq</u> <u>fi</u> <u>al-qarn</u> <u>al-tasi'</u>
<u>'ashar</u> (Biographies of the Famous Men of the East in the
Nineteenth Century). Cairo, 1910.